NARRATIVE RESEARCH

Applied Social Research Methods Series
Volume 47

APPLIED SOCIAL RESEARCH METHODS SERIES

Series Editors
LEONARD BICKMAN, Peabody College, Vanderbilt University, Nashville
DEBRA J. ROG, Vanderbilt University, Washington, DC

Other volumes in this series are listed at the back of the book

NARRATIVE RESEARCH

Reading, Analysis, and Interpretation

Amia Lieblich
Rivka Tuval-Mashiach
Tamar Zilber

Applied Social Research Methods Series
Volume 47

SAGE Publications
International Educational and Professional Publisher
Thousand Oaks   London   New Delhi

For information:

SAGE Publications, Inc.
2455 Teller Road
Thousand Oaks, California 91320
E-mail: order@sagepub.com

SAGE Publications Ltd.
6 Bonhill Street
London EC2A 4PU
United Kingdom

SAGE Publications India Pvt. Ltd.
M-32 Market
Greater Kailash I
New Delhi 110 048 India

Printed in the United States of America

Library of Congress Cataloging-in-Publication Data

Lieblich, Amia, 1939-
    Narrative research : reading, analysis and interpretation / by
Amia Lieblich, Rivka Tuval-Mashiach, Tamar Zilber.
    p. cm. — (Applied social research methods ; vol. 47)
    Includes bibliographical references (p.) and index.
    ISBN 0-7619-1042-5 (cloth)
    ISBN 0-7619-1043-3 (pbk.)
    1. Discourse analysis, Narrative—Research—Methodology. 2.
Methodology. I. Tuval-Mashiach, Rivka. II. Zilber, Tamar. III.
Title. IV. Series: Applied social research methods ; v. 47.
P302.7 .L538 1998
401'.41—ddc21
                                98-9071
This book is printed on acid-free paper.
    00 01 02 03 04 10 9 8 7 6 5 4 3 2

Acquisition Editor:	C. Deborah Laughton
Editorial Assistant:	Eileen Carr
Production Editor:	Wendy Westgate
Editorial Assistant:	Lynn Miyata
Typesetter/Designer:	Rose Tylak
Cover Designer:	Candice Harmon

Contents

Acknowledgments

This book is the outcome of intergenerational cooperation. Rivka and Tamar first met Amia as students taking her course, joined in her research projects, and became her graduate students. While learning about narrative research from personal contacts is a special privilege, the three of us hope that the book captures some of this experience for the benefit of our readers.

We would like to thank the Israeli Foundations Trustees, Grant Ag. 92 (1992-1994), the Ministry of Education and Culture, and the NCJW Research Institute for Innovation in Education for their generous support of the original research project within which the life stories presented in this book were gathered. In addition, the Frankenstein Fund supported the work involved in writing this book.

Special thanks to Orna Shatz-Openheimer and Sara Blank Ha-Ramati for joining us in conducting the interviews and discussing them. Irit Ha-Meiri also took part in some of these enlightening meetings.

Any researcher who uses taped material knows the importance of good transcriptions. We were lucky to have the assistance of Guy Lederman, Maty Lieblich, Einat Lerner, Hila David, Noga Sverdlick, Mirit Naor, and Michal Nachmias, who diligently transcribed the taped interviews.

Michal, intrigued by the material, wrote a beautiful analysis on the subject of first memories. We thank her for sharing it with us (see the second part of Chapter 4).

Many thanks to Yael Oberman, who translated some parts of the book from the Hebrew, read and edited the manuscript, and made numerous thoughtful comments.

We warmly thank Naama Levizky, who assisted us in many different ways during the writing period, and especially in compiling the bibliography. Efrat Yitzhaki helped us with proofreading, and the Department of Psychology at the Hebrew University of Jerusalem was a comfortable home for the project.

Finally, we would like to thank all our interviewees. By telling us their life stories, they contributed to our understanding of high school experience, the special teaching program, and narrative analysis. Beyond that, they gave us the opportunity to write this book together—an experience that enriched the stories of our own lives.

1

A New Model for Classification of Approaches to Reading, Analysis, and Interpretation

During the last 15 years, the concepts of narrative and life story have become increasingly visible in the social sciences. Gradually they have earned a place in the theory, research, and application of various disciplines, among them psychology, psychotherapy, education, sociology, and history. Citing Kuhnian terminology, some have termed this historical evolution "the narrative revolution," while others have viewed it as a manifestation of the demise of the positivistic paradigm in social science (Bruner, 1990; Sarbin, 1986). The use of narratives in research can be viewed as an addition to the existing inventory of the experiment, the survey, observation, and other traditional methods, or as a preferred alternative to these "sterile" research tools. Either way, narrative methodologies have become a significant part of the repertoire of the social sciences.

Concomitant with the rise of the narrative paradigm and the growing number of narrative research reports (see publications in the *Journal of Narrative and Life History* and the series The Narrative Study of Lives[1]) has been a noticeable need for studies dealing with narrative methodology in social science. In fact, the use and application of this research method seems to have preceded the formalization of a philosophy and methodology parallel to the practice. Frequently, moreover, narrative study has been criticized as being more art than research: It seems based predominantly on talent, intuition, or clinical experience; defies clear order and systematization; and can hardly be taught.

We believe that the future development of the field of narrative research requires a deliberate investment of effort in the elucidation of working rules for such studies. These would necessarily focus on approaches to analysis of narrative material and the development of techniques that could be employed in relevant studies. This book tries to address this need.

At first glance, such aims are in stark contradiction to the basic tenets of the narrative approach. Narrative research (which will be defined later in this chapter) differs significantly from its positivistic counterpart in its underlying assumptions that there is neither a single, absolute truth in human reality nor one correct reading or interpretation of a text. The narrative approach advocates pluralism, relativism, and subjectivity. Nonetheless, we believe that researchers are responsible for providing a systematic and coherent rationale for their choice of methods as well as a clear exposition of the selected processes that have produced their results. These aspects of narrative research can and should be taught and learned.

This book deals with the methodology of life-story research. It will focus on the stage of reading the text, analysis of data, and topics often absent or neglected as a main focus in the publications on qualitative research. Our aim is to instruct the reader in reading, analysis, and interpretation of life-story materials through a presentation of a new model for the classification of types of readings and a demonstration of techniques and procedures used by us in our empirical work. Although we hope to convince the readers of the wealth and significance of narrative research, we do not see our presentation in this book as a final prescription or cookbook for doing narrative studies but as a perspective on the current state of the art with its unfolding possibilities. The book is aimed at a wide spectrum of readers—scholars, students, and researchers interested in narrative study of lives—yet it is written by three psychologists, so that our terminology and examples are drawn mainly from our field. We hope that this presentation will introduce new ideas and methods for researchers' use and encourage readers to contribute their own creativity to this developing field.

WHAT IS NARRATIVE RESEARCH?

While qualitative studies freely use the terms *narrative* and *narrative research*, it is quite rare to find definitions of these terms. *Webster's* (1966) defines a *narrative* as a "discourse, or an example of it, designed to represent a connected succession of happenings" (p. 1503). *Narrative research*, according to our definition, refers to any study that uses or analyzes narrative materials. The data can be collected as a story (a life story provided in an interview or a literary work) or in a different manner (field notes of an anthropologist who writes up his or her observations as a narrative or in personal letters). It can be the object of the research or a means for the study of another question. It may be used for comparison among groups, to learn about a social phenomenon or historical period, or to explore a personality. Our proposed model can be used for the analysis of a wide spectrum of narratives, from literary works to diaries and written autobiographies, conversations, or oral life stories obtained in interviews. Naturally, such studies belong to several disciplines: literature, history, psychology, anthropology, and so forth.

BRIEF LITERATURE REVIEW

Traditionally, published literature and electronic sites, reports, and databases all point to the conclusion that the use of narratives in research has grown tremendously in the last 15 years. In the fields of psychology, gender studies, education, anthropology, sociology, linguistics, law, and history, narrative studies are flourishing as a means of understanding the personal identity, lifestyle, culture, and historical world of the narrator. This is clearly presented in Figure 1.1, which demonstrates the significant rise in the number of publications in the field.

The figure has been reproduced from the Internet "Resources for Narrative Psychology" site (Hevern, 1997) and is based on a database of 2,011 bibliographical resources—articles, book chapters, books, and doctoral dissertations—located using the keywords *narrative and life history, narrative and psychology, storytelling and psychology,* and *discourse analysis.* The distribution of these items by year of publication is also illustrated in Figure 1.1.

This wealth of material can be roughly classified into three main domains, according to their contributions to the field.

Studies in Which the Narrative Is Used
for the Investigation of Any Research Question

This category is the most common and varied, and includes the majority of work in narrative research. Narrative inquiry may be used as a pilot study in the process of formation of objective research tools, or in a combined strategy of using objective surveys for a larger sample and narrative methods for a smaller group to provide more in-depth understanding. In some cases, however (as in the research presented in this book), the entire evaluation of a real-life problem may be tackled by a narrative approach (see Greene, 1994).

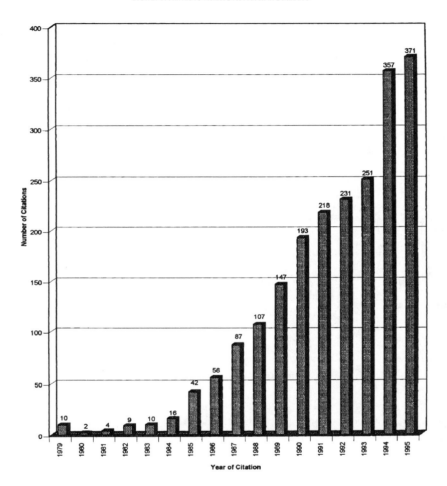

Figure 1.1. Resources for Narrative Psychology
SOURCE: Copyright © 1997 Vincent W. Hevern. Used by permission.

In psychology, education, and medicine, narratives are used for diagnosing psychological and medical problems or learning disabilities (Capps & Ochs, 1995; Herman, 1992; Wigren, 1994).

In many studies in sociology and anthropology, the narrative is used to represent the character or lifestyle of specific subgroups in society, defined by their gender, race, religion, and so on. From a social, cultural, or ethnic point of view, these social groups frequently are discriminated-against minorities whose narratives express their unheard voices. (On women's issues, see, for example, Gluck & Patai, 1991; Josselson, 1987; Personal Narratives Group, 1989. On girls' voices, see Gilligan, Lyons, & Hammer, 1990; Gilligan, Rogers, & Tolman, 1991. On Palestinian women, see Gorkin & Othman, 1996. On gay life, see, for example, Curtis, 1988; Plummer, 1995.)

Narratives are also used in developmental psychology and sociology to study special age groups and cohorts in society. Many studies concentrate on children's narratives as a method for studying their cognitive and social development (e.g., Nelson, 1989; Sutton-Smith 1986). Thompson (1994) uses narratives to study adolescents, and Kemper, Rash, Kynette, and Norman (1990) and Koch (1990), for the study of aging. Other work adopts narrative research for investigating specific periods or transitions in the life cycle: for example, Farrell, Rosenberg, and Rosenberg (1993) on the transition to fatherhood; Riessman (1990) on divorce; Murray (1992), Ochberg (1994), and Wiersma (1988) on careers or vocational development; Lieblich (1993) on the transition of immigration; and so on.

In cognitive sciences, the narrative method is employed to study memory, development of language, and information processing (Hartley & Jensen, 1991; Neisser & Fivush, 1994).

In applied work, clinical psychology uses the narrative in the context of therapy. Restoration, or development of the life story through psychotherapy, is considered the core of the healing process. (Epston, White, & Murray, 1992; Omer & Alon, 1997; Rotenberg, 1987; Schafer, 1983; Spence, 1986; and others).

The studies mentioned above demonstrate that narrative inquiry can be used in both basic and applied research. Because research methods should be always selected to best fit the research question, when researchers are asked by various social agencies to address real-life problems, to contribute their expertise to public debates or decisions, it may be advisable to approach people whose lives are relevant to the issue in an open manner, exploring their subjective, inner experience on the matter at hand. Narrative methods can be considered "real-world measures" that are appropriate when "real-life problems" are investigated (Bickman & Rog, 1998).

Studies That Investigate the Narrative as Their Research Object

In this category we refer to work about the narrative itself rather than narrative as a means for studying other questions. Studies of this kind are prevalent in the theory of literature, communication, and linguistics, and relate to different facets of the story, its nature, structure, or quality (Frye, 1957; Rimmon-Keenan, 1989). Many of these studies are focused on formal aspects of the narrative rather than its contents, such as the structure of the story, the development of the plot, or various linguistic aspects of the narrative. (See, for example, Gergen & Gergen, 1988; Labov & Waletzky, 1967.)

Studies on the Philosophy and Methodology of Qualitative Approaches to Research and, Among Them, Narrative Research

Although these topics are connected, much more has been written on the philosophical perspectives represented in narrative research than on its methodology. Among the most important philosophical contributions are those made by Bruner (1986, 1990, 1996) on the narrative as one of the two human modes of cognition; by M. Gergen (1992), K. Gergen (1994a), and Giddens, (1991) on postmodernism, identity, and the narrative; and on a variety of philosophical issues by Alasuutari (1997), Fisher-Rosenthal (1995), Howard (1991), Mitchell (1981), Polkinghorne (1988), Runyan (1984), Sarbin (1986), Widdershoven (1993).

Emphasis on the subject of narrative methodology as a primary concern, comprehensive models for analysis or reading of narratives, and work on the classification of methods is relatively rare in narrative research. Some relevant papers have been written within larger works on qualitative research methods (Denzin, 1978, 1989; Denzin & Lincoln, 1994; Riessman, 1993). Researchers have proposed specific tools for focusing on certain aspects of the story or for reading a story as a whole. Meaningful contributors of this kind are, among others, Gilligan and her coworkers (Brown et al., 1988), Linde (1993), and Rosenthal (1993). Our review of the literature, however, located almost no comprehensive models systematically mapping the variety of existing methods of reading narratives.

Two recent publications do provide, nonetheless, a wider perspective on various aspects of narrative research. Ochs and Capps (1996), citing more than 240 publications, present an extensive review of the work in this field focusing on the relation of narrative and the self. Mishler (1995) proposes a typology for the classification of narrative studies according to their central research issues. His typology includes three categories or perspectives on the narrative: *Reference and temporal order* refers to the relationship between order of events in real time and their order of narration; *textual coherence and structure* deals with linguistic and narrative strategies for the construction of the story; *narrative functions* relates to the wider contexts of the story in society and culture. Our own model, which aims to systematize various readings, analyses, and interpretations of narrative research, will be presented later, after we have introduced our basic theoretical position.

OUR THEORETICAL POSITION

Why should one conduct narrative studies? Put differently, what is the place of the narrative about oneself (self-narrative), or life story, in psychology today?

People are storytellers by nature. Stories provide coherence and continuity to one's experience and have a central role in our communication with others. Our theoretical position, based on some of the literature reviewed above, is that along with its interest in the *behavior* of humans and animals, and its goal to *predict* and *control,* the mission of psychology is to *explore* and *understand* the *inner world* of individuals. One of the clearest channels for learning about the inner world is through verbal accounts and stories presented by individual narrators about their lives and their experienced reality. In other words, narratives provide us with access to people's identity and personality. In the same manner that many theorists, notably Freud, formed their views about mental life, the personality, and its development—from "case studies" of women and men in psychotherapy—so too can the researcher interested in normal identity construct it from self-narratives gathered in research interviews (McAdams, 1990).

In the forefront of psychology and sociology today, Bruner (1991, 1996), Fisher-Rosenthal (1995), Gergen (1994b), Gergen and Gergen (1986), Hermans, Rijks, Harry, and Kempen (1993), McAdams (1993), Polkinghorne (1991), and Rosenthal (1997), among others, advocate that personal narratives, in both facets of content and form, *are* people's identities. According to this approach, stories imitate life and present an inner reality to the outside world; at the same time, however, they shape and construct the narrator's personality and reality. The story *is* one's identity, a story created, told, revised, and retold throughout life. We know or discover ourselves, and reveal ourselves to others, by the stories we tell.[2]

Not everybody fully adheres to this view, however. In the summary of their introductory chapter to their excellent handbook of qualitative research, Denzin and Lincoln (1994) contend, "The field of qualitative research is defined by a series of tensions, contradictions and hesitations"

(p. 15). The crux of these tensions is the nature of "truth," "knowledge," and "research"—topics that are far too deep and broad for our work in this book. Against the postmodern views presented above, one may still find, in current scholarship, realistic, essentialist, or historical perspectives that examine the story, or any verbal account, as a (better or worse) representation of internal and external reality. Within this contested domain, our position takes a middle course. We do not advocate total relativism that treats all narratives as texts of fiction. On the other hand, we do not take narratives at face value, as complete and accurate representations of reality. We believe that stories are usually constructed around a core of facts or life events, yet allow a wide periphery for the freedom of individuality and creativity in selection, addition to, emphasis on, and interpretation of these "remembered facts."

In the context of life-story research in psychology, the broad issue of the linkage between story and reality can be translated to (among other things) the relationship of self-narrative and personal identity, which "resides" in the hidden domain of inner reality. Life stories are subjective, as is one's self or identity. They contain "narrative truth" (Spence, 1982, 1986), which may be closely linked, loosely similar, or far removed from "historical truth." Consequently, our stand is that life stories, when properly used, may provide researchers with a key to discovering identity and understanding it—both in its "real" or "historical" core, and as a narrative construction.

A life story that is provided in an interview (or any other particular setting) is, however, but one instance of *the* life story, a hypothetical construct that, for two reasons, can never be fully accessed in research. This is so, first of all, because the life story develops and changes through time. When a particular story is recorded and transcribed, we get a "text" that is like a single, frozen, still photograph of the dynamically changing identity. We read the story as a text, and interpret it as a static product, as if it reflects *the* "inner," existing identity, which is, in fact, constantly in flux. Moreover, each procured story is affected by the context within which it is narrated: the aim of the interview (for example, getting a job or participating in a study), the nature of the "audience," and the relationship formed between teller and listener(s) (for example, Are they similar in cultural background, or of the same or different gender?), the mood of the narrator, and so forth. Hence the particular life story is one (or more) instance of the polyphonic versions of the possible constructions or presentations of people's selves and lives, which they use according to specific momentary influences.

Notwithstanding the debates about its factual grounding, informative value, or linkage to personal identity, the life story constructs and transmits individual and cultural meanings. People are meaning-generating organisms; they construct their identities and self-narratives from building blocks available in their common culture, above and beyond their individual experience. The constructivist approach, as advocated by K. Gergen (1991) and Van-Langenhove and Harre (1993), for example, claims that individuals construct their self-image within an interaction, according to a specific interpersonal context. We join these scholars in our belief that by studying and interpreting self-narratives, the researcher can access not only the individual identity and its systems of meaning but also the teller's culture and social world.

SOME BASIC FEATURES OF CONDUCTING NARRATIVE STUDIES

The use of narrative methodology results in unique and rich data that cannot be obtained from experiments, questionnaires, or observations. We refer the readers elsewhere for the issues of how to formulate a research question, build the research tools, and collect the data.[3] This advantage of the narrative study also generates its main quandaries, which stem from the quantities of accumulating material, on the one hand, and the interpretive nature of the work, on the other.

In spite of the fact that most narrative studies are conducted with smaller groups of individuals than the sample size employed in traditional research, the quantity of data gathered in life stories is large. A single case study may be based on several hours of an interview, and many more hours are required for listening to its record and transcribing it to a written text. There are often hundreds of pages of exact transcription of an interview. Even when researchers limit the breadth of their questions, or the time of the interview, or use written narratives, the quantity of material in such studies is always surprising. Moreover, no two interviews are alike, and the uniqueness of narratives is manifested in extremely rich data. The global structure or organization of the interview may aid the researcher in providing a preliminary order or orientation, yet narrative materials can be analyzed along myriad dimensions, such as contents; structure; style of speech; affective characteristics; motives, attitudes, and beliefs of the narrator; or her or his cognitive level. Furthermore, as mentioned above, the data are influenced by the interaction of the interviewer and the interviewee as well as other contextual factors. These dimensions and influences are often hard to detect in the first reading, and the meticulous work of sensitive reading or listening is required for gaining understanding pertinent to the research questions. Even after long experience in conducting narrative research, every new text retains the air of an enigma, a vivid mystery that generates a mixture of excitement, challenge, and apprehension. Another feature of narrative research concerns the place of hypotheses in the study. The investigator usually has a research question or general direction that leads to decisions regarding the selection of interviewees or tellers as well as the procedures for obtaining the story. However, in narrative studies, there are usually no a priori hypotheses. The specific directions of the study usually emerge from reading the collected material, and hypotheses then may be generated from it (Glaser & Strauss, 1967). Furthermore, the work that is carried out is interpretive, and an interpretation is always personal, partial, and dynamic. Therefore, narrative research is suitable for scholars who are, to a certain degree, comfortable with ambiguity. They should be able to reach interpretive conclusions—and change and rechange them, when necessary, with further readings.

Working with narrative material requires dialogical listening (Bakhtin, 1981) to three voices (at least): the voice of the narrator, as represented by the tape or the text; the theoretical framework, which provides the concepts and tools for interpretation; and a reflexive monitoring of the act of reading and interpretation, that is, self-awareness of the decision process of drawing conclusions from the material. In the process of such a study, the listener or reader of a life story enters an interactive process with the narrative and becomes sensitive to its narrator's voice and meanings. Hypotheses and theories are thus generated while reading and analyzing the narratives, and—in a circular motion as proposed by Glaser and Strauss's (1967) concept of "grounded theory"—can enrich further reading, which refines theoretical statements and so on in an ever growing circle of understanding. Thus the construction of an identity by an autobiographical story, and the process of theory building by empirical research, parallel each other.

In its most prevalent forms, narrative research does not require replicability of results as a criterion for its evaluation.[4] Thus readers need to rely more on the personal wisdom, skills, and integrity of the researcher. Yet interpretation does not mean absolute freedom for speculation and intuition. Rather, intuitive processes are recruited in the service of comprehension, which examines the basis for intuiting and should test it repeatedly against the narrative material. Interpretive decisions are not "wild," in other words, but require justification. While traditional research methods provide researchers with systematic inferential processes, usually based on statistics, narrative work requires self-awareness and self-discipline in the ongoing examination of text against interpretation, and vice versa. Needless to say, these attributes of narrative studies mean that they are highly time-consuming for the researcher.

HOW CAN ONE LEARN
TO DO NARRATIVE RESEARCH?

A balance of academic studies and experience is necessary for all learning. Narrative research, like psychotherapy, we believe, can be learned best via experience and supervision. Taking part in a research group that conducts narrative studies, or participating in a research seminar on the use of narratives, provides opportunities for gaining experience, interacting, consulting, and getting feedback from other researchers who work in the same area, with similar materials, and thus grapple with similar problems. In the United States, for example, Gilligan has collaborated with her colleagues and students in narrative work that emphasizes listening to various voices in the text, an ongoing project that has resulted in a manual for reading interview materials (Brown et al., 1988). In Europe, Rosenthal and Fisher-Rosenthal conduct training workshops for students and scholars in which they use local demonstrations to teach the use of autobiographical materials for studying individual identities. As part of the growth of interest in and wider application of narrative research, more university courses, training workshops, and other opportunities will be offered to provide hands-on experiential settings for learning.

Clearly, however, not everyone has access to direct learning experience of this kind, and this is our reason for offering this book. Our aim has dictated the book's content and character. This book does not deal with the entire process of narrative research. Its focus is the process of reading and analyzing a narrative—constructing tools for this task and applying them to the narrative. More than in most academic writings, we have tried to share with you our thoughts on the process of narrative processing, our considerations and doubts when selecting a method, and our own criticism of our interpretive work. For this purpose, two life-story interviews are presented almost verbatim (in Chapter 3), and many additional examples are provided, so that you may accompany the process and judge the inferences against the materials.

This book is the outcome of a continuous dialogue between the three authors.[5] As participants in such a "live" conversation, we gained a lot from the exchange of opinions, the examination of different ideas, and the comparison of viewpoints on the same texts. Dialogues, however, are not

confined to actual meetings between scholars but exist in the realm of books
and journals, authors and readers. We will share our experience with you,
hoping that this book will become a voice in the fruitful dialogue on
narrative research.

A MODEL FOR THE
CLASSIFICATION AND ORGANIZATION
OF TYPES OF NARRATIVE ANALYSIS

Upon looking at different possibilities for reading, interpreting, and
analyzing life stories and other narrative materials, two main independent
dimensions emerge—those of (a) *holistic versus categorical* approaches
and (b) *content versus form*. At the polar ends of each of the two, clear
differentiation can be made, but, as we will see throughout this book, many
possibilities for reading a text represent middle points along these dimensions.

The first dimension refers to the unit of analysis, whether an utterance
or section abstracted from a complete text or the narrative as a whole. This
distinction is somewhat similar to Allport's classic comparison between
"idiographic" and "nomothetic" types of research (1962) and very similar
to the distinction between "categorization" versus "contextualization" as
proposed by Maxwell (1996) and Maxwell and Miller (in press). In working from a categorical perspective, as in traditional content analysis, the
original story is dissected, and sections or single words belonging to a
defined category are collected from the entire story or from several texts
belonging to a number of narrators. In contrast, in the holistic approach,
the life story of a person is taken as a whole, and sections of the text are
interpreted in the context of other parts of the narrative. The categorical
approach may be adopted when the researcher is primarily interested in a
problem or a phenomenon shared by a group of people, while the holistic
approach is preferred when the person as a whole, that is, his or her
development to the current position, is what the study aims to explore.

The second dimension, that is, the distinction between the content and
form of a story, refers to the traditional dichotomy made in literary reading
of texts. Some readings concentrate on the explicit content of an account,
namely, what happened, or why, who participated in the event, and so on,
all from the standpoint of the teller. Another content-oriented approach
aims at getting to the implicit content by asking about the meaning that the
story, or a certain section of it, conveys, what traits or motives of the
individual are displayed, or what a certain image used by the narrator

symbolizes. On the other end of the spectrum, some readings ignore the content of the life story and refer to its form: the structure of the plot, the sequencing of events, its relation to the time axis, its complexity and coherence, the feelings evoked by the story, the style of the narrative, the choice of metaphors or words (passive versus active voices, for example), and so forth. While the content is often more obvious and immediate to grasp, researchers may prefer to explore the form of a life story because it seems to manifest deeper layers of the narrator's identity. In other words, as the formal aspects of a story are harder to influence or manipulate than its contents, form analysis may be advantageous for some purposes.

We may visualize these two dimensions as intersecting, resulting in a matrix of four cells, which consist of four modes of reading a narrative, as follows:

HOLISTIC-CONTENT   HOLISTIC-FORM
CATEGORICAL-CONTENT   CATEGORICAL-FORM

The holistic-content mode of reading uses the complete life story of an individual and focuses on the content presented by it. When using separate sections of the story, such as the opening or closing sentences of the narrative, the researcher analyzes the meaning of the part in light of content that emerges from the rest of the narrative or in the context of the story in its entirety. This kind of reading is familiar in clinical "case studies."

The holistic-form-based mode of analysis finds its clearest expression in looking at the plots or structure of complete life stories. Does the narrative develop as a comedy or tragedy, for example? Does a story ascend toward the present moment in the narrator's life or descend toward it from more positive periods and situations? The researcher may search for a climax or a turning point in the story, which sheds light on the entire development.

The categorical-content approach is more familiar as "content analysis." Categories of the studied topic are defined, and separate utterances of the text are extracted, classified, and gathered into these categories/groups. In this mode, quantitative treatment of the narrative is fairly common. Categories may be very narrow, for example, all sections in which narrators mentioned a certain political event that occurred in their lifetimes, or broader, when all sections referring to political events are withdrawn from the texts for analysis.

The categorical-form mode of analysis focuses on discrete stylistic or linguistic characteristics of defined units of the narrative. For example, what kind of metaphors is the narrator using, or how frequent are his passive versus active utterances? Defined instances of this nature are collected from a text or from several texts and counted, as in the categorical-content mode of reading.

Each of the four modes of analysis is related to certain types of research questions, requires different kinds of texts, and is more appropriate for certain sample sizes.

The reader should bear in mind that these fine distinctions are not always clear-cut in the reality of conducting narrative research and interpretation. Form is not always easily separated from the content of the story. In fact, the word *idea* in classical Greek refers to both content and form. Some may view the form of a story as an embodiment of its content, a more subtle manner for conveying a message, not too different from using symbols (whether consciously or unconsciously) in a story. Furthermore, we are aware that conclusions regarding separate categories as exemplified above, such as the narrator's use of a more passive voice for explaining her life events, may be highly significant for understanding an individual as a whole. Our classification refers, however, to the manner of reading in this categorical fashion, which concentrates on separate sections rather than the story as a whole. These fine distinctions will be clarified in the following chapters (Chapters 4-7), which will provide detailed examples of the various types of reading and analysis from our own research. A more complete discussion of the model, and its value and limitations, will be presented in the last chapter (Chapter 8) of the book.

DEMONSTRATION OF THE FOUR
TYPES OF READING FROM PREVIOUS WORKS

In the following section, we attempt to provide examples for the four cells of our model from previously conducted narrative studies. As the proposed model provides a new systematization of the area of narrative research, the authors of these studies have obviously had no exposure to it, and have not, on their own accord, tried to design their work along its dimensions. In looking for appropriate examples, we aimed to select research that might be considered as prototypical for each of the four cells. Most of the narrative studies, however, analyze the material from several perspectives, combining strategies of several cells—a topic to which we will return in our discussion in Chapter 8.

The Holistic-Content Reading

This type of reading takes into consideration the entire story and focuses on its content. Thus Lieblich (1993) presented the life story of Natasha, a young Jewish woman who had emigrated from Russia to Israel. In several conversations with the author, Natasha narrated the story of her life and adjustment to life in Israel. The analysis concentrates on one major theme: change, as manifested in many areas of Natasha's life—her external appearance and dress code, her language, her manners, her attitudes toward her family members and relationship with her parents, her friendships with girls and boys of her age group whether immigrants like herself or native Israelis, her occupational choices, and her views concerning gender and equality. Cultural changes due to immigration are superimposed on the issues of Natasha's adolescence to create a rich picture of a unique individual at a crossroad.

While Lieblich dedicated her study to a single case, Bateson (1989) relates the stories of five women, including herself, all of them American women with careers in the creative arts. Her book cannot be simply qualified as "research," nor is it her goal to draw systematic conclusions from the lives of her protagonists. Rather, this is a fascinating literary work that combines stories, conversations, and impressions on the part of the author to discover the similarities and dissimilarities in the lives of the women to whom she listened. The foci of the story are femininity, partnership, caretaking, self-actualization, commitment, and so forth. Bateson's major message is that women's lives are composed of fragmented areas and identities as well as an ongoing creative process of improvisation to put them together. Her book demonstrates that working from a holistic perspective need not be limited to a single case study.

This is also the nature of Josselson's (1987, 1996b) follow-up study of a group of women through the last 20 years. On the basis of a holistic-content perspective, and using Marcia's (1966) typology of "identity statuses" at the transition to adulthood, Josselson characterized her interviewees as being in the category of "Identity Achievement," "Foreclosure," "Moratorium," or "Diffusion." In consecutive interviews, during the following years, she traced the patterns of these women's lives to look at their various developmental trajectories. While clear-cut differences between life stories of the groups, as defined by their past identity status, were not easy to detect, this work can be taken as a demonstration of the holistic-content approach for the study of groups.

The Holistic-Form Reading

This type of reading also looks at the complete life story but focuses on its formal aspects rather than its contents. According to Gergen and Gergen (1988), every story, whether oral or written, can be formally characterized by the progression of its plot, which can be discerned by "plot analysis." Three basic patterns or graphs are progression, regression, and a steady line, while an individual story is usually a combination of all three. In one of their studies, individuals who belonged to two cohorts provided life stories, including indications of high and low points in their lives. Plot analysis was performed on these stories and the individual graphs were combined to generate an average graph for each cohort. The authors report that the stories of the older cohort can be characterized as having the form of an inverted U-curve, namely, an ascent, leading to a peak, followed by plateau, and a gradual decline. On the other hand, the young adults' stories have the form of a "romance," namely, a U-shape curve.

The perspective of holistic-form reading can be further demonstrated from works in narrative approaches to psychotherapy. White and Epston (1990) developed a method that uses a person's life story as an instrument for changing his or her psychological reality. In their book *Narrative Means to Therapeutic Ends,* they develop their theoretical outlook regarding narratives and their use in psychotherapy. The methods they offer for changing a person's (initially presented) life story refer mainly to its form rather than its specific content, for example, making the narrator a hero of his or her story instead of a victim of circumstances, or leading to the externalization of the problem as the narrator's "enemy."

Omer (1994) shares the belief that psychotherapy constitutes the joint creation (of client and therapist) of adequate life stories. He has proposed additional structural criteria to distinguish between "bad" and "good" life stories in this respect, referring, for example, to the existence of gaps or leaps in the initial story—"the patchy narrative"—versus the achievement of coherence, taking into account the chronological sequencing of life events, its beginning or end points, or whether it is a "closed" or an "open" story.

Categorical-Content Reading

This type of reading, traditionally called "content analysis," focuses on the content of narratives as manifested in separate parts of the story, irrespective of the context of the complete story. The study of Feldman,

Bruner, and Kalmar (1993) demonstrates the use of a narrow category, namely, specific words. The investigators presented subjects of three age groups with stories and asked them a series of interpretive questions about their contents (e.g., "What is the most important thing I've told you so far?"). The transcripts of the subject's answers were the data of this study. Some of their conclusions regarding interpretive patterns at three ages were based on a quantitative analysis in which the frequency of certain words was counted and compared across age groups.

While Feldman et al.'s research used counting of specific words, Schulman, Castellon, and Seligman (1989) referred to a broader category or unit, namely, "event-explanation units," in which narrators provide attributions to various events in their lives. Such units are analyzed according to three scales based on Seligman's model of attributional styles, namely, "internality," "stability," and "globality." This method leads to the detection of individual attribution styles based on rich and varied narrative materials such as quotations from political speeches, therapy transcripts, diaries, and personal letters.

McAdams, Hoffman, Mansfield, and Day's (1996) work demonstrates a categorical-content perspective that deals with a large number of broad categories. Beginning with Bakan's (1966) theory about the two basic modes of human identity—agency and communion—McAdams et al. (1996) develop various tools for the evaluation of these two broad dimensions. They define four content categories for communion—namely, love/friendship, dialogue, care/help, and community—and for agency—self-mastery, status, achievement/responsibility, and empowerment. In their article, McAdams et al. detail the procedure for finding and quantifying these categories in autobiographical texts.

Categorical-Form Reading

The last cell of the model refers to narrative reading, which looks at formal aspects of separate sections or categories of a life story. Farrell et al.'s study (1993) can be used to demonstrate this approach. Like Gergen and Gergen (1988), they also conducted plot analysis of his material but attended only to parts of the text, namely, the description of the transition to fatherhood in his narrators' life stories. Similarly to Gergen and Gergen (1988), Farrell et al.'s work distinguished among three prototypical graphs representing this transition.

Another study that belongs to the categorical-form type was conducted by Tetlock and Suedfeld (1988), who developed a method for the assessment of individuals' "integrative complexity" based on their form of argumentation, irrespective of its contents. Their measure is composed of two dimensions: "differentiation" (the number of dimensions of a problem that are taken into account in evaluating or interpreting events) and "integration" (the development of complex connections among differentiated characteristics). Tetlock and Suedfeld claim that this method can be used for a variety of verbal behaviors, procured from different sources, such as diplomatic communication, speeches, interviews, magazine editorials, and so on.

Linde (1993) also analyzes formal aspects of life stories, namely, the way in which coherence is built into a story. Linde performed an analysis of 13 interviews on choice of profession, examining different means for the creation of coherence, among which are temporal order, causality, and continuity. In this part of her work, Linde focused on the morphological and discourse levels of the texts rather than the stories in their entirety, and on the form rather than the contents.

Above and beyond the classification offered by our model, the various demonstrations from studies quoted in the last part of this chapter represent the wide range of subjects investigated in work done under the broad title of "narrative studies." Moreover, they also exemplify very different scholarly and methodological approaches, from the detailed quantitative research of Tetlock and Suedfeld (1988), through Omer's (1994) clinical approach, to Bateson's (1989) literary work.

ABOUT THE BOOK

In the following chapters, after the presentation of the narrative of our own research project, which provided the data for this book (Chapter 2), each one of the four modes of reading and interpreting a text will be fully demonstrated. Prior to this, however, the third chapter will present the life stories of two of our interviewees, a man and a woman, who participated in the research. Their narratives will be used in the following chapters for various demonstrations of our analyses. They are presented in full so that readers may compare our interpretations against the text and actively try analyzing the stories on their own.

Chapters 4-7 will then provide readings, interpretations, and analyses of our narrative data from the four points of view included in our model. Each of the chapters consists of two demonstrations of the same model's cells. Although they represent the same mode of reading in our typology, they differ in its application, namely, in the actual research tool that is described. Each of our examples is accompanied by sharing with the reader some of the process of the researchers' work, including various considerations, doubts, and self-criticism that were part of the individual route taken by each of the authors as well as the ongoing dialogue among us. Some of the analyses that will be presented were indeed part of the processing of the research results (as reported to the funding agencies) and will be reported in full, while others are specifically offered for the demonstration of our model in additional applications and will be briefly presented, without empirical conclusions. In the light of these, the final chapter of the book will go back to some of the theoretical issues relevant to narrative research and discuss the model, the options it opens for narrative inquiry, and its limitations.

This book is the joint product of the three authors, an outcome of long cooperation in the study and many conversations. However, throughout these processes, we managed to maintain independent perspectives, as manifested in the chapters of this book. While the general approach for the book grew out of our joint work, each one of us developed her own tools for reading and analysis. The second section of Chapter 5 is the only example of analysis developed and conducted by the three of us together. Tamar Zilber focused on categorical-form analysis. Within this mode, she developed an instrument for the evaluation of cognitive functioning in a narrative and suggested means for the detection of emotional expressions in a text. Rivka Tuval-Mashiach became immersed in plot structure analysis of the story as a whole. She also developed a content analysis for understanding the family dynamics of our interviewees. Michal Nachmias, a senior research assistant of our team, contributed her own section about early memories and their place in a holistic-content reading. Finally, Amia Lieblich wrote the two case studies of the narratives presented in Chapter 3 as a demonstration of the holistic-content cell and developed the content analysis of high school memories in our participants' life stories. These chapters, and the analyses presented in them, were written independently by each of the authors and provide a variety of readings and perspectives on the same narrative material. You, the reader, are thus invited to compare and integrate these various pieces, together with your own attempts to develop your skill throughout the book, into the rich collage that resulted from our group's work.

NOTES

1. The *Journal of Narrative and Life History* has been in publication as a quarterly since 1991 (by Lawrence Erlbaum). The series the *Narrative Study of Lives* has been published yearly since 1993. See Josselson and Lieblich (1993, 1995), Lieblich and Josselson (1994), Josselson (1996a), Lieblich and Josselson (1997).

2. The issues of the relationships between life, life story, and identity, as well as text and interpretation, are highly complex and cannot be adequately represented here. For further reading, see McAdams (1990), Rosenwald and Ochberg (1992), Widdershoven (1993), Alasuutari (1997).

3. For planning narrative studies, please refer to Glaser and Strauss (1967), Yin (1984), Denzin and Lincoln (1994), and Maxwell (1996). For reading about various approaches to interviewing in the context of narrative research, please refer to Denzin (1978), Spradley (1979), Kuale (1983), Mishler (1986a), McCracken (1988), LaRossa (1989), and Chambon (1995). On the subject of transcribing and editing interview materials, see Mishler (1986b) and Blauner (1987). A comprehensive review on interviewing with many additional references is Fontana and Frey (1994).

4. The topic of criteria for narrative study and analysis, and their rationale, will be dealt with in Chapter 8.

5. Conversation among investigators of a certain area has also recently become a form for writing about research. Please refer to *Conversation as Method* (Josselson, Lieblich, Sharabany, & Wiseman, 1997).

2

The Narrative of
Our Own Research

The various procedures for reading, analyzing, and interpreting narrative material will be demonstrated in this book through life stories collected in the framework of a large applied research project conducted in Israel from 1992 to 1995. As we previously have argued that life stories are always context related, the purpose of this chapter is to provide a brief review of the study, its aims, sample, and procedure, as background for the narrative materials and analyses that will be consequently presented. Our aim, in other words, is not to engage in comprehensive description of the study, its theoretical background, and its results (as was done in a technical academic report submitted to the foundations that supported it; Lieblich, Tuval, & Zilber, 1995) but to highlight these aspects that are relevant in terms of the purpose of this book.

BACKGROUND

A massive immigration of Jews from many countries, many from developing countries, marked the first years after the establishment of Israel as an independent state in 1948. One of the unique approaches developed for coping with the cultural-educational gap created by this immigration was Carl Frankenstein's (1970a, 1970b) theory of "rehabilitative teaching."[1] In concrete terms, the problem of the "underprivileged" became apparent through significant differences in school achievement and academic motivation and in a variety of what were then considered inappropriate behavior patterns. These characterized children of families of low SES and educational levels (often illiterate), most of whom had immigrated from Middle Eastern and North African countries.

Teachers, administrators, and scholars, influenced by educational experiences in other parts of the world, proposed various analyses and remedies for the educational gap in the school system (see, for example, Amir, Sharan, & Ben Ari, 1984; Eshel & Klein, 1995; Klein & Eshel, 1980). Integration was the policy most frequently adopted by Israeli public school institutions to provide equal opportunities for all students. Frankenstein, a prominent authority in education, however, proposed an original and controversial pedagogical program that, in practice, led to the segregation of the underprivileged students into separate classrooms. According to his theoretical conceptualization, the educational gap was a syndrome of "secondary retardation" caused by the poor home environments of immigrant, low-SES, families. To repair students' "damaged intelligence," according to Frankenstein, "rehabilitative teaching" was required. Consequently, he developed a comprehensive teaching method for all academic subjects, which was to be applied in separate classes teaching 12- to 18-year-olds of the target population.[2] As practiced, students of the program were gathered from different city zones, separated from the regular high school classes, and given extra help and care from teachers specifically trained to guide the students toward gradual recovery of their intellectual functioning. Academically, rehabilitative teaching may have seemed potentially beneficial for the underprivileged student; however, its substantial personal price, in terms of the student's social stigmatization and isolation from "normal" youngsters, was undeniable. The original plan was, in fact, to integrate all underprivileged students back into regular classrooms after two years of separate studies. But, due to many unforeseen difficulties, this plan did not materialize either in the early implementation of the program or in later years. It should perhaps be added that Frankenstein developed his theory and method in the 1950s and 1960s within a social-intellectual climate that greatly differed from our contemporary one and under the pressure of a vast number of immigrant students that the Israeli school system had to absorb.

Without further evaluation of the method and its theoretical basis, which do not directly concern us in this book, suffice it to say that due to its apparent contradiction of the "melting pot" ideology, Frankenstein's program was never widely implemented. One exception, however, has been its use since 1966 at one of the best high schools in Israel, to which we will refer hereafter as Elite High School. The first two classes of this project were viewed as an educational experiment and accompanied by evaluation research (Frankenstein, 1970a), which generally indicated notable academic success. The social and personal aspects of studying in separate classrooms for the entire high school period, however, were not directly evaluated in the original study. Following this experiment, and up to the present, Elite High School has implemented the project of rehabilitative teaching in one or two classes of specially selected students every year—a policy that is often a topic of public debate and criticism.

THE GENERAL APPROACH TO
OUR STUDY AND ITS SAMPLE

In the course of repeated attempts to justify this controversial policy, in 1991 Elite High School officials approached Amia Lieblich with the general idea of conducting a follow-up study of its rehabilitative program graduates. Rivka Tuval-Mashiach was invited by Lieblich to help in designing and carrying out the proposed study.

After studying the relevant literature, and repeated meetings with teachers and other school officials, we decided to employ a qualitative approach for the study (Greene, 1994), which could tap into the more unique and profound positive as well as negative effects of participation in the rehabilitative teaching program. We planned, however, to include in the study demographic measures of current life attainment as well as a few objective tests for relevant personality traits and values.[3] In light of Frankenstein's (1970a) assertion that the process of change allegedly produced by this educational intervention is long-lasting and may even appear only later in life, we decided to approach adults in two cohorts—graduates of the class of 1970 (the first "experimental" class) and of 1982. At the time the interviews were performed (1992-1993), the average age of our participants was either 41-42, about 22 years after high school graduation—a group we termed *midlife*—or 28-29, about 10 years after their graduation—namely, *young adults*.

To broaden the scope of the study and allow for some comparisons, same-age individuals originating from similar backgrounds who had graduated from other schools in the same city were also investigated. The original request of the school was to locate a "control group"—underprivileged pupils of similar developmental potential who had studied in integrative classrooms (as opposed to under the segregated policy of Elite High School)—and to evaluate the program by a series of comparisons between the two graduate groups. The idea of "control groups," however, is foreign to the model of narrative research as presented in the former chapter,[4] and we refrain from using this concept here. Moreover, in practice it is impossible to assess precisely how similar or different were youngsters of the selected cohorts in terms of their educational potential before they entered their respective high schools.

Using lists of graduates of two integrative high schools in one city, as well as Elite High School, candidates for the study were identified. The actual location of graduates of the selected classes for the research was extremely problematic due to the mobility of the population and changing family names, especially among married women. Upon location, the initial telephone contact was aimed at obtaining agreement to participate in what was presented as "a study about life stories of individuals in your age group, for the purpose of writing a book." This very general goal was presented to avoid putting initial emphasis on high school experiences and to receive a spontaneous picture of this period as part of a comprehensive self-narrative instead. In this telephone conversation, the candidates were told that two meetings, of about one-and-a-half hours each, would be conducted at their convenience. Those who raised the issue of confidentiality were assured, even at this early stage (as well as later when the meetings took place), that their story, if included in a future book, would first be given to them to review, comment on, and correct and that they would have the right to decide not to be quoted. When this matter did not come up at this stage, it was usually brought up by the interviewer toward the end of the meetings.[5] In general, only about 40% of the individuals approached via telephone agreed to be interviewed for the research. The remaining 60% refused, usually because of lack of interest or time.

A total of 74 individuals participated in the study and were divided into four research groups—two cohorts, as defined above, from two different high school settings, which will be descriptively termed *segregative* versus *integrative* settings. Their distribution into research groups by age, high school settings (and gender) was as follows:

Midlife, segregated—19 (7 females, 12 males)

Midlife, integrated—17 (7 females, 10 males)

Young adult, segregated—18 (10 females, 8 males)

Young adult, integrated—20 (10 females, 10 males)

THE LIFE STORY INTERVIEW

The research procedure will be described only as relevant to the purpose of this book, concentrating on the life story interview.

Each interviewee was scheduled for a first meeting with one of five trained female interviewers (the three authors of this book and two volunteers[6]), preferably in the interviewee's home. A minority of the interviewees asked to conduct the meeting at their workplace, claiming that they would have more quiet and privacy there than at home. In most cases, the life-story interview took up one meeting, and a second (or, rarely, a third) was scheduled for its completion. When the complete life story was obtained, several questionnaires were administered (see Note 3). One interviewer took responsibility for all telephone contacts and interviews with a particular interviewee. All conversations were tape-recorded. Notes about the setting as well as various other impressions on the part of the interviewer were recorded as well.

Given the large number of participants included in the study, our chosen method for procuring a life story presents a compromise between the wish to obtain free and rich self-narratives, on the one hand, and the need to limit allocated time and the amount of material per person, on the other. As will be demonstrated in the following chapters, this kind of interview facilitated some kinds of analyses while limiting others. Similar procedures for life-story interviews have been reported by Scarf (1981) and McAdams (1985, 1993).

In opening the interview, the interviewer introduced the task of "stage outline" as follows:

> Every person's life can be written as a book. I would like you to think about your life now as if you were writing a book. First, think about the chapters of this book. I have here a page to help you in this task. Write down the years on the first column—from zero, from the day you were born. When did the first stage end? Write it here. Then go on to the next chapters, and put down the age that each one begins and ends for you. Go on till you reach your present age. You can use any number of chapters or stages that you find suitable to your own life.

The one-page form that was handed to the interviewer included two columns—the left for the delineation of the stages by age, and the right for providing headings for each one. The directions for the second task were given when the chapters were all recorded, as follows: "Now, please, think about the title you would give each one of these chapters, and write it in the next column."

When the interviewee had completed the stage outline, the interviewer placed it where it would be visible to both of them and said, "I will be asking you several questions about each one of the stages you proposed." Our instructions led the narrators to focus on four questions/directions for each stage:

1. "Tell me about a significant episode or a memory that you remember from this stage."
2. "What kind of a person were you during this stage?"
3. "Who were significant people for you during this stage, and why?"
4. "What is your reason for choosing to terminate this stage when you did?"

While these were the precise instructions, the majority of the interviewees provided, in addition, a general descriptive report concerning each one of their life stages. For many, the narrative flowed through the various perspectives listed above, and for others, without specific directions from the interviewer. The interviewers added probes and questions to achieve more clarity in the stories or to encourage the narrator to continue.

When the entire stage outline was thus worked through, three final topics were introduced: (a) Additional elaboration regarding high school memories was procured from those interviewees who did not talk much about this stage. This request followed the divulgence of the specific goal of the study, namely, our original interest in following up the graduates of various high schools in the city. (b) Future life expectations of the participant were explored. (c) For those who were parents (all the midlife interviewees and about half of the young adults), a question was introduced regarding their future expectations from their children.

The interviewers were trained in this procedure and were instructed not to be too mechanical and formal in their attitude but to be open and flexible toward the teller's line of narrative so that an authentic life story would be obtained. As a result of this orientation, coupled with the normal individual differences among the interviewers as well as the narrators, and the type of interactions that emerged in each dyad during the conversations, protocols of the interviews varied a great deal from each other. Some were monological and provided an almost undisturbed narrative. Others were more dialogical and consisted of many question-answer transitions.[7] Some interviewers were very precise in pursuing the four topics for each chapter, while others let themselves be carried away by the teller's stories. Such variations are to be expected whenever strict formality is limited for the sake of authenticity.

TAKING CARE OF THE FINDINGS:
COLLABORATION WITHIN THE TEAM

As more people were contacted and interviewed, we augmented the process of data collection in two major ways. On the technical level, each interview was submitted to complete transcription. With the aid of a Dictaphone and a word processor, several assistants typed verbatim records of the conversations. Unintelligible sections were returned to the interviewers for their assistance. We instructed the transcribers to record everything they had heard, including repetitions, nonwords, incomplete utterances, pauses, and affective expressions (laughs, sighs, weeping, and so on). An important part of the selection and training of transcribers was to assure that they understood the personal nature of the interviews and would abstain from talking about their contents. To guarantee accuracy, a comparison of the typed transcripts with the recorded conversations was undertaken for selected parts of the interviews. The total number of typed pages of the 74 interviews is more than 4,500 pages.

While this monumental job was carried out, ongoing weekly group meetings of the interviewers were taking place. This is where concerns were shared, questions were raised, feedback was given to the newcomers by the veterans, and the first seeds of the analysis and interpretation process were planted. These meetings were particularly important for interviewers who were in between sessions with their interviewees and who, by talking about their recent experience, gained perspective for subsequent meetings. An issue that was often raised, for example, dealt with interviewees who were extremely inhibited or laconic, or (more often) with those who could not restrain their discourse to the required framework. The give-and-take of these weekly meetings was enormously meaningful for sustaining our interest in the project, improving our interviewing skills, and encouraging and enriching us all. The convergence or divergence of our viewpoints— women from a variety of ages, life experiences, research expertise, and backgrounds (clinical psychology, social psychology, developmental psychology, and education)—produced the fertile ground necessary for this kind of research. It seems to us that doing this kind of study single-handed would have been very hard, if not impossible.

These discussions, and the processing of the data accumulated, resulted in our research report (Lieblich, Tuval, & Zilber, 1995) in which an attempt was made to evaluate the positive and negative long-term effects of the two kinds of school settings on our participants. This report, in its turn, resulted in a dialogue with Elite High School officials regarding the future of the program of rehabilitative teaching. Although we will not enlarge on these issues here, some of their repercussions can be discerned in the following chapters. Experiencing, as we did, the wealth of the narrative material we had gathered, on the one hand, and the scarcity of work that may provide directions in reading and analyzing it, on the other hand, we decided to embark upon the current project, namely, this methodological book.

NOTES

1. Most of Frankenstein's work, as well as that of his followers, has not been translated into English. The main publications in Hebrew are Frankenstein (1970b, 1972, 1981). Additional presentations of Frankenstein's method were published by Eiger (1975) and Eiger and Amir (1987).

2. It is interesting to note that although most of the proposed interventions or enrichment programs for the underprivileged are usually aimed at very young children (see, for example, reports about Head Start; Zigler & Valentine, 1979; Barnett, 1993, also referred to most recently in Bruner, 1996), Frankenstein's rehabilitative teaching program was targeted at junior high and high school students.

3. The variables tested by objective tests were self-esteem (Spence, Helmreich, & Stapp, 1975), hardiness (Kobasa, 1982), locus of control (Rotter, 1966), and value system (Schwartz & Bilsky, 1987). The use of these tests for the analysis of data was limited because of the small sample size, and the results concerning these tests will not be reported here.

4. For additional reading about the topic, see Runyan (1984) and Crabtree and Miller (1982).

5. The issue of ethical considerations regarding narrative research is beyond the scope of the current volume. See Josselson (1996a).

6. Please see Note 3 above.

7. Such variance in the nature of conversations produced in the interviews should be taken into account in some of the analyses—see, for example, analyses of cognitive functioning in Chapter 7.

3

Demonstrative
Life Stories

This chapter presents two life stories from our midlife group that were obtained in the study. These stories will be used in following chapters to demonstrate various kinds of reading and analysis. All names used in this chapter, as well as in the entire book, were changed to protect the narrators' privacy.[1]

SARA

Sara is 42 years old. She was interviewed by Amia Lieblich.

The interview, in two sessions, took place in Sara's house in the suburbs with her young children coming and going around her as we talked.

The following life story is based on the recorded transcription of the conversations in three parts:

Part A: An accurate and complete transcription of Sara's and the interviewer's speech, including all verbal utterances.

Part B: An almost-verbatim transcription of Sara's speech. Unfinished sentences and repetitions are omitted from the text.

Parts A and B together present the first session of the interview. Because Sara (a teacher by profession) is very clear in her speech, the difference between the style in parts A and B is not very noticeable, as it might be for other interviewees.

Part C: An edited and slightly abbreviated version of Sara's speech in the second session of the interview.

The choice of a complete or an edited transcription is directed by the intended uses of the text, by consideration of the reader (a full and redundant text is harder to read), as well as by practical matters such as space limitations. When a formal linguistic analysis is undertaken, all speech utterances are important (see, for example, Rosenthal, 1993). When the text is used to understand broader features—such as the order of life events, psychological motivations, major themes in the life story—an edited version is more useful.

Several symbols appear in the text below (as well as in David's life story, below) as follows:

- Brackets [-] signify the addition of a missing word or phrase by the author.
- Parentheses (-) signify the addition of a descriptive or explanatory word or phrase by the author.
- Three periods— . . . —signify a pause in the flow of speech.
- Three periods in brackets [. . .] signify the omission of a sentence, several sentences, or a paragraph from the text. This was done for abbreviation purposes, usually when the omitted part substantially repeated a former one.
- Quotation marks signifies dialogue reported by the narrator. Often, this has been inferred from the context.
- New paragraphs in part C signify stops of the flow of conversation or change of subject as inferred by us.

Sara's stage outline was as follows:

Stage 1: From birth to 6, titled Childhood
Stage 2: 6-12/13   Elementary school
Stage 3: 13-18   High school
Stage 4: 18-20   Army[2]
Stage 5: 20-30   The work of teaching as a single woman
Stage 6: 30-40   Building a family

Part A

I: So, will you please say few words about the first stage, something about your home, your parents, and so on.
S: Well, uh . . . I will give you the general background. Uh . . . My father is from Iran and my mother from Turkey, and we are a family of four kids, so that I'm the firstborn, my sister is two years younger than me, then . . . uh, my brother is seven years [younger], and then, later, when I was already at high school, my sister, the child of their old age, was born, who is 26 today, but

she was the child of their old age then. A very normal childhood, home, uh
. . .

I: Where did you live?

S: We lived in C (name of city) in BG (name of neighborhood), uh . . . nursery
school, the usual—we stayed at home till the age of 4, with mom, with mom
spoiling, and then pre-kindergarten, as it was called then, and kindergarten
for 2 years, which were nursery schools uh. . . . I have very good memories
from kindergarten, I even really remember the names of my teachers,
because I enjoyed myself so much there, had really great fun. My mom,
didn't then—that's actually never—work. Later on she used to take care of
children but that was already—and in our home, when we were older. So
that I always used to come back to a home full of joy, with a cooked meal
and mom who's home, who's there for us, welcomes us, uh . . . That's it. I
remember that she always cooked such very good food, that it was a joy to
eat. Father always worked hard.

I: What did he do?

S: He was, at this age he was still a policeman, part of this age, and later—an
accountant-policeman, an accountant, and still later—he continued to work
as an accountant but in other workplaces. But often he had to take two jobs,
and [work] late into the evenings, so that we would be provided for
hon-honorably. This is more or less what I remember, so, actually.

I: Can you recall a specific episode perhaps, something that stands out?

S: Something very, that is a thing, an experience, an experience in quotation
marks, which was very unpleasant. That . . . I think I was then really in
kindergarten still, yes, when a sister was born to us, and I don't remember,
she was a year old, or about, she passed away. I don't remember the period
when she passed away, but I remember the shiva,[3] which remained a very
unpleasant memory for me, what I remember is that . . . the commotion, it
was a small house in an immigrants' housing project, before we moved to
another flat, and I remember the experience, the so-called "experience,"
again I'm saying, a house full of people—

I: Was she already 1 year old?

S: She was about a year old when she passed away, I think 10 months or a year,
the girl. As much as I remember from my mother, she passed away of some
disease actually, a children's disease which probably developed into something more that it, so—it's not really clear what, hepatitis if I'm not
mistaken, if I remember correctly. So [I recall] the commotion of lots of
people lying on the floor, coming and going, and I'm pretty much lost
within all this and I go out to play in the neighborhood, and then I even
didn't understand what had happened, and then one of the older girls of the
neighborhood then said to me: "Do you know why your home was full of
people, because your sister died." And this was such a shock to me, and
then really only uh . . . I asked more questions. So this experience really
stands out for me.

I: But this wasn't the girl born right after you, this was really the third sister—

S: (together with I's question) This was after the sister, she was the third, yes.

I: Yes.

S: She was the third girl, uh . . . That's it. So this was sort of a very traumatic experience. That's it. Then, towards first grade exactly we moved to a new apartment, really, I was, I think, the beginning of first grade, we moved, and this was uh . . . a very pleasant experience. I clearly remember how the truck came and loaded our stuff, and they came for me from school—I studied also at (name of neighborhood, name of school) and they came in the middle of my school day to say—here, that's it, we are moving. I still remember my sister, the nursery school was really uh . . . touching the house, so she was still because she is two years younger, she was 4 then. She was still there till the very last moment of the . . . loading of the stuff, and then, later on, we found out in retrospect that she'd been very alarmed, she saw the whole house being packed, and thought that she would be left behind in kindergarten, and that we wouldn't take her with us (laughing). So that's it. And then we moved to a new apartment, and there was also this experience of children from my class who suddenly saw me in the new neighborhood: What are you doing here? You don't belong here. And then I had to explain that I'd moved—and I remember this as if it happened yesterday.

I: So you stayed in the same school, you didn't have . . . ?

S: I stayed in . . . During this stage I still stayed in the same school.

I: Just one last question about this stage, because we are moving into the next one—

S: Yes, the next one.

I: Who are the people you remember around you? The significant figures, uh. from the age of zero to 6, as you did in the first stage?

S: That's it, I don't know if they belong only to this stage, or also to the next one—the people to whom I was deeply attached were really my grandpa and grandma on my mother's side.

I: Did they live close to you?

S: They did not live near us, they lived, they lived in MD (another neighborhood), but the relationship was very close, and . . . And I remember us going there all the time, that's we used to go there a lot, taking the bus with not much uh . . . great joy—we were not spoiled then. Really a joy. And they also used to come to us a lot, that's both during this stage and later, when I was in elementary school already, so it was really a very close contact with them.

I: Why was it so joyful with them?

S: (Silence) I don't know, I, also, perhaps because I am the firstborn, all the time I was the daughter that's . . . spoiled, in quotation (laughing) that is I was a daughter of the home,[4] and a daughter that's very uh . . . I received a lot of attention, a lot of love. Something more, I think also that even at this age there was also an aunt, who was at the time single, so many times she really even ordered a taxi, Oh God, now I recall, bless her memory, she already passed away several years ago, three years, so since she was single, she was my dad's sister, she used to take me to her place for Friday and Saturday. On the way there she stopped, we stopped at the center, and she always used to buy me a book or some toy. I even remember that I had a tricycle then, I liked it so much that she was willing with the taxi to load the tricycle, to take me—everything to give me fun, and to give her, really, fun so that I would be with her and she would not be alone. That's it, I know . . .

I: So if you had to characterize yourself at this first age, you would describe yourself as a child, a preferred child?

S: I think that, I think yes, at every age, really at every age.

I: Yes.

S: In Spanish[5] we say *Bechorika*—the beloved firstborn girl that . . . I also was, I think that I knew how to return this love. I was deeply attached to the family, a family was for me the . . . to this very day I think, this is what seems to me the most important, all other things pale in comparison.

I: Yes, but anyway at every stage I will ask you how you saw yourself perhaps it does change. But I'm simply curious, when you say firstborn—is it also related to gender? If the baby is male, a boy?

S: No, not at all, because at the time—

I: No, with you it isn't.

S: No, because at that time, my father, for example, he also today—My mom told me at the time that my dad was thinking all the time, he was sure that a boy would be born to him, so, for example, when he bought the first clothes, he bought a buttoned shirt for a boy and such, and so it really wasn't relevant I'm the daughter the . . .

I: Yes.

S: God forbid, this does not mean that they did not relate to everyone—each one of the kids had his special place. But really, because I am the firstborn I think that I always am related to . . . all in all there was something of a relation, uh . . . somewhere yes, preference towards me, I really cannot even name it, but really I got the best treatment of all.

I: Fine, so this stage is to the age of 6, because you moved home or because you went to school?

S: No, because we entered, we moved then, this I'm telling you [happened] exactly in first grade, we moved and also elementary school, in which I remember, first of all, really, very favorably the teacher from the first and second grades. I remember her name. I remember the plays in which I acted, even the parts I had to say, since she always included me among the actors. She also uh . . . She, at the time, that is, she saw my parents, how they came to the new neighborhood. My mother had been very young when she married, a woman, to this day—she is a very pretty woman, but at that time

she was really a beauty and she stood out on the background of the . . . My
father who's dark, he's from Iran, and she is light with blue eyes, a blond,
she had long hair, a youngster, so uh . . . At the time even Mom said that
she saw her [and asked] "what are you doing here in the neighborhood?"
In other words, the contact was made directly even before I became her
student, even when she just arrived in the neighborhood. And later I became
her student,[6] and really it was always something very uh . . . I still remember a trip I took with her to the zoo, and how she assigned a boy from the
class to be my permanent partner, or the plays I participated in. I remember,
for example—I never made spelling mistakes but then, in first grade—Dad
was still a policeman—and I remember this special dictation exercise in
which I spelled the word policeman wrong! "And how did this happen, and
you go and make an error in 'policeman'?! Your father is a policeman and
you misspell the word policeman?" That was it, I still remember those
words. I always helped her decorate the classroom, I helped her in the class.
First and second grades were really an experience, really. Third and fourth
grades were very regular, that is there were teachers that I also uh . . .
remember them and I went to visit them because one of them had a baby
and we had good relationships. And then in fourth, fourth or fifth grade
they built a new school already next to our home. I then had a problem that
I had to transfer to the new school, and my parents, and I had good friends
and I liked my class and I didn't want to move so much. And I remember
that my parents fought for me and they succeeded, and we received a letter
that I don't have to move to another school, and it was great, so, to stay
with my class, with my friends, etc. However, right after it was clear that
I could stay, another letter arrived: "No, you have to be transferred anyway,
according to the zoning law, there is nothing to be done." But at that time
quite a number of children moved, from the neighborhood and the class,
and today, if I look back on it, I am very happy that I transferred, because
social life in my first school, today when I look on it, or at later time when
I looked, became rather snobbish, and today when I think how it turned to
be, and how (in the new school) I discovered the youth movement, in which
I was very active, and later became a counselor, and at a later stage went
to the army with the youth movement *gar-in*[7]—I don't regret this move for
a moment, in other words, that I changed society and school.

Part B

[. . .]
The new school was real close to our house, so in class, also, I was very active.
    I don't think I was outstanding as a student, I wasn't brilliant, but I liked
    to work and study. In fifth grade I joined the youth movement, and I really
    became very active there. [. . .] I didn't miss single meeting. When we
    had meetings on Friday night, and since my parents were not religious,

traditional,[8] I would participate in the Shabbat prayer, and then go to the meetings of the youth movement. There were different projects that I volunteered for, even in elementary school—like painting the place. About field trips—although I was the firstborn, and a daughter of the home, I was never restricted. I remember every trip. The first one was when I was in fifth grade, and my sister in third grade—she was not a member of the movement yet. We went for three days in the mountains, sleeping in sleeping bags outdoors, and I took my sister along; they were very glad to let us go. On Saturdays we used to go on hikes, they let me go, they didn't restrict me. Look, conditions are different today. Today I would not allow my son to go on a daylong backpack hike alone with his friends. We used to get organized with the youth leader to go pick wild fruits, have a field day, build tents—we were really independent. As much as I was a girl of the home, I was very independent. There is always this contradiction—a daughter of the home, and at the same time very autonomous and very active in the movement.

I: What do you mean by calling yourself a daughter of the home?

S: Very attached to the home. For example, during the summer vacation I was very active, I would go out on field trips, and do different projects, like selling old newspapers to fish stores, to make money I-don't-remember-for-what purpose. But I always got up early and helped my mom at home first. My mom married very young, when she was 16 or 17, and she gave birth to me when she was 18. So our home was very . . . lots of friends would come and when we played she joined us. And my father used to make a Sukkah,[9] so all the children from the neighborhood would come with colored paper to help us decorate it, we were all together, it was a feeling of togetherness. In other words, I was extremely attached to my home, yet also socially very active. When I was in seventh or eighth grade I became a counselor, that is a youth leader—my experiences from the youth movement could make a story in themselves, with all the trips and the work camps.

I: But this was probably during high school.

S: Yes, but starting in eighth grade. Today I ask myself how I did this. I was a youth leader of children two years younger than me, and I would go to their parents to persuade them to let them go on a trip. How did I take this responsibility to go with the older counselor from house to house, convincing the parents to send their kids with us on a trip. Today, as an eighth grader, I would never dare take on such responsibility.

I: And who were the people that were significant for you at this stage?

S: Beside my parents, the male and female counselors.

I: Were they the same people for some time?

S: No, they changed often. But with one of them I used to correspond until I went to the army. She was from a kibbutz, and we maintained our relationship, she sent me letters and I to her, she sent me her picture and I did mine, and then she used to visit. With a male counselor I also maintained a long relationship. In other words, if I gave myself to the youth movement, I did it with my whole heart, and I still remember them. At the end they got married, these two, and we remained friends. And of course grandma and grandpa—it all continued. I visited them, and they knew that I liked certain kinds of sweets or foods, so they always kept them for me in their kitchen closets. I remember their house—it was an old Arab building with huge rooms, and this iron key that was once in use. The kitchen was outdoors, yes, I remember the courtyard, sitting and chatting there, or sitting there with my grandma and the grinder, helping her to grind almonds. My grandfather used to wait for us in the bus station to help mom, everything so that we would come and visit.

I: When did they immigrate, was your mother born in Israel?

S: No, she was born in Turkey.

[. . .]

My mother was the youngest daughter, and closest to her parents. I don't think her sisters were as close to them. My mother was very loved by her parents. And my father didn't have parents, I mean his father died abroad, before they immigrated, and his mother a little later, I don't remember exactly when. So he used to call my grandpa and grandma, father and mother, and they called him our son. They gave him a feeling that he was their son, and that is how he treated them. When they died, it was him who arranged everything for their funeral, and he always marks the anniversaries of their deaths. Later on, when I was in ninth grade, and it was the the Six Day War,[10] it was grandpa who took care of us. He brought us rice and potatoes so that we would have food at home. He also loved films, so we went together to the movies. Since he couldn't read Hebrew, he used to say: Come here, teach me to read and write. We used to sit together.

I: But what language did you speak?

S: Hebrew, with a little Spanish. Grandpa spoke Hebrew better than grandma. They spoke to me also in Spanish, and I answered them in Hebrew, which they understood. It was a really close relationship. Grandma became very heavy later, when I was at high school, and it was hard for her to move around. So I was the one always ready to run to the bus station to wait for her, to hold her hand, and to assist her in climbing up the steps. I was always willing to help, and at the same time they always gave me something—a sweet, a good word or a good feeling.

I: That's nice.

S: When my sister was in high school, she was more stubborn than me, and less willing to obey. She had many confrontations with our parents. So who would she run to when she was mad at our parents? To grandpa and grandma. And where did she go to cry? To grandpa and grandma. It was this kind of a relationship that she could go to grandma and complain about mom. And I remember when my brother was born, who went shopping for the bed cover and the blanket and all the pretty things—it was grandpa. He did not work then, he was retired and lived on a tiny pension from the post office, but who bought me my first bicycle? He did. So there was a feeling of a great relationship.

I: Okay, so you say this stage is up to the age of 12 or 13—

S: Yes, we finished elementary school, and had to select a high school. At that time it was decided to start an experimental class at the Elite High School, a program designed by Prof. Frankenstein—I was in the first class of this program. They took a group from various schools and had to select students for the program. We took so many tests, as if we were going to college at the very least. They started from hundreds of children and picked out our class. In later years they used a different procedure—they accepted whole classes to the program from certain elementary schools. In the first class we were really a great group. I can see today how every one of us made something of themselves. At that time, they called children of this class "underprivileged"—I don't know if my parents belong to this category, maybe since my father never studied. You know, the definition of under-privileged was based on the education of the parents, and the second criterion was origin of the parents, I think. Today I don't agree to this at all, because my father was always terrific in mathematical calculations, and he had a fantastic memory for facts and figures. I could ask him anything and he answered me right away. My mom—not, her education was elemen-tary. She could read Hebrew, but had many spelling mistakes in her writing. She loved to read, she could read for hours. Anyway, their definition was to select students with potential from underprivileged families—that's what they called it—to see how far we could get. So four children from my class went to the tests, two boys and two girls, and the girls were chosen. That's it. So my transition to high school was something of a jump.

I: How was this period for you?

S: Again, my high school was really good for me. First of all our class was very cohesive because, how can I put this, we formed a class within the best high school in town, and in the beginning, they used to peep at us, especially during the first year, as if we were monkeys in a zoo. They wanted to see who were these new kids who had arrived. Later I found out that there were children who always felt disturbed by this, as if they were odd, but I did not look at it this way. First of all, I continued as a leader in the youth movement, in the company of friends with whom I went later to the army, and second—I think that this high school really invested in us above and beyond our expectations. We received help with our homework.

I: At school?

S: Yes. Now, when I look back at this group there was a girl whose father was an important administrator, really, the two of us and several others could not be labeled underprivileged, whatever the professors may say. But others certainly were, and when I think what they invested in them, and where it brought them—it is simply incredible. Some were from slums, their fathers were alcoholics, the bottom of the barrel, from the worst neighborhood in town. Very very poor students. They really invested—that is, if someone had any difficulties. For me, for example, history tests based on memory were a nightmare. Math was my strong side at the time, but in history I had this problem. If I did not feel prepared, I would simply not take the test. This was one of my weak points during high school. Today I think that no other school would have treated the problem like they did. They invited the parents to discuss the matter and find out what the problem was. They formed a study group with the history teacher. I used to go to his home—I didn't pay anything for that—and he helped me prepare for the test, so that this barrier of fear and the blackout [would not occur]. Since this was the defense [mechanism] I employed: "I don't know so I am not taking the test." Later on, I had some problems with English, so they took me and a group of students to study English at the teacher's home—it was fun to work with her. I had this teacher N.M. who just recently died—did you hear about her?

I: Yes.

S: She was our homeroom teacher. Today I think she was a model teacher. Education was something for her. Look, today I see things differently. At that time we had a teacher, we had a head of the program, and a social worker. So, for example, I just remember—there were two girls who fought and pulled each other's hair. One called the other a whore. So they took it so seriously. That girl was not a whore, God forbid, but she was easy with the boys and she came from a very poor home. I remember that the offender was treated so severely that nobody called that girl any names ever again. She was actually one of the poorest students and was later on put in a foster home with one of the other students' family, a very good home—therefore I'm saying that not everybody who went there deserved the definition of underprivileged.

I: Someone from the same class provided her with a foster home?

S: Yes, from the same class. They had a nice house, and only a son and a daughter, so they took her, and gave her a room for herself, and warmth and everything. They took good care of her. In the army she became a military social aide and now she is a social worker, taking care of people. So that is what I mean. The majority—except one with whom they had no success, and I hear very bad things about him. We have among our class graduates a movie producer, an artist, an occupational therapist with an M.A. degree. One who was very good in math became a teacher for students with learning disabilities—she is a Ph.D. or something. In other words—everyone became something, except one, out of the 30 pupils. Two dropped out; they really could not be rehabilitated. One of the graduates is a lawyer, one is a top bank manager, it is simply incredible.

I: Yes. And did this program start at ninth grade?

S: Yes. We studied four years together. There were two tracks, a humanistic and a biological one—I was in the humanistic—but we were all in one class all the time, two tracks that belonged to the same class.

I: And you said you were cohesive?

S: Yes, very. We had those evenings—at first it was sort of artificial. They brought counselors to get us going. For example, the social worker returned from a trip in Kenya, so she gave us a slide show—you understand? So at first it was really artificial, but gradually [relationships] were established. Gym classes and some of the biology labs were for all the students together, so some of us—not many but some—formed relationships with students from the regular classes. But we were cohesive [in our own class]. Now I remember something which warms my heart. Towards the end of 10th grade, there were students who could already move up, they had such good grades that they could be integrated in the regular classes. This was brought to a class meeting, and a very stormy discussion followed. Look, some of the students didn't want to move because of insecurity—how can I leave this class suddenly, a real hothouse, and move to a new class, be integrated there? Other students did not want to move only because they thought of all the unfortunates who would not be integrated, and how would they face everybody? Since this was the situation. We had made it and we could move to the normal classes, while a core which could not move up remained [in the special class]. And if we were all regarded in the first year as a zoo—what would happen next? It was a very tough debate, but there was no way we would agree to that. We took a vote and decided.

I: Decided to remain as a separate class?

S: Mind you, those who could move up were outstanding students, and we stayed with the others in the class not to create . . . I am telling you frankly, some of us were afraid to cope, after this hothouse, to cope with a different class, where you had to prove yourself again etc. Another part of the class had this other concern—not to take apart our class, not to hurt those who could not move up.

I: Were you among those who were offered to move up?

S: I could move up, yes.

I: So this means that the studies were not terribly difficult?

S: Not too difficult. I'm telling you—I had this complex that I couldn't stand the memorization tests, lots of material to remember would stress me out. But at some stage I overcame.

I: Wasn't there a great gap between your level in elementary school and this high school?

S: No, I'm telling you—in the first year only. People would open the door to our classroom and stare at us to see who are they in this special class. I am not hiding these things. It's true, it's not a secret. But soon enough—we had breaks together, and some created relationships while others didn't. I didn't care much about this—my best friend was in our class, and for social life,

the youth movement was much more suitable for me. In the regular classes
there was only a small minority in the youth movement, while most were
more into disco—which was not for me. I did form relationships with them,
some were "high society" really. In 12th grade I sometimes joined their
parties.

I: But you continued being a counselor in the youth movement?

S: Yes, and I cared a lot, I cared a lot about this. We moved to another location,
and we, the older kids, prepared and painted the clubhouse—I still wonder
how we did all this, how we took all these tasks upon ourselves. In the old
location, I was in charge of the library—I organized the library and lent
books out to the members. Then we started to get ready for our military
service in the kibbutz.[11] We had trips and walks—I took each one of them,
and every work camp. We would just organize and go.

I: And don't you remember any special problems of adolescence, problems with
your parents?

S: No. I really think it is a matter of one's character. I almost didn't have
[conflicts] because I am obedient by nature. I wasn't the type who goes out
and disappears either. When I went to the youth movement they trusted me,
I never overdid things—when the meeting was over, we either took a stroll
or I would go home. They trusted me, I almost never had confrontations
with my parents, I really didn't.

I: Who were your friends during that time?

S: I had a very close girlfriend at high school, who is still in touch with me. She
was not in the youth movement with me, however. A quiet girl, it was nice
to be with her. Today we see each other less, but we speak on the phone,
or when we have something to celebrate. There was another friend who
moved to a village. She was married with children, while I was still single,
and I used to go to visit her in the village. The three of us were always
together.

I: And you didn't have a boyfriend?

S: In 11th grade I had one, he was from my class. Today I think we were just
babies, one day together and one—not. We used to write letters to each
other (laughing). He wasn't a member of the youth movement, we were
opposites, he liked disco. To find a middle road, sometimes he would join
me at the meetings of the youth movements, and sometimes I would join
him at the disco parties—which I really disliked. But it was important for
him. So this was my boyfriend.

I: For how long?

S: With twenty thousand breaks—we were together for about a year and a half.

I: And how were your matriculation tests?[12]

S: Highly pressured. Today I am disappointed by my results, because, for some
reason, I had higher expectations. I don't know what happened that I got
such grades. I was disappointed. Apparently, I had exam anxiety at the time.
For example in math, which was my strongest subject, I used to get always

9 or 10 [out of 10], I used to help everyone in school. Then, when the test came, I had a blackout. I felt like getting up and leaving, and I would have done so—but my teacher came and just said, "Sit down, you can do it, read it, it is not difficult." She really encouraged me. I didn't get a good grade, but I didn't fail. And I was ready to leave! I completed my entire matriculation, I didn't have to repeat any of the tests, but the grades were not good.

I: Yes.

S: All in all we had an atmosphere of learning. We took our studies very seriously, most of the kids did. The truth is they rehearsed with us, they invested, really invested above and beyond. You know what, had they invested so much in usual high schools, there would be no dropouts. It was incredible, the dedication of these teachers. Look, I'm a teacher today and when I was single I was more dedicated than today, and I do care—but that was much more. And it was education—boys didn't grow long hair or put earrings, no miniskirts for girls. Such things show that you care. They also invested in the teaching materials above and beyond, it is simply incredible. We had many visitors to our program at high school. And, at the end we had a conversation—what did we learn, and the conclusions were very positive. In retrospect, most students said they would have been ready to do this program again. In other words they didn't regret it, that they belonged to the experimental class, although later on there were some who were ashamed. They were just a few who denied; when they were asked, they just gave the name of the high school. They denied belonging to our program—this was very sad. They ignored it, and didn't want to be reminded of it, they were ashamed to say "I am from the experimental class."

I: And your reactions?

S: It didn't disturb me. [. . .] And at the end most of us made progress, we were very successful, each of us has established a nice family and a career. You can see, you know, everyone has three children, four children, everyone has built a family and has a respected occupation. Some would have made it anyway, but not all. I myself profited from the encouragement of my teachers who showed me I was capable of success. Who would have looked at me in a regular class? Either I would have had to struggle and exert myself, or I would have dropped out at some stage. It might be that I wouldn't have had enough power to cope. Children coming from problem families couldn't cope. [. . .] I don't tell everyone that I studied in the experimental program, but if I'm asked specifically—I wouldn't deny it. I'm not ashamed.

Part C (Second Meeting)

I: Tell me about your next stage—the army.

S: I went to the army in the framework of my youth movement—to the Nahal.[13]

I: Yes.

S: I went with my gang, some of whom were people I had been with together in the youth movement for years, and some were people who joined us from another town, and we got to know them during 12th grade. We, the girls, had basic training for two months, it was very tough. Today I wonder how girls get to do such hard training, with nightly hikes and lots of physical stress. Then came one of the most beautiful periods—we founded a new settlement in a desert border area, we were truly the first to be there. It was some sight! We were 10 girls, we lived in tents. Our dining hall and the club were in large tents—everything was in tents there. We girls learned how to get along with each other, although it was not that simple sometimes, because some girls were less . . . But we had lots of experiences. For example, there were many sand storms in the area, so when we wanted to eat, we used to prepare big pails of water, and dip the plate in water right before we put the food on it. To wash the dishes we used these pails, too, until some kitchen sinks were built later on.

I: What year was this?

S: I was drafted in 1970, so this was in 1971, more or less. It was a very beautiful period.

I: It seems that you enjoyed your service.

S: Yes, very much so. In spite of the fact that we got leaves to go home like the men—one Saturday in a month or in six weeks. If someone was brave, she could invent excuses for a special leave, but if someone was naive like me, it was sometimes six weeks that I didn't go home. This was a really good time. From the settlement we went to a kibbutz, where I worked in the kitchen. I enjoyed myself a great deal, although gradually everybody split up. The boys went on to more military training, and the girls were offered different courses, none of which interested me. So at that time I asked to be transferred to a military base near my home. In fact, from the kibbutz I used to visit my mother quite often. If I didn't have to take turns in the kitchen, I would hitchhike on Friday afternoon, and spend Shabbat until noontime at home. Then I got my transfer, and became a secretary in a storehouse near my hometown, so that every day at 5:00 I went home—this was great.

I: Can you give a general evaluation of your time in the army?

S: My time in the army was very nice. First of all, when I was with my friends—it was great because I didn't go to a new place, everything was familiar. And the period in the settlement was just a terrific experience, because it was all new. For example, since we had our club in a tent we were really close all the time, and living together with boys and girls that we grew up with—some of them at least—we felt a sense of togetherness.

I: Did you gain anything personally from this?

S: What did I gain personally? Well, I don't know if it gave me anything new, except reinforcing what was already there, because from a very young age

I was very active, it was really a continuation of that, and the fact that you're really responsible. For example, we girls worked mostly in the kitchen and the dining room, so our task was to prepare food and invent new dishes so that it would be interesting for the boys. The boys had guard duty in the area, so when they returned to the settlement, even at night, we would get up to prepare a meal for them, so that they would have . . . to create an atmosphere of helping, of doing this really together. And I liked life in a kibbutz, and considered settling in one, although this particular kibbutz wasn't it, it wasn't much fun. There was a rather large group of South American immigrants, and I saw many kibbutz parasites, namely, people who didn't work much and took advantage of the kibbutz. It was not a kibbutz that attracted me to stay. Later on, in the office, I felt really appreciated, and was given a lot of responsibility by my boss. I became friendly with him, and so did my parents. He used to come to our family parties, when invited. He sort of adopted me, and didn't treat me as a secretary but as a daughter. He used to protect me from his male soldiers, who tried to have fun on base. So that's it. I was released from service after a full two years, and I started studying at the teacher's seminary right away.

I: When did you decide to become a teacher?

S: I think that I always, in other words very early—I remember seeing myself as a teacher whenever we had to fill out all kinds of questionnaires regarding "what do you want to do when you grow up." I think it was a continuation of my role as a youth leader in the movement. So I went to the admission tests . . .

I: Just a second, before we go into this period, can you tell me who were the significant people for you during military service?

S: I think that my parents once more. But I had great times with my friends in the army, and one of them was my boyfriend in the settlement—although he left later on and went to the armored corps. That's it, there is nobody else. With my commanders it was normal relationships, nothing special, and I had a good friend, a girl who worked in the kitchen with me—but she didn't influence me or anything.

I: How would you describe yourself during that period?

S: (Thinking) As I told you, as much as I was close to my home, I think I was independent. In other words, I assumed responsibility. In the settlement, for example, if there was something to organize, I would do it. In the kibbutz I was more with my friends in the room—the kibbutz did not interest me that much, I withdrew more to the shell of my group, and we organized our own social life from time to time. In fact, I now recall that life in the kibbutz was comfortable because I had family there, two sisters who were cousins of my dad, were members of that kibbutz. So I didn't have to get adjusted to a new family.[14] Well, I did adjust, since I didn't know them so well before, but it was very comfortable, and they treated me like a family member, even more than expected. I went to see them in their room every day. Some girls didn't visit their [adopting] families that often, while for me it was great fun to go, and chat, and listen to music. They had kids about my age, so a good relationship was established. One of the women was very open and talkative, while her husband was rather closed. The other husband had a great sense of humor, so it was real fun and laughter all the time. My parents knew that I was with the family, so it made them feel good, too, that I wasn't among strangers. So that's it.

I: Okay, fine. So we have a long stage now—from 20 to 30, teaching and being single.

S: (laughing) It starts in the seminary where I studied for three years to become a licensed teacher. And of course all of the students were girls. I specialized in early childhood, and I had a very very good friend there, with whom I became really close, at one mind, you could say.

I: And where did you live?

S: I lived at home, at my parents'. In the seminary, some of the students[15] came right from high school, postponing their military service, and I could see how childish they were, while we who came after the service were serious and really wanted to study and become teachers. I don't know if I enjoyed my studies so much, I enjoyed the practical side much more. I had the opportunity to do my student-teacher practicum with good teachers, so that I learned something from every one of them. The most significant part, my great surprise was when, during my third year, I was selected to practice as a student teacher at the model school within the seminary.

I: This shows great estimation.

S: I think so, since it is one of the most important projects of the seminary. I was really afraid I would be under a magnifying glass all the time, but the senior staff from the seminary provided close supervision, and I think I gained a lot from this year, both from the point of view of self-confidence as a teacher and regarding the work with children themselves. When I was working in second grade, their home teacher had to go to the hospital for an operation, and for a period of six weeks I was her replacement. I did have an assistant, but just the same it was a great challenge. By the way, that is where the method of small group instruction was developed at the time, all this was happening at our model school then. We served as an example for all the other schools that sent teachers to see us. I think that I really learned a lot there.

There was one peculiar incident that I remember. At the graduation party, with all teachers and parents present, I was surprised to be presented with flowers by two of the small children I taught at the model school. None of the other graduates received flowers there, and I vaguely remember an argument about this later—was it fair that only I got flowers. I didn't make much of all this. So that's it.

Then I had to decide. We had a relative on my father's side who was a senior officer in the Ministry of Education. My parents suggested that I talk to him so that he could find a good school for me to work, somewhere close to our home. It was known for a fact that new teachers who are single are sent to schools far out of the city, and my parents wanted me very much to be nearby. I decided, however, not to ask for help from anyone. I believed that wherever I was thrown would be for the best. Today I am not only glad, I am really happy that I didn't pull these strings. Because if I'm a teacher today, someone with confidence, with a direction, and with good team orientation—since I work in teams today also—it is all thanks to that experience of working in GG.[16] I was assigned to GG and I taught there for three years. The first advantage was that we were all young beginners, so that I wasn't working with senior teachers who might have given me a sense of inferiority or lack of confidence, because evidently they know more and have more experience than me. The second advantage was that since GG was a faraway school, they invested a lot in education there, and sent the best supervisors to work with us. We were given a study day every week, on which we went to do observations in a top school in the center, and had instruction and discussions on what we observed. We were accompanied by experts all the way, and we did great projects in our school. This brings me to another advantage—today I think that it was a plus to start teaching as a single woman, because I was able to dedicate incredible amounts of time, I could work until 12 or 1 at night. I mobilized my entire family, even my little sister, to help me, making flash cards and games and projects—I remember them all. We had lots of money for materials and stuff, the school principal never said no to any of my requests—something that I encountered later on my way. [. . .] This principal was a kibbutz member and she emphasized the participation of parents in our work, it became like a community project. We used to stay in school late in the evenings for our projects, we even took a shower in the teachers' hall sometimes. I saw that for one of the teachers, who was married and had a daughter, it was much harder to keep up with us. Good relationships between the teachers were formed here too. With some of them I'm still in touch. This was the outcome of the long workdays and also the long trips on the special bus which took us back and forth every day from the city center to GG.

So this is really the school which gave me the tools to become a teacher, and I had wonderful supervisors, too. After three years, however, I became tired of commuting and I asked for a transfer. My social world was also constricted, because I saw only the teachers,[17] and some of them got married in the meantime. I didn't go out and I was most of the evenings at home, dedicating myself to work. So I wanted a change.

Since my sister was at that time a member in a kibbutz far in the south, and I also loved the kibbutz, I applied to a kibbutz for a teaching job. I wanted to find a kibbutz near my sister's, so that even if I was far away from home, I would be close to her. I managed to find a position like that and went to work as a hired teacher in a southern kibbutz for a year. From the teaching perspective it was ideal—I had a class of 15 kids, with the best conditions. I could really work separately with each of the students, according to their personal level. It was great, and the relationship with my sister was good—I visited her a lot, and she visited me.

[. . .]

I was teaching first grade, and again I was lucky—I think I find people that really help me in life. The principal of this school, M., was the sister of Israel's president at the time—a personality in her own right. There were only two hired teachers in this school. The two of us became very good friends, and our principal M. treated us as her daughters. She cared so much for us that it was unbelievable. She understood that I missed my family. In the beginning I was told I would be able to visit home once a month. I said this would be difficult so she understood and allowed me to go once in three or even two weeks. This meant that I couldn't arrive on time to teach on Sunday, but she never took that day off my salary. She knew that I worked evenings, and she never counted my hours at school. She gave me a feeling that I was one of the kibbutz members—it was incredible. Until recently I used to call her from time to time, and I went to visit her new grandchildren. I got acquainted with her daughter-in-law too. It was really a nice relationship.

I: Just the same you stayed only for a year?

S: I left after a year because there were no people my age in the kibbutz either. I was 25 years old already and I saw that if I stayed there I would remain single. So I decided to leave the kibbutz and return home. But I didn't go to live at my parents' place, I rented my own apartment. My parents helped me to find an apartment close to them—after a year by myself it was hard to find place for all my stuff at home, and my parents didn't even have a room for me. At first I lived alone, I wanted to be alone and was afraid I wouldn't be able to share an apartment with a roommate. I had my meals at my mom's, I worked in the same elementary school in which I myself had studied as a kid, and my rented apartment was close to both my parents' home and the school. But then M's daughter-in-law came as a student to town and offered to share my apartment. It worked out very well, she was a very nice girl. When she moved out, I lived with another woman, a childhood friend who had also been in the army with me. It was nice not to have to find a new roommate. I think we lived together for two years, until, at the age of 30, I met my husband and got married.

I: How did you meet him?

S: That's a funny story. We both lived in the same neighborhood since childhood, we both grew up there, we were both 30. I met him at the local bakery which belonged to his aunt. He was studying printing technology in the evenings, and working at the bakery during the day to support himself. I used to visit my mother's friend who also worked at the bakery, and I met D., and within three months we decided to get married. We were both 30, we felt the time had come, and in six months we were already married. I'm laughing because we each moved in a circle in the same area, yet I never saw him before. So this started a new period.

I: Where did you live?

S: Oh, I had bought a new apartment a while before, because it was a waste to pay rent rather than the mortgage. It was a new building, in a new development area outside the city, and about to be finished just as I got married. A month after the wedding we got the keys to this apartment, so I moved in as a couple,[18] and I'm so glad, because the place is full of young couples and small children, and as a single I don't know how I could have taken it. There was one single woman here for two years, and she left.

That's it. Right then they opened the new school here, and my district inspector asked if I would be willing to transfer and teach here. I had my doubts because I liked my former school, and the population was great there, but commuting on the bus to my parents' neighborhood was very difficult, and I hate to come to work stressed out at the last moment. So I finally decided to accept the offer and started to work here.

The year after I became pregnant, I was due a sabbatical, and took the year off. We went to visit my husband's sister in the USA and took a long trip there. When I came back I returned to work in the school here, that's what I have been doing since then, and it's great.

I: And the family?

S: Oh, that's the greatest part. You have seen them.

I: So tell me about them.

S: Well, our oldest son, A., is about 8½ years old now. He was born normally, it was easy, a joy. Then our daughter B. came, she is a year and half younger than him. The beginning was very difficult, with two babies in diapers in the house, but after the first year it turned to be real fun. They have a very nice relationship, they play with each other like friends. Now, when B. was 4 years old, my youngest son, C., was born. Some periods were not easy. A., as an infant, he used to suffer from severe breathing problems, and he gave us many frightening moments—I don't wish it upon any woman, not even my enemies.[19] We were at the hospital with him many times. But all in all he is a very good kid. Often I was too afraid to leave him with the caretaker, so I brought him along to my class to spend the day with me. Both my older children used to come with me to school from time to time, when they were small and had a cold or something. They played quietly in class, or participated in the class activities. My students knew them, they didn't disturb us at all. They were kids of the school,[20] everybody knew that. With my youngest, I don't dare, it's simply impossible (laughing)—he is too jumpy, and disturbs the class.

I: You kept working all these years?

S: More or less. I was able to take a sabbatical year once, and after every birth I received the regular three months' maternity leave. Then I found a caretaker for the children, and returned to school.

I: And your husband, does he help you around the house?

S: You see, he works outside all day. He used to shop in the market for me, but lately he almost doesn't do it anymore. He would come and drive us in the car when we need to go to the doctor, that's about it.

I: You don't drive?

S: No, not yet. But God gave me a great gift—speed, this is my luck, and I hope I will be able to keep up my pace. My friends make fun of me and say that all I need are roller blades. I have so many errands a day, taking the children back and forth to their activities, so that they will not cross the streets alone. But it is somewhat easier lately.

I: Can your mother help at all?

S: You see, she lives far away, but, first of all, on every birth she came with me to the hospital, assisted me during labor, and then she came home with me and helped in cooking and everything, she would take a bus and come here every day to help. Several years ago I had an operation, and was hospitalized for few weeks, so she came and took care of me in the hospital all the time, while my husband did extremely well at home, tending to the children and the house.

I: You seem to enjoy both being a teacher and being a mom.

S: I really love teaching very young kids, only that. I have good experiences all the time, I have wonderful relationships with my schoolchildren. When I once replaced a teacher with teenagers, I didn't enjoy myself at all—I said that this was my first and last time. I love the spontaneity of the first and second graders, for better or worse. Sometimes they make comments which are rather unpleasant to hear, but you know that when they are happy they will compliment you, tell you they have a good time. That is the type of relationship I have with them. If they have fun, they will say, "What a nice day we had together, Sara, how lovely our homeroom is today, how pretty are the paintings that we did together." They may comment on how I look, if I have a new dress or more makeup than the usual, they'll say, "What happened? Where are you going after school today?" In other words, our relationship is very personal. If they dislike something they will immediately complain, however, but I accept this because it's true. And my own children also give me pleasure, may they be healthy. They are good children, they study well, they are interested in things. The young one is a little wild sometimes, maybe it's his nature, or because, being the youngest, we spoil him more than the older ones. We may want to have another child, but who knows, we aren't so young anymore.

I: Yes.

S: Now, you probably want to hear about my religious way of life.[21] (laughing)

I: Yes. Was your husband religious?

S: No, nor his family. But a couple of years ago, I don't remember quite how many, his sister, who was 16 at the time, was run over by a car, and she died. So his parents and brothers started saying the mourning prayers for her, and gradually, each one in his way, they all returned to the Jewish religious way of life. One is even ultra-Orthodox, he studies in a Yeshiva[22] all day. And so my husband also, about five years ago, started to adopt some religious habits. He started to pray every morning, at first separately at home before going to work, and then he said, "If I pray already, why not go to the synagogue," and so, things started slowly to evolve.

The truth is that in the beginning it was very hard for me, because we were used to going every Shabbat for a family meal at my parents', but as an Orthodox family we could not do this anymore, since we don't drive a car on Saturday. I tried to invite my parents to come here for the holidays, but it is too crowded for all of us, and it was hard for them. This part is still difficult for me. In all other respects, however, gradually I . . . I'm not sorry about that. My children's education, for example, is far better in their Orthodox schools.

I: But you teach in a secular school as before?

S: Yes. And when I see the decline of discipline there—I am a conservative person myself—I am very happy that my children go to another kind of school. I also enjoy my rest on Shabbat, after my hard work all week. Saturday is my real day of rest. Still, my husband is much more observant than I am. He goes to prayers twice a day, and also attends daily classes in Jewish religion. I don't define myself as "religious," but I do what is necessary at home. Actually, my parents were traditional in their habits, too. They had a Friday night blessing of the wine, and always went to the synagogue on holidays. And gradually, I understand more about all that. Whatever I need to do as a member of the family, I do, but the more personal requirements are up to me.

I: So you didn't feel pressured to go along in this direction?

S: No. My husband went about this change very gradually, and it took a long time. There were no changes that happened all of a sudden. I am a type that gives in, and I care a lot about the family harmony. The only thing I complained about, in the beginning, was being unable to visit my parents and family on Shabbat. But I see that it's good for the children, and that's what is important for me.

I: Okay, and what are your plans for the future?

S: This is the first year I feel it is difficult for me to be a teacher. I mean, I cannot see myself in another profession, just the same, but our work becomes really more difficult. Children are less disciplined today, even at this young age, they have more problems. Gradually I am losing my patience for teaching kids when all they want is to disturb in class. After all, 19 years in the profession are quite a lot. If I have another child, I will be perhaps able to take a year of leave—and I think I'd enjoy that. On the other hand,

I don't know if I will be capable of staying at home all the time. But I would
be ready to have a time-out for rest, I believe.

DAVID

David is 42 years old. He was interviewed by Tamar Zilber. The interview was conducted in two sessions in his office at the hotel where he
works.
David's stage outline was as follows:

Stage 1: From birth to 18—Childhood and youth—Studies
During the interview, he proposed to subdivide this chapter into three
subsections: before elementary school, elementary school, and high school.

Stage 2: 18-22   Army[23]
Stage 3: 22-26   University
Stage 4: 26-32   Work in Israel
Stage 5: 33-36   Work in Africa
Stage 6: 36-today (42) Work in Israel

The following life story is slightly edited and abbreviated to eliminate
most of the repetitions and unfinished sentences from the original transcript. Some of David's longer descriptions of his experience, especially in
stages 3 and 4, were omitted due to limitations of space.

D: I remember my childhood as being normal. A child, just a regular child, living
  in a good, nice home.
I: What did your parents do?
D: My father, that is . . . My mother, in principle, she has always been a
  housewife, she almost never worked outside. Sometimes she used to teach
  French in the army, but nothing special. My father, he worked for a travel
  agency. But it was really a period of freedom from worries, I don't know,
  going to the beach, picking wild grapes, spending time with other kids—
  nothing out of the ordinary.
I: Do you have siblings?
D: I have a sister older than me, and one younger than me. She was born when
  I was 5. But I, at least, don't remember this as a traumatic event in my life.
I: What kind of a child were you? Naughty?
D: Not really, no. I was shy, I think, I was sensitive, I was a cry-baby, that is who
  easily took offense, very . . . Nothing more.
I: And who are the people you remember from this period?

D: Mostly the family, some uncles, some friends. That is, I remember very little. What I remember is that, when I was 8, we moved to another city, and this was rather exciting. Suddenly my whole life changed. I remember the class, the new kids, the structure of the school, which was different. The weather was somewhat different. I was sick a lot, yes. It was in second grade, and the middle of the school year. It took me a couple of months to adjust, I think, but then I fit in very well and was rather popular in my class. I had good friends and was elected to the class council here and there, I don't know.

I: Why did you move?

D: We followed my father from job to job; he was transferred to another agency, in which he became a partner.

I: And did you like school?

D: I wasn't an outstanding student. I was a mediocre-plus student, but I rather liked school. I was very obedient, a good kid, doing my homework, but not making too much effort. My teachers' comments were always, "Had he made more effort, he would have achieved more." But I didn't make more effort, they never convinced me to. I was average, that's all. Our class was very cohesive, and we had a teacher who educated us in real values—like honesty, not cheating on exams, and friendship, and mutual aid. I was one of the flag-bearers in this respect, so I was assigned to two or three weaker students, and used to help them with their homework. I took it very seriously, and was able to be of help. I remember myself as popular and happy most of the time, but there were naturally also periods of feeling more introverted, and more . . . Now that I have my own children, I see this as all normal, crises that everyone experiences. I remember these moods somehow, however, and I think that it helps me today with my kids.

I: Were they related to special events, or just passing moods?

D: Not around events, no . . . Perhaps falling in love for the first time, social relationships . . . Not about studies. In this area things were quite stable, without any serious effort on my part. But, there are times when a kid is more popular—then it was better for me; when you're less popular, then . . . [it was worse]. Our family relationships were warm and good, but not too open. In other words, when I had problems, I preferred to tackle them all alone, I didn't share them with my family—this does not diminish any of its warmth in my eyes. But sometimes it was . . . I can't remember particular events. I just had these moods, and I'd say "Okay, I'm expected to be more with people, so I'll go to look for a friend to be with," but nothing more than that.

I: And after elementary school, where did you go?

D: I went to B.D. High School, and I kept up to the same pattern, that is, I wasn't among the best in class, and therefore I couldn't go to one of the best high schools to begin with. Actually, I didn't even try, because I knew that it would be difficult for me, and I might not succeed. So I went to B.D.—a mediocre school, reasonable, and I stayed there, and indeed, as was to be expected, everything went well and I graduated. Again, socially it was easy, I was very popular, a member of the school council and so on.

I now remember that during this period I was into my volunteer work. I volunteered to work with children with polio, I really became addicted to it. I went to this children's hospital daily, I rarely skipped a day—it was total addiction. For example, if a child needed to go home for the weekend, and for some reason his family didn't pick him up, I would take the wheelchair, and, in a bus, bring this child home. Then I might stay with him for the weekend, and take him back on the bus once more. As a child, I did all this, and it really amazes me! The public transportation in buses, all this Via Dolorosa.[24] Later I also used to take these disabled children to the theater, which obviously provided me with free tickets—so that's part of the same period.

I remember one girl from the hospital that had to get to the radio station to be interviewed for a teenagers' program that was running at the time. There was nobody to take her, so I did. We went on the bus and I made it somehow to the station. After they interviewed her, there was some time left, so they asked me to do something, and I did. From then on I was addicted to this radio program. I used to appear as their youth reporter almost . . . I think it was twice a week at the time. I used to go and interview people and prepare programs, I don't remember exactly, but I did many things in the radio sort of accidentally. Every time I used to find something of this sort, often without neglecting my other activities, [I dedicated myself] until things began to conflict so that gradually it declined. In other words, it always started intensively and then another project came, getting gradually more intensive, and then I let go [of the first thing]. Not really, because I maintained some contacts [with my former activities], but not with the same enthusiasm.

At high school we also organized a radio system. We had this loudspeakers' network in the classrooms, so that the principal could make announcements. So we took advantage of this, and every day at lunch break we broadcasted a program to the entire school. I remember that we had lots of arguments whether it was appropriate to use a Beatles song for our opening, or not, was it in conflict with our school values, or not; and at the end we won. We had these kind of battles, that's it.

I: Who were the significant people for you at the time?

D: The truth is I'm not good in keeping up relationships, so there are no people from that stage that I'm still in touch with. But I remember many people, friends. Recently we had a class reunion, even our class from elementary school had one, which is pretty unusual. I wasn't among the organizers, but I went gladly. It's difficult for me [to answer your question] . . . Look, there are some teachers that I remember, but they weren't significant for my life. Only my elementary teacher was, she really instilled some values in me, values that even today I find hard to give up. Honesty is very very important for me, maybe I absorbed it more than the others. I think it came from there. Other significant people? I never entertained big hatreds. I had many girlfriends. It started in eighth grade. Each girlfriend that I had was for a long time—never just a week or two and then it's over. I always had a regular girlfriend, it was rather nice, and it helped me. In other words, it wasn't "just like that," but a pretty serious thing. I used to go to their homes, and they used to come to my home, as if it was all in the family.

I: What sort of a person were you then?

D: What can I say? Sensitive, spontaneous[25]—not really. The only definition I can give is that I was a normal child, a little more sensitive than the others. I was popular, so that means I was a nice person, I suppose. I can't attach any stereotype to myself, I certainly wasn't the street bully, but I wasn't the underdog either. On a scale from 1 to 10, I was between 7 to 9 in the group, always in a good place.

And then I had to make a decision about military service, and I decided not to go with my youth movement group, but as an individual. I went to the paratroopers, and then saw it was too difficult for me, so I joined the infantry, which was still really tough. But I had no other choice.

I think I completed my training honorably. I had this image of the guys who did it before my eyes, and all the time I kept telling myself, "If he could do it, and he could, so can I."

Later, I wanted to become an officer, but the tests said my standing was not quite good enough. So I said, "Okay, there is nothing to cry about, I'm not looking for a military career, I'm fine as I am." But then, it turned out that they needed more people for the officers' course, and I was called up to go. At first I said, "No. no. When I wanted to go—you rejected me." They said, "Come, just the same," and I agreed. So I went, and graduated successfully enough to be retained as a training officer in the course afterwards. It was very nice in comparison to my infantry unit.

Just then the Yom Kippur War[26] broke out. It was a traumatic event, but it didn't affect me too much. All I can say is that I lost an uncle in the previous war. I remember mourning for him, and after the October war, the trips to the Golan Heights to visit the place were he'd been killed in battle. As for me, since I was part of the officer's school personnel, we weren't sent to the combat zone, but we participated in some brief attacks, and . . . a friend of mine got wounded in one of them. That's a story. We were asked to send reinforcements to one of the military actions, they needed two teams. [When they formed the teams,] I remember that it was either me or this friend, so we tossed a coin to see who would go, and he won. He went to the battle, got a head wound, and is an invalid to this very day. So that's fate, I tell myself. I could have gone in his place, would I have been wounded too? Anyway, I didn't, and I completed my military service very well.

I: And who were the significant people for you at the time?

D: What comes to mind is a friend from elementary school who died at the time. He had leukemia, and I remember this because it was the winter I did my training in the infantry. We were at some northern post . . . I remember it affected me deeply, and I wanted to visit and talk to him. I called his home and they told me that he wasn't there. So I asked when would he come, and they told me he wouldn't be there anymore. That's how I remember it. We didn't study in the same high school but we had a good relationship. Afterwards I used to go and visit his parents, it was important for me to maintain these contacts. He was an only child. Aside from him, I had many friends, but nothing special. One man that I keep meeting in the reserves every year I still consider my good friend.

I: What sort of a person were you then?

D: I used to keep a low profile, not to stand out. I did it purposely—I never took the first place in line, so I wouldn't be called. I wanted to live in peace, to be mediocre. In other words, I wanted to be good enough, never to excel. Maybe because of the former periods in which I got carried away too far with all my voluntarism, as if I couldn't tell where to stop. So perhaps this is why later I said, "No, studying is too hard for me, I should stick to my mediocre level. It is important to be among the good ones, but not the best."

So after the army I took a job in a tourist office, which was rather nice. I was going to restaurants and staying in hotels, to report about the quality of the service. At the same time I applied to the university, and was rejected by the law school, so I went to my second choice—economics. I managed to work full time and study full time, and I graduated in time. But I didn't want to go on studying. A B.A. was enough for me, all I wanted was the degree.

I remember this as a very stressful, intensive period of work. All the same, as usual, I had a girlfriend, and when I was 23 I met the woman whom I married about a year later. She was a receptionist in one of the hotels I visited for my work. We lived together in my apartment.

I: Where was this?

D: In L. (name of neighborhood).

I: And who were the significant people for you at this stage? Was your wife significant?

D: She was, without doubt. She helped me a lot in my studies. The mere fact that I had a cozy corner to return to at night, and I didn't have to go out again and look for entertainment, when I was so busy working and studying [was good for me]. It was a task I took upon myself, and I did it. Again, I finished in a mediocre place, I remember calculating the minimal number of home assignments I had to submit in order to pass. Only the minimum grade needed for passing, that's all I expected of myself.

At first, my wife and I decided we would wait with children. She worked in an airline company, she does this today also, which allowed us to go abroad freely. We used this privilege for short weekends in Europe—Rome, Zurich. It was a nice way to let off steam. What else can I tell you about this period? I got a good promotion at work. From a simple clerk I was made vice-manager of my department, and was put in charge of tourists' complaints. I never lived the social life of students, I had no time to sit in cafés. I had no time. I bought a car and ran from one place to the next. At work, as I said before, I was promoted, and . . . I was highly thought of, which I think I deserved. Undoubtedly so.

It didn't take me long to see that I wouldn't be able to make an impact with the work I was doing. I wasn't going to put up with that, and so, a year after I finished my studies, I started to look for another job. I wanted to work in a place where I would make a difference—not in a large organization like the one I had been in so far. How could I get ahead? A career?

I found a hotel to work in, and resigned from the office. Just as I handed in my letter of resignation, the director offered me a promotion. I didn't know what to do. I consulted my father—I always liked to consult him—I talked to others, what to do? At the end—namely, a moment later—I said, "What the hell, I will go my own way." I went to work in the hotel.

It was a tremendous leap for me, an ambitious leap, which is . . . a thing I think I always do. I got an important managerial job in a hotel although I knew nothing about hotels, aside from having been a guest. It was a relatively important managerial job. Okay, I was a university graduate in economics, but what good was that training for? Here I needed to take a lot of financial responsibility. I found some of my father's acquaintances, and another relative that had some experience in hotel management, and, in three weeks, in the evenings, after work, I learned from them all I could about this new job. It reminds me of when I was 16, and I claimed that I knew how to drive a tractor, and then went and, in half a day, taught myself to really do it.

Anyway, it was hard work, but I did this hotel job very well, and was well appreciated for it. After three years I started to feel that this was too small for me. I needed to learn more about hotels—it's a big world—and there are new methods developing all the time. Just at that time an American chain was opening a small new hotel in the city, and I saw this as a new beginning, so I applied for a job there. I was given an opportunity to choose one of several positions, and I chose a very minor position in comparison to what I had held previously, and I remember all my friends asking "Tell me, how come from being the third ranking man in your previous hotel, you are suddenly going to be the most simple clerk here?" I said "I'm not afraid, I believe in myself and I am ready to learn," I believed I would be discovered and promoted from this minor position.

Anyway, they were just opening the hotel, and there were millions of things to do. They asked me to stay in the hotel overnight, so I agreed only if my wife could also come, and I think that we stayed there for two weeks or so. I worked hard, but it was very good, very interesting, I was highly thought of and received the first award for excellence in this hotel at the end of the year. And naturally, like in other things, I was carried away and put everything I had into this business. With time, I became one of the main managers there.

Here I have to stop, however. At that time we were trying to get pregnant, and it didn't go so well. My wife went to all sorts of treatments, it was very, very hard. And then we had one of the hardest decisions to make, that we would adopt children, and the sooner the better. The problem is to admit you have a problem. It was easy for me, but very difficult for my wife to admit. After this, we had a terribly long period of waiting for our turn to get a child to adopt—it took about three years and was extremely nerve-wracking. So then, three weeks after we got the baby, the Lebanon War[27] broke out and I was mobilized to the army. I said, "What if I . . . How am I to behave now?" As if the whole world was on my shoulders. Of course, I obeyed and went "to protect my country." I didn't do anything stupid, but I remember how bad I felt. It was also difficult for my wife and my parents, it was just awful. For about three weeks I was even unable to call home from Lebanon. I had these feelings, after all this time of suffering and waiting, what if something happens to me and they may decide to take the child away from my wife, a single mother, for the good of the child—who knows. Anyway, I returned home safely.

In the meantime, at work it was a very stormy time, because of great financial difficulties, but I managed to keep my place and stay honest, and was appreciated by all sides. I had been working for five years there already, and heard about a position in Africa in another hotel chain. But I felt that I owed my loyalty to my own chain, so I went to my employers and told them about this opportunity. They said, "Are you ready to go to Africa?" And I said, "Yes." So they said, "Don't worry. Find somebody to replace you here, and we will find a place for you." This suited me, I am not the kind who leaves scorched earth behind.

So then we went to Africa. My wife had her doubts, but I told her that a place which runs a hotel like this cannot be a jungle. This was how I saw it, although I didn't know all the details. That's how I am, I tend not to worry, I'm ready to go. She took the challenge and came along with me. We really arrived in the middle of nowhere, with a 3-year-old son and all of a sudden we needed to speak French, which I knew, but just the same, [it wasn't easy].

I could write a book about this period of two and a half years in Africa. I learned something new every day. The Third World is entirely different from anything we know, that we are able to imagine. Even though I can talk about it, I cannot transmit in words the depth of my experiences there. For me, honest as I am, it was startling to see all the corruption, and right in the open. It was a dictatorship, and anyone who lives in a democracy cannot fathom it. All in all it was a fascinating experience.

For example, there are these native inspectors all the time, they come to the hotel and just say, very openly, "We want money." "No, I cannot give you any money, but I have some hotel T-shirts." They take the T-shirts but say, "We cannot eat this." So I go and make a food parcel for them. These kinds of interactions. I didn't give them money so that it wouldn't be considered bribery, but for me, personally, these little gifts were also bribes, but not really. To compromise with the conscience, with reality, somehow.

(Here David gives more examples about his experience in Africa in great detail.)

I: You seem to have learned something there.

D: Oh, sure. Look, from a personal perspective, this period really changed me. Not completely, yet it gave me a lot of maturity. This period, it taught me to say, "No. But no!" Because you are facing people of such unbelievable misery, for example, the workers of the hotel, who ask you for loans. You give them, from the hotel cash—not my personal money, although I did this too sometimes—out of pity. And then this man, who could not return the loan, comes and asks for another one. You feel somehow that you need to educate the person, and to say no. But how can you? I would have never managed to live on such a sum of money, and they do. They have 10, 15 children in a family. But I learned to say no, even in those cases that were very difficult for me personally, because I identified so much with these people and their problems. I learned about another world, so different than ours.

Another topic is health—you know that if anything happens to you, it may be fatal. Appendectomy is 90% fatal there. Poisoning, infection, AIDS, everything is happening. Murder is fairly common, people talk about it freely, and everyone knows that a criminal may be released from jail after two days by bribing the warden. And all these problems of whites and blacks! My black assistant was blamed for cooperation with a white man—me, so they found a reason to arrest him. I had to go and fight the police for him, but who am I, just a small citizen, I have no power, no authority. You may be blamed for anything, and then—go prove your innocence. I wasn't afraid for my life, but certainly for my career and the safety of my family. About AIDS—the lifeguard was, my son, he was there, we used to go to this swimming pool. My son used to help him to take the chairs out, things like that—he was 3-4 years old. We left for a summer vacation, and when we returned—he [the lifeguard] wasn't there. I asked where he was, and they said, "He's dead." "What did he die of?" "Of AIDS." Suddenly I realize, wow, my child was walking hand in hand with him, and he had AIDS. That is, suddenly you ask yourself, "Why am I doing all these things? Why, what, why should I, why should I risk my family? Risk myself, for that sort of thing?" So okay, he was tested later, and he is not a carrier, he is fine, but still—I have amazing stories like this, hundreds and thousands of them. Does it interest you?

I: I've understood this period more or less. Just one more question. Who were the people who were meaningful for you at the time?

D: I'd say everybody in Africa, all my workers who helped me and taught me so much. They taught me that if I give them—I get a lot in return. These are people that really, I can truly say that they influenced me in forming my personality, in spite of my age then. This includes the white managers with whom we became very close. We all lived together in one wing of the hotel, like a kibbutz. I was with them, but I was more—I was above them. And I took care to keep distance, not to participate in interpersonal tensions or gossip. It worked out very well, and my wife also went along with me. We took a lot on ourselves, you may say, and didn't ask much in return, and this attitude empowered our status there among the others. You may add also the Jewish community in the city, and their rabbi, who was a very special man. Generally, I look on this period as tremendous. Difficult, again, but something that I'm happy I did, that enriched me incredibly. I learned a lot—about myself, society, relationships, small communities and a totally different world I would never have known otherwise.

I: And this lasted for about two and a half years?

D: Yes, and I gained a reputation and a second award—I was elected man-of-the-year of the hotel chain in Africa and Southeast Asia. I really turned this hotel inside out. Obviously they wanted me to stay there, but I refused. I wanted to go back to Israel. How come a person so attached to this country decided to live elsewhere anyway? So I said that I couldn't continue. It was hard for my family also. The chain looked for an appropriate job in Israel for me, but couldn't find one. Meanwhile I waited a long time. They offered me all sorts of places around the world, but I came up with a story that they had to accept—that we were in line again for adoption of our second child, so we had to return to Israel. Finally I agreed to take a job below my managerial level in Israel, just so that I could return.

It was supposed to be for a short time, but lasted longer and longer. In fact, I enjoyed this—I had less responsibility, work was easy and familiar for me, and I had enough time to build our new home with the money I'd made in Africa. It worked out well, it really suited me. I didn't care for advancing my career then and rejected all kinds of alternatives.

Finally a man came to me, who had built a hotel far in the South, and the place was not running so well. Right then it was closed, and he wished to reopen it. He tried to convince me to accept this project, and somehow I was tempted. I went to see the hotel and was somehow pulled in—not with enthusiasm or any intention of getting involved, but I did. In fact, the chain that had been so good to me all the time, was suddenly not so good anymore. Once I rejected their offers to go to all sort of places, it was over. I asked to reduce my job to half-time, managed to convince them to agree, and then started commuting three days a week to this hotel in the South. I worked very hard, long hours, but it brought challenge into my life, and also gave me additional income. That's it, so I helped to open this hotel. That's an experience—to make something out of nothing, or almost nothing, to start an organization which then works and functions. You have to understand how hotels work—it's a system that works on time. On money also. You cannot postpone anything for tomorrow, since the guest who needs a certain service today, won't be there tomorrow. He wants it now. And you need to bring him exactly what he asked for. It's not like any other office. It's a great challenge. And it's always teamwork. So that's what I did for a year.

About this time we got our daughter for adoption. It was very exciting— the waiting, then going to receive her. We went with our son. It's a matter of coping, these are traumatic experiences in their own right. I was trying to divide my time between the old hotel, and the new one, and my new daughter, all that. It was very pleasant, until I understood that I can't spread myself thin like that. Right then, I heard that a superior manager in another hotel had been fired, and I proposed myself as his replacement. I got the job immediately. Since then I'm here. I think that I introduced many changes here, and brought the hotel up to a standard that it had never reached before. I can't take all the credit, but I really think that the methods I introduced, my analysis of the situation, have been successful. I'm highly appreciated here, and loved a lot, and I enjoy myself. It's a challenging job, a large hotel, one of the most successful in town. I've been here almost four years. No one before me was able to stay in this position for as long as me. Again, it's a matter of coping with the company and all the directors above and alongside me. This is where I'm rather good, so I can stay on the job, as I could also in the former hotels I worked in, in spite of all the conflicting interests. So that's my life, in brief.

I: And the people that have been meaningful for you in this last period?

D: Look, it's hard . . . The people that I work with daily are very important to me, but I . . . I don't have any models that I follow, there is no man that . . .

I: It doesn't have to be that. From my point of view it can be your wife and children also.

D: Look, my wife and children were always most important to me, above myself. That is, I made certain steps only when my wife agreed to take them with me. Everything I did was after consulting my wife, and the children are now one of the most important things. In other words, if a child is sick, I don't go to work. There's nothing to it, I can always do my work at night, that's the advantage of a place which runs 24 hours a day. I do work long days, perhaps, but I love the children very much, and they love me. We like to be together. I take them for trips abroad and enjoy every minute. When my wife went for two weeks to visit her sister, I had no problem with that. The children go to school, I am always available on the phone, I cook for them, feed them, play with them. All in all my relationships with the children are very very important, and my family is the most important thing to me. From time to time I have had tempting positions offered to me, but I didn't take them because it wasn't convenient for the family. You see, today I can pick where I want to go—I'm pretty sure of this. I know how good I am professionally. I know the work, I have experience.

I think that . . . An important thing in my life is the computer! Don't laugh. In spite of the fact that I learned to use it at a pretty late age—I'm not a child anymore—I have a good grip of it, I like it. It likes me, too. We have good relationships. I understand its language, and language, so I've learned, is the most important thing in the world.

NOTES

1. In the process of writing this book, Sara's and David's complete life stories were sent to them and received their approval for publication.

2. The research subjects were all Israelis, and in Israel, military service is obligatory for all Jewish citizens: two years (18-20) for a woman and three years (18-21) for a man.

3. *Shiva* means seven, referring to the Jewish tradition of seven days of mourning after the death of a family member. During this week, relatives and friends visit the mourning family, and—if they are Orthodox—prayers are conducted at home.

4. The term *daughter of the home,* and sometimes *girl of the home,* is not idiomatic in Hebrew. It is used by Sara as a unique form of expression, influenced by Ladino, a vernacular Judeo-Spanish jargon spoken in the past by Jews in several countries.

5. Ladino word—see Note 4.

6. The reader may notice a certain inconsistency in details or order regarding the timing of the meeting between the teacher and Sara's mother, and Sara's entry into elementary school. Slight inconsistencies of this sort appear at other points of the story.

7. *Gar-in*—literally "kernel"—refers to a group of youth movement graduates, who go together to serve in the army, in the framework of the "Nahal corps"; see Note 11 below.

8. Jews in Israel vary in the extent to which they follow Jewish practices or observe religious laws in their lives. *Traditional* usually refers to a moderate level of observance. Toward the end of the story, Sara tells about her own family move toward a more observant, namely, an Orthodox, way of life.

9. A booth with a roof of branches and leaves that is built, according to Jewish tradition, for eating and sleeping in during the holiday of Sukkoth.

10. A war between Israel and its Arab neighbors, June 1967. Some combat activity took place in the part of the country in which Sara grew up.

11. Part of the military service in the Nahal corps used to take place in a kibbutz; see Note 13 below.

12. Matriculation tests are final national exams prior to high school graduation. They are normally taken by all high school students in Israel toward the end of 12th grade.

13. Nahal stands for "Fighting-Pioneering Youth," which is a military corps in the Israeli Defense Force. Until recently, the Nahal consisted of youth movement graduates who formed "kernels," namely, small groups who went through the military service

together. The period of military service in the Nahal was divided into military training, work in a new collective settlement, and work in an existing kibbutz.

14. Single or young individuals who come to a kibbutz for a period of time are usually assigned to "adopting families" that form the personal link between the newcomer and the kibbutz community.

15. The Hebrew language has different noun and verb forms for masculine and feminine. In the account of Sara's studies and experience as a teacher, she always refers to her classmates and teachers, as well as, later on, to the teachers in the schools in which she taught, in the feminine form. This makes it very clear that she is speaking about an all-feminine experience.

16. GG is a the name of a small development town, about 30 minutes' drive from the larger city in which Sara lives.

17. This is stated in the feminine form—see Note 15.

18. This sentence is highly irregular in its grammatical form, which is especially salient in the context of Sara's high level of verbal fluency. Its significance is explained by the holistic-content analysis; see Chapter 4.

19. In feminine form—see Note 15.

20. It is interesting to note the similarity of this phrase to the one used often by Sara for the description of her place within her family as *daughter of the home.*

21. Sara refers to the fact that her house has features and her children display dress and mannerisms that signify a Jewish religious way of life, while she herself is much less so. The interviewer asked her about this at the end of the first interview, and she promised to return to this point at the end of her story. The population in Israel is roughly divided into Orthodox and secular groups, and the move from one to the other is fairly common. The story of Sara's husband and family in this regard is a common example of what is titled "return to Judaism."

22. A school for Orthodox Jewish studies.

23. The research subjects were all Israelis, and in Israel, military service is obligatory for all Jewish citizens: two years (18-20) for a woman and three years (18-21) for a man. When a male soldier volunteers for officers' course, he commits himself to an additional year of service, fully paid. This was the case with David.

24. Literally "the way of suffering," referring to Jesus's last march.

25. This mockingly refers to a famous matchmaking TV program running at the time of the interview in which most of the men presented themselves with these two adjectives.

26. A war in which Israel was attacked by Egypt and Syria, October 1973.

27. A war between Israel and its northern neighbors—Lebanon and Syria—June 1982.

4

The Holistic-Content Perspective

This chapter presents our holistic-content approach to the life story. The chapter is divided into two sections: (a) reading a life story from a holistic-content perspective and (b) early memories as a key to holistic-content approach.

READING A LIFE STORY FROM A HOLISTIC-CONTENT PERSPECTIVE: AMIA LIEBLICH

In our reading of the entire story (pp. 30-60), we tried to form a holistic-content picture of Sara's and David's selves as presented in their interviews. This will be presented in full for Sara and briefly for David.

The process of reading for content in a holistic manner can be summarized as follows:

1. Read the material several times until a pattern emerges, usually in the form of foci of the entire story. Read or listen carefully, empathically, and with an open mind. Believe in your ability to detect the meaning of the text, and it will "speak" to you. There are no clear directions for this stage. There are aspects of the life story to which you might wish to pay special attention, but their significance depends on the entire story and its context. Such aspects are, for example, the opening of the story, or evaluations (e.g., "it was good") of parts of the story that appear in the text.

2. Put your initial and global impression of the case into writing. Note exceptions to the general impression as well as unusual features of the story such as contradictions or unfinished descriptions. Episodes or issues that seem to disturb the teller, or produce disharmony in his or her story, may be no less instructive than clearly displayed contents.

3. Decide on special foci of content or themes that you want to follow in the story as it evolves from beginning to end. A special focus is frequently distinguished by the space devoted to the theme in the text, its repetitive nature, and the number of details the teller provides about it. However, omissions of some aspects in the story, or very brief reference to a subject, can sometimes also be interpreted as indicating the focal significance of the topic, as will be demonstrated below.

4. Using colored markers (following the method applied by Brown et al., 1988), mark the various themes in the story, reading separately and repeatedly for each one.

5. Keep track of your result in several ways: Follow each theme throughout the story and note your conclusions. Be aware of where a theme appears for the first and last times, the transitions between themes, the context for each one, and their relative salience in the text. Again, pay special attention to episodes that seem to contradict the theme in terms of content, mood, or evaluation by the teller.

Discussion of the case with other independent readers can be highly productive, but as this is interpretive work, do not expect to obtain "inter-judge reliability."

Sara: Global Impression

Sara's life story lends itself easily to the formation of a global impression as it evokes a strong sense of continuity from early childhood throughout her growth into adulthood. As a reader, I never felt great surprise at any of the developments in Sara's life, with the exception, perhaps, of her late conversion to an Orthodox way of life.[1] The consistent manner in which Sara constructs her life story is characterized by a positive, optimistic worldview and evolves in the interpersonal rather than the intrapersonal realm.

To begin with the latter characteristic of her narrative, Sara's is a relational story,[2] constantly referring to others, both in the context of describing her relationships with them and also as asides about these others—her parents or high school students from her class. According to a rough estimate, such interpersonal descriptions form from half to three-quarters of the text of her narrative. "Others" in Sara's world are very often women and children while men who are not family relatives are seldom presented. Statements about the "I" as a separate individual are rare and often refer to the "remembering self"—I, Sara the adult, am looking and reflecting on these past events. For example: "I still remember this sentence," or "Today, as an eighth grader, I would never dare take on such responsibility." Other rare examples of reference to the "I" are when she depicts herself as unusual in some respect, in comparison with her peers or siblings, such as " because I am the firstborn I think that I always am related to . . . all in all there was something of a relation, uh . . . somewhere yes, preference towards me." However, these type of utterances are actually taking into account the existence of others, as they form some standard for comparison. Finally, there are rare personal statements in which Sara describes her traits: being active, responsible, or "not brilliant."

In addition to its predominantly relational nature, Sara's story is positive in its outlook on herself, the people around her, and the world. Negative feelings or events are extremely rare. By her account, all the people she met in life, whether relatives or not, individuals or groups, were good and nurturing toward her. In the second meeting, when Sara herself probably becomes aware of this pattern in her story, she comments: "I think I find people that really help me in life" and defines it as "being lucky." From the vantage point of the present, Sara's past life events are always described as beneficial, even if their positive nature might have been questionable when they occurred. About her transfer to another elementary school, for example, against which she struggled as a child, she says, "I don't regret this move for a moment." Negative moments in her life story are reversed so that they exemplify something positive. This can be demonstrated by her description of her segregated high school experience as an opportunity, if not for herself then for other students. Or, regarding her test anxiety, which, in the context of her narrative, Sara used to praise her school for giving her individual attention and assistance: "Today I think that no other school would have treated the problem like they did." Finally, even in talking about her present life, with the extremely difficult tasks of mothering three young children (one of whom is not entirely healthy) and being a full-time teacher, with minimal help from her husband or parents—she never complains. She says: "God gave me a great gift—speed, this is my luck, and I hope I will be able to keep up my pace."

Two exceptions stand out and actually reinforce the benevolent nature of Sara's constructed life story. The first is her earliest memory of the death of her sister (an episode that will be interpreted from several angles in this book), and the second is her personal disappointment by her grades at the end of high school: "Today I am disappointed by my results, because, for some reason, I had higher expectations. I don't know what happened that I got such grades."

Finally, the combination of the two aspects of the global impression of Sara's story—its positive and relational nature—finds its strongest and most direct expression in the frequent appearance of "good relationships" throughout her life story. With these in mind, we now turn to the examination of central foci in her narrative, some of which will, as expected, elaborate further on the global impression summarized above.

Major Themes

Sara's life story suggests four themes that appear repeatedly in the various stages. These themes present the uniqueness of her life story and may be viewed as four different perspectives for reading the story as a whole.

(1) Belonging and Separateness. When Sara presents herself at the beginning of her interview, she tells about her parents, her siblings, and her place in the family. "My father is from Iran . . . My brother is seven years [younger]" and so on. Right away she is telling the interviewer: I am a family person, I have a strong sense of belonging to my social unit. Yet, in the same set of first sentences, she adds: "I'm the firstborn," an attribute that forms the basis of her separate and unique status, as will be elaborated below. Thus the first perspective of the story is voiced very clearly in Sara's introduction.

As she describes her life during childhood—what she calls "a very normal childhood"—Sara often speaks in the plural: "we stayed at home till the age of 4, with mom," for example, or "a sister was born to us." The primary unit she refers to is the family, characterized by its nurturance and warmth. In Sara's case, the family also includes her grandparents, who are described in great detail. Additional family members (e.g., an aunt) are added on to the caring network that is holding Sara and providing security. Throughout her life, Sara tends to see (or construct in her narrative) other social units that she encountered as similar to her family in that respect. This happens when nonrelatives are attached to the family or when nonfamily units are perceived, remembered, and/or presented in the story as familylike.

For example, Sara's narrative attaches her beloved first-grade teacher to her family by emphasizing her contacts with, and affection for, her mother—"the contact was made directly even before I became her student." In elementary school, Sara speaks of her friends as having special relations with her family. Her young mother joined the kids in their play: "Lots of friends would come and when we played she joined us." When her father prepared for the Sukkoth holiday, "all the children from the neighborhood would come" and join in the festive preparations of her family. "It was a feeling of togetherness," she concludes in this description. A strong sense of attachment to the family seems to characterize Sara's mother also, regarding her family of origin. At the same time, family boundaries seem to be flexible; Sara's father is considered a son of her maternal grandparents, and the concept of "adoption" appears numerous times in the following life stages.

Similar affectionate connections are carried over to the youth movement in which male and female leaders assume the roles of part-parents, part-older siblings: "At the end they got married, these two, and we remained friends." In line with the merging boundaries between family and the external social realm, she tells how she took her young sister along to one of the youth movement trips, a step that is rare in such age-segregated organizations. Later in life, she tells about very cohesive class relationships (so that, as in a family, students gave priority to their loyalty and belonging to the class rather than to individual advancement); about home visits to her high school teachers, who gave her tutorials for free; about a familylike unit of her friends in the army settlement (here, again, she uses the same words as in her childhood: "we felt a sense of togetherness"); about remote family relatives who are suddenly discovered in the kibbutz where she does her military service and who adopt her; about the military commander who "sort of adopted me" for a daughter and used to join her family in festive occasions; and, when she became a teacher herself, about the group of teachers who form intimate group relations, and about the kibbutz school principal who (again) took her and the second teacher as her daughters; "she cared so much for us that it was unbelievable." Sara's attraction to the kibbutz, which is revealed in several stages of her life story, may be taken as another manifestation of her view of the social world as familylike. Thus strangers become integrated into the family network or form a simulated family for Sara, and all contribute to the creation of the warm, safe, relational world that surrounds her.

Sara herself seems to contribute to the selection and formation of the units or networks that surround her—although that part of her story is usually muted. She tends to play down her role as a good partner. She says, "I was lucky—I think I find people that really help me in life." Once, in a story about her grandparents, she refers to the reciprocal nature of her relationships, saying, "I knew how to return this love"—but uses the word *return* rather than a term reflecting personal agency. Later, she also tells how she used to help them, to teach them, and so on. Such active reciprocation, however, is rare in her presentation of self.

In her brief reference to her own young family, Sara describes her children also from the same perspective, namely, as a unit of warm and positive contacts. Rather than describing their different traits, she says, "They have very nice relationship, they play with each other like friends." Her workplace as a teacher assumes some familylike characteristics—she brings her young children to work with her on many occasions and calls them "kids of the school." At the same time, her relationship with her mother maintains its place and intensity. It is her mother who assists her in labor when she delivers her three children and takes care of her when she is hospitalized for an operation. Generalizing, she says, "I was deeply attached to the family, a family was for me the . . . to this very day I think, this is what seems to me the most important, all other things pale in comparison."

Within this supportive network, however, with all the emphasis on belonging, Sara remains an individual with a separateness and uniqueness of her own. As mentioned above, in her introduction, she says, "I am the firstborn," and later refers to herself as *Bechorika,* a term from her native tongue that means (in her words) "the beloved firstborn girl" or "a daughter that's very uh . . . I received a lot of attention, a lot of love." In a consistent manner, she conveys the picture of being a chosen individual, at the same time that she herself apologizes for this immodest view: "God forbid, this does not mean that they did not relate to everyone—each one of the kids had his special place." Yet Sara "got the best treatment of all" and was preferred by her grandparents and her aunt, a position in which she gets more (sweets, toys, "a good word or a good feeling") but also gives more to the others. She describes well how she was different from her siblings, especially the sister following her in age—this being her way of self-definition. "She was more stubborn than me, and less willing to obey." The traits she presents at the core of her uniqueness are being very *active,* a word that appears in many contexts as characteristic of herself, *fast* (a trait that she presents as her major luck in life as an adult), *hardworking,* and *responsible.* These traits make her a *leader* in the youth movement. Her uniqueness is further defined by Sara in a negative manner, by what she is not—namely, a brilliant student who enjoys academic work.

In telling her life, Sara often sees what happened to her as a unique development; she is the "first" not only in her family but in many of her experiences. Similarly, she conveys the sense of being "chosen." Sara was given lead parts in the school plays. She was picked out of the entire class, with three others, to take the tests for a highly prestigious high school, and she is accepted to the school—to be in the first class in an experimental program. This class to which Sara belonged was unique as a unit, and its educational outcomes were "simply incredible." Within this class, Sara sees herself as one of the "outstanding students." This, incidentally, may be why she is disappointed by her final grades. In the army, she has the experience of pioneering, "we founded a new settlement in a desert border area, we were truly the first to be there." As a student in the teachers' seminary, again, she is selected to teach at the model school and is the only graduate presented with flowers during the graduation ceremony. With her husband, she goes to live "in a new building, in a new development area outside the city," and is immediately offered a job in the new school that is opened there. Her uniqueness, which is sometimes blurred with her independence, changes its nature somewhat after her marriage. Now, a mother of three, a homemaker, and a full-time teacher, she tells the interviewer that she is blessed by a more practical trait: "God gave me a great gift—speed, this is my luck."

Within the theme of belonging and separateness, one anomaly is Sara's struggle with the title of "underprivileged" for herself and her family. Related to this is Sara's awareness that being special is not always desirable. Throughout her story about high school, Sara expresses her ambivalence about being named as a lower level student, which is, of course, a contradiction to her sense of being "chosen," or may be interpreted as being chosen for the wrong reasons. She argues that her family did not deserve this offensive title, yet at the same time she is thankful for the individual attention she received in the special enrichment program. Being special may become a cause for shame—not for her, she says, but for other students in the "experimental class"—as when she describes how students from the regular classes "used to peep at us . . . as if we were monkeys in a zoo." In Sara's case, however, her sense of worth is so solid that the episode remains isolated in a story that stresses being unique, special, and chosen.

(2) Closeness, Remoteness, and the Experience of Moving. Concepts of location and movement, in particular being near to or far from a certain place, usually where her family lives, abound in Sara's life story. It may be seen almost as a story about gravitation; until the age of 30 it is her parents' home that serves as the lodestone for her movements, while in the last decade the center gradually becomes her own home, where her children are growing up. On another level, home and closeness to home is Sara's way of speaking about femininity. Although Sara has been a working woman all her life, she usually only describes men as going far from home, driving cars out of the home territory, and staying out for many hours a day.

Generally, the stages of Sara's life story follow a similar pattern: She lives close to mother (or another nurturing figure or figures) and from this safe home base dares venture outside on her own. Her close environment is not restricting; on the contrary, the receipt of care, love, and security empowers her to move out, at least for limited periods of time. In later stages, this pattern is simulated with nonfamily individuals, friends and commanders in the army, or school officials and teachers who work with her. She prefers to remain in a familiar environment, yet often she takes daring steps and moves out, where she, once again, manages to re-create familiarity in her new location.

The introduction of this perspective suggests a paradox: Would a child whose mother stays at home with younger siblings, whose home environment is described as so nurturing, be as happy to go out into the foreign world of kindergarten? Apparently so; this is the dynamic of Sara's development, along the line of Mahler, Pine, and Bergman's (1975) concept of refueling: It is a loved child who separates with greater ease. And so Sara tells us that, after staying with mother at home till the age of 4, she was happy in her nursery school, and "I always used to come back to a home full of joy, with a cooked meal and a mom who's home, who's there for us, welcomes us."

The world outside is foreign, and Sara mentions several times that she prefers old acquaintances and does not look forward to meeting new people. However, moving to a new apartment with her family is remembered as a positive episode. To express Sara's tenuous security (or her own fears) of moving, she compares her experience with that of her younger sister: "[She] thought that she would be left behind in kindergarten, that we wouldn't take her with us." This follows a more distant separation, from the baby sister who died, a formative experience that probably contributed to Sara's need to gather her loved ones near. As she comes to the new neighborhood, Sara is threatened by the experience of being a newcomer, but this evaporates as she meets children from her school. Movement is a challenge and requires the overcoming of hardship and fear—but all ends well, as she remembers from elementary school: "I don't regret this move for a moment."

As a child, life for Sara evolves within a small parameter—her school and home are very close. So is the youth movement club, which allows Sara to be present at home for the Shabat services and in the club for her meetings. This is repeated later in life—when she is a single teacher living next to school and her parents' home in the city or, at present, where she teaches in her new neighborhood.

But, from childhood, due to the love and permissiveness of her family, Sara ventures greater distances with ease. She fondly recalls her field trips in the youth movement as she reflects on this apparent paradox: "Although I was . . . a daughter of the home, I was never restricted." A little later she repeats: "As much as I was a girl of the home, I was very independent." It should be noted that the phrase *girl (or daughter) of the home* is unusual in Hebrew and is an invention by Sara for her self-presentation. When the interviewer asks Sara to explain this term, she defines it as being "very attached to the home," yet her story implies that she is emotionally attached but, in practice, highly autonomous. She dares to go far on her own and, in addition, to assume responsibility for younger children, as if her home environment empowers her to do so. The trust that allowed her autonomy to flourish is reciprocated, according to her story, by her natural obedient and responsible behavior: "I am obedient by nature. I wasn't the type who goes out and disappears . . . I never overdid things [such as staying outside for fun]."

Sara went to the army "in the framework of my youth movement," namely, with former friends she had known for years. She goes to a very new place, together with familiar people. The matter of home visits is highly salient in her story about the military service and, indeed, in her entire story as an adult. In the army, for example, she was able to live far from her family and not visit except once every six weeks—which is uncommon for young women in the Israeli army, who get leaves to go home frequently. But after some time, the pull from home overcame her need for autonomy, and she asked for a transfer "so that everyday at 5:00 I went home—this was great." Again, as a new teacher, she is happy to work in a distant school and names many advantages of the distance (in spite of the fact that her parents preferred that she worked closer to home)—yet she commutes and continues to live at home with her parents.

Sara's most daring move out of her parents' territory is when she finds a teaching job in a southern kibbutz. (This is a voluntary move, while the army service is compulsory.) Yet she goes to a kibbutz near her sister's, and in the kibbutz establishes, again, a semifamily for herself. The matter of visits at home is once more clearly voiced in the story. At the end of the year, going back to her home town, and to a teaching position in her own former elementary school, Sara describes some conflicts regarding living in an apartment of her own. She ends up choosing a place very close to both her parents' home and the school. This is her last location as a single woman before moving to her permanent place in a flat of her own, as a wife, soon to be a mother.

Talking briefly about meeting her husband, she again presents a map, a story about locations: "We both lived in the same neighborhood since childhood . . . I met him at the local bakery . . . we each moved in a circle in the same area, yet I never saw him before." After her marriage, when a safe haven for life as an adult has finally been reached, Sara takes her longest trip outside her local territory, doing this, however, in the company of her husband: "We went to visit my husband's sister in the USA and took a long trip there." So throughout her life, close locations of home, work, and family provide Sara with the security she needs and employs so as to travel from time to time.

In this perspective also, there is an episode that stands out because it does not follow the pattern, a negative instance—the story about her infant sister's death. If going far away is both a threat and a challenge in Sara's life, death is of course the farthest possible "trip." It is hard to determine whether security issues remain so central in Sara's life because of this early episode or whether the memory of this premature loss is brought up and given its prominent place as a result of her consistent reconstruction of her life story.

(3) The Meaning of Teaching, or Teaching as Care. Sara dedicates a large—perhaps the largest part—of her story to her memories as a pupil and her various experiences as a teacher. Teachers and classmates have remarkable presence in her story throughout her life and are often portrayed as extensions of her family. Teaching and learning, in Sara's life story, are embedded in nurturing relationships more than in an academic, achievement-oriented world.

As Sara's story demonstrates, she retains clear and predominantly positive memories from each phase of school life. Starting with the earliest period, she says, "I have very good memories from kindergarten . . . I enjoyed myself so much there." This repeats itself when she talks about first and second grades: "I remember (. . .) very favorably the teacher from the first and second grades. I remember her name. I remember the plays . . . she always included me." She talks about her move to a new elementary school as a transition from one good experience to a better one. Even her high school experience, which was traumatic for some of her peers, is remembered as being dominated by many caring teachers and officials.

But as she traces her growth as a student in memory, Sara reflects, "I don't think I was outstanding as a student, I wasn't brilliant but I liked to work and study." Even when she is selected for a high school program based on her potential, and later on when the same high school offers her a transfer to a higher level class, she does not seem to give herself credit for academic excellence but instead presents herself as responsible, active, and hard-working, one who likes to help her teachers and organize different activities for her friends. Her teachers are also not described as extremely talented in teaching per se; they are commended by Sara for personal attention and assistance to students, for not charging money for extra tutorials given in their homes, for encouraging her during tests, saying that "this high school really invested in us above and beyond." In a different context, she says, "And it was education—boys didn't grow long hair or put earrings, no miniskirts for girls. Such things show that you care."

The lower priority given by Sara to academic excellence and a competitive approach, both as a student and as a teacher, is epitomized in her story about giving up her chance to be promoted from the experimental class to a far better class because of purely social considerations. The same motives are repeated when she talks about herself as a teacher to younger children and about her own children's experiences in their schools.

Again we find here an exceptional instance that emphasizes the basic pattern by its deviation from the norm. At the end of high school, regarding her matriculation tests, Sara says, "I am disappointed by my results . . . I had higher expectations." Significantly, this admission is evoked as an answer to the interviewer's direct question, after a very long description of her high school experience that did not include this point. In her spontaneous account, Sara describes her entire school experience under the heading "My school was really good for me." She repeats several times her view that the positive outcomes in the future development of the program's graduates should be attributed to their teachers' investment in them. The graduates' achievements or success is not defined only in professional or academic achievements but also in family life (which, in one of her two references to this point, comes first in the sentence):

> And at the end most of us made progress, we were very successful, each of us has established a nice family and a career. You can see, you know, everyone has three children, four children, everyone has built a family and has a respected occupation.

As a teacher, Sara strives to provide her young pupils with the same individual care and nurturance that she remembers being given by her own teachers. She says that she decided to become a teacher very early in life, in continuation of her role as a youth leader. Her life story as an adult refers to her professional life much more than to any other aspect of her experience, in spite of her clear statement that her family is by far the most important thing in her life. She also speaks about tremendous investment of time and energy in her profession, especially when she was single. She describes herself as a teacher who is "someone with confidence, with a direction, and with a good team orientation." She enjoyed working in a small class, in the kibbutz school, where she could give individual attention to each of her students, and she always refers to "good relationships between the teachers." Finally, she says that she really loves "teaching very young kids," with whom she is able to develop a relationship that is "very personal" and "true."

To summarize this voice in Sara's story, she put great stock in her experiences and identity as a student and a teacher—both roles that she describes as being focused around giving and receiving personal care, somewhat as an enlargement and generalization of family relations into the occupational sphere.

(4) Men, and the Threat of Remaining Single. In reading a life story for its meaning, the topics that stand out are usually characterized by their high frequency of appearance, proportional length, or vividness in the text. However, meaningful components of a life story sometimes manifest themselves through silences, namely, nonelaboration in the narrative. Their force in the story is implied by their lack, by what may seem like avoidance, or by abrupt flashes of intense nature.[3] This phenomenon is demonstrated by the final (and missing) focus of Sara's narrative.

Men play a minor role in Sara's life story, which evolves between and around women and children. Her father is given less space in the story than her mother; her only brother is not mentioned at all; and her boyfriends and husband are an enigma. It seems that in the same fashion that men are absent from the household due to their leaving home for work, they are also missing from Sara's account of her life. About her father she says, "Father always worked hard . . . Often he had to take two jobs." As compared with her relatively absent father, brother, and husband, Sara's grandfather has high salience as a nurturant figure in her childhood account, proving that—in Sara's construction of her life and world—when an older man retires from the job market, he is once more allocated a space in women's world and in her story. Although Sara does work as a professional, her work is marked by being nurturant in its nature and close to home in its location. The significance of the gap between men's world and women's space is epitomized by the fact that Sara does not drive a car, and the family car is used solely by her husband.

In the same vein, only in response to a direct question does Sara tell the interviewer about her high school boyfriend, mostly denigrating this childish relationship—which stands out in comparison with all the other relationships that she cherished. Her second boyfriend, from the military settlement, is mentioned only in passing. As for her husband, other than rescuing her from the state of spinsterhood—a topic to which we will turn later—the story gives him only one role of relative prominence in Sara's life, namely, his initiative to adopt the Orthodox Jewish lifestyle. In choosing orthodoxy, he takes a step to change the life of his family together with his own so that, from this perspective, his life is depicted not as outside the family and Sara's life space but right at the center, influencing a change that affects them all. This, however, is accepted with good nature by Sara—she has always described herself as an "obedient" individual. For Sara, evidently, the harmony of her family takes precedence over daily habits and behaviors that may divide it. Typically, she sees her children's chance for better education as a beneficial outcome of this change. Here again we find Sara's central trait of living through relationships; her conformity to her husband's religious requests has little to do with a deeper sense of spirituality or religiosity in herself. "I don't define myself as 'religious,' but I do what is necessary at home . . . the more personal requirements are up to me."

While men seem to play a marginal role in Sara's narrative, for a woman of her strong familial orientation, the threat of remaining unmarried emerges as a major theme. Her story indicates that the world is divided into single and married people. She introduces this motif in an early childhood memory about a "single" (this adjective is mentioned twice in two following sentences) aunt who used to take her in a taxi to spend the weekend in her house "to give her [. . .] fun so that I would be with her and she would not be alone" for the weekend. A single woman alone for the weekend is thus depicted as a clearly negative life condition. The relatively late age at which Sara herself got married amplifies this childhood memory and is apparent in her naming of her 20-30 life stage as "teaching and being single."

Yet being single for a while is not all bad: In several places Sara refers to the advantages of being unattached at the beginning of her teaching career. "When I was single I was more dedicated than today," she says. Or "Today I think that it was a plus to start teaching as a single woman, because I was able to dedicate incredible amounts of time." The prefix "Today I think" may introduce the evaluation as a present reconstruction of former experiences, but the same feeling permeates statements without such a prefix, as in the comparison she makes: "For one of the teachers, who was married and had a daughter, it was much harder to keep up with us."

As she tells about her life after 20, Sara is candid about her concerns around meeting men for the purpose of eventual marriage. For Sara, the important transition is between single life and having a family—the couple relationship of love, attraction, and so on has no place in her narrative. Whether this is due to modesty of speech or to her attitudes toward heterosexuality is impossible to say. She tells the interviewer about the difficulties of achieving her aim due to the nature of her profession, that is, that all the students at the teachers' seminary were females, and so were the young teachers in schools where she taught. After three years in such an environment, she says,

> My social world was also constricted, because I saw only the teachers [females], and some of them got married in the meantime. I didn't go out and I was most of the evenings at home, dedicating myself to work. So I wanted a change.

Sara is active in her search, which even leads her to a year in a remote kibbutz and back to the city because "there were no people my age in the kibbutz either. I was 25 years old already and I saw that if I stayed there I would remain single."

Sara was 30 when she met her husband in the same neighborhood she had grown up in. Very soon they got married and settled down. Her sense of accomplishment in this personal act, and her escape from a miserable fate, are revealed by her last comment about being single, in reference to her new apartment:

> A month after the wedding we got the keys to this apartment, so I moved in as a couple [a strange phrase], and I'm so glad, because the place is full of young couples and small children and as a single I don't know how I could have taken it. There was one single woman here for two years, and she left.

Evidently, Sara's fate is different, and in talking to the interviewer in her home, with her children coming and going around her, she projects a sense of gratitude for her lot in life.

Concluding Remarks. The holistic-content presentation of Sara's story has depicted a self that emerges from her interview as being relational and positive. Four major foci referred to allow for a comprehensive representation of the story. The themes are not easily extricable from one another, especially the first two, which are interconnected at one pole: Being a family member is examined in the first perspective in comparison with being a unique individual, while in the second it is contrasted to going far from home. In general, the first perspective deals with Sara among people, while the second, with Sara's movements between various locations. The term *closeness* is common to these two polarities: In the first it refers more to intimacy or warmth of a relationship, while in the second, the word *close* means near in physical space. The third perspective in the story relates to Sara's experiences as a student and a teacher, and the last one, to the place of men in her world and her fear of not achieving what she sees as her major life task—to create a family of her own, which brings us back full circle to the first theme of the story.

At this point it is important to introduce the concept of "interpretive level," which is relevant to the differences between the three first foci of Sara's story and the fourth one. Reading and interpreting a life story may vary in the extent to which theoretical understanding plays a role in interpretation. At one extreme is the phenomenological stand, which takes the report of the teller at face value as a presentation of his or her life and world, and reads or listens to it naively, respecting the explicit narrative as is. At the other extreme, we may come to understand a story armed with a variety of theoretical assumptions (unknown to the interviewee, of course). Such reading suspects the teller's presentation and is searching for silences, gaps, contradictions, symbols, and other clues to the underlying or implicit contents that the interviewer is concealing, often also from him- or herself. This kind of reading is prevalent among clinical psychologists, especially those working within the psychoanalytic framework. Various shades of interpretive levels can be characterized between these two extreme poles. The position one takes on this dimension is reflected also in the type of questions that are asked and comments that are made in the interview itself (a topic that we will not discuss in this volume).

While many of the researchers of life stories advocate relatively naive, nonjudgmental reading, and refrain from extensive theoretical interpretation, every reader is inevitably bringing her culture, language, experience, and expectations into her interactions with others or with texts. I try to be a "naive listener," respecting the subjectivity of my interviewee, but my feminist and existential systems of values, for example, certainly permeated my reading of Sara's story as well as my attitudes toward her during the interview. From this general position, however, there is a difference between the three first foci of her analysis, which are based mostly on the explicit account, and the fourth, which is directed more toward the implicit level.

While each personality and life story is unique, the analysis presented above demonstrates what may be learned in reading a narrative from a holistic-content point of view. It is not proposed as a "true" reading but as one possibility, based on the inference process documented above. Not all the points mentioned in the introductory instructions were used in this presentation of Sara. The reader is invited to try her or his additional applications of the method to both Sara's and David's life stories.

General Impression and Main Foci of David's Life Story

Without going into detail as we did for Sara, some of the central aspects of David's story will be outlined. The reader might stop and try to write down her or his impressions from David's story before continuing to read this section. Afterward, while reading the following description, the reader might look for quotations in the interview to support the claims made or to test their shortcomings. Both for lack of space and to supply the reader with this exercise, no quotes are supplied in the following summary.

David is a hardworking man. Since childhood, he has often held several jobs or pursued several activities at once, which he describes as being a challenge. His life story is very much a story of a career, with all the various positions he held, in different places, while climbing on the managerial ladder. Different stations in his work life are clearly depicted as progressive or regressive. While success and evaluation by himself and by others are major themes of the story, David's work is described with great affect, stressing his personal involvement and dedication, to the point of naming some of his activities as "addictions." Furthermore, the criteria of progress and success are equally applied to the organization, namely, the hotels, in which David works.

From childhood onward, David measures and evaluates himself on a scale of worth and is concerned with his place on the many scales he employs for this conceptualization. In his youth, he often refers to himself as mediocre, someone whose alleged goal is not to exert himself, not to excel, not to stand out. This tendency changes as he grows up and finds his occupational field, where he discovers—and reveals to the interviewer—his ambitions and investment. The style of his story also changes; from initial understatement and a reserved manner of speech, he allows himself more extensive and declarative statements about his projects and achievements. Yet, altogether, David's story consistently emphasizes an ongoing evaluative process, which he applies to each of his moves in life. When he is not making head-on progress for a while, he rationalizes by claiming involvement in other areas of his life, and seems to convey the message that it is out of his own choice, in other words, that he is in control of his life.

Clearly, David's narrative is the story of an individual, one man, perhaps a loner—and an organization. His story gives a broad and deep picture of himself as a separate person. In other words, his "I" takes up a large space in his story. Parallel to this perspective, it is also a story of a culture, the organizational world of the hotel and the hotel chain, with some of its specific features and dilemmas. Only after these two major components, or heroes, of the story do we find other people, in supplementary roles. David conveys the sense that others, especially his wife and children (and at one time his father), are very important for him, and he loves them. But he takes them for granted. They provide the ground for his figure to emerge from, namely, his individuality.

David admits he is not good at maintaining relationships. This is further epitomized by the small place others occupy in his life story. Others appear mostly in response to the interviewer's direct questions. Even so, we never hear anything about his mother or sisters, for example, and very rarely about his father, whose business is quite similar to David's own career. A seemingly exceptional pattern emerges at two points of the life story when David—of his own initiative—tells the interviewer about the adoption of his first child and then his second child. However, in both cases he returns promptly to the main line of the story—namely, his career, and even in this very personal and painful matter of childlessness, David presents his story within the discourse of problems, decisions, solutions, and achievements. In a similar fashion, his girlfriends are described as resources—they assist him in various ways. Even when we hear about his outstanding voluntary activities on behalf of handicapped children, the altruistic motivation is totally muted and the episode is presented as an addiction on his part. Similarly, when we hear about his involvement with the African workers, it is presented as a test of his honesty and an educational endeavor on his part.

On the other hand, when asked directly, David presents himself as a sensitive man, more than others, according to his evaluation. If we take David's claim seriously, we may conclude that the minor and detached manner in which others enter into David's story, as well as the major place of the "I" and the organization in it, manifest his public voice, his chosen way to narrate his story, perhaps in accordance with some masculine norms that he senses around him. It may be possible that, being a sensitive man, he keeps the more intimate and personal matters to himself. In completing his story with the half-humorous reference to the computer as a "significant other," and to the matter of language as a most important thing in life, David may be telling us that he is used to the language of doing, evaluating, and achieving but lacks language for talking about feelings and relationship.

EARLY MEMORIES AS A KEY TO
THE HOLISTIC-CONTENT APPROACH:
MICHAL NACHMIAS

The subject of early memories has gained much theoretical and empirical attention in psychology. In the following section I will demonstrate a detailed interpretation of the early memories of two interviewees from our sample (Sara, see pp. 29-50, and Jacob, both aged 42) and show their significance in the context of the story as a whole.

Alfred Adler's ideas about early memories were at the core of his psychological theory (Adler, 1929a, 1929b, 1931, 1956). Freud, too, discussed early memories in his writings yet did not attribute unique significance to them in his psychoanalytic theory (Freud, 1899/1950, 1901/1960). According to Adler, memories are always emotionally significant, even when they do not seem to be important. Memories are personal creations; they consist of choices, distortions, and inventions of past events in a manner that befits the individual's current goals, interests, or moods. "There are no 'chance memories': out of the incalculable number of impressions which meet an individual, he chooses to remember only those which he feels, however darkly, to have a bearing on his situation. Thus his memories represent his 'Story of My Life' " (Adler, 1931, p. 73).

Memories therefore are, according to Adler, an efficient tool for making inferences about an individual's personality and lifestyle. Early childhood memories, in particular, and especially the first one, are of unique significance for Adler. They display the individual's basic view of life and can therefore be used as an effective instrument for the evaluation of personality.

Many empirical studies have been inspired by Adler's theory, although most, unlike the present study, were conducted in a clinical setting or collected early memories separately (see, for example, Bishop, 1993; Bruhn, 1985; Mosak, 1958; Watkins, 1992) rather than within the framework of life-story research. The application of Adler's ideas to memories derived from life stories requires several interpretive decisions. The major dilemma is how to locate the "first memory" in this context. Is it the earliest memory on a chronological dimension, or the first memory narrated in the interview? This dilemma relates to the understanding that a life story is a text and, like any text, is constructed of a beginning, middle, and end that carry special significance. In other words, the life story is not just a chronology of ordered events, which can be derived from the text, but also the specific kind of organization according to which the narrator chooses to tell his or her life. Furthermore, the first memory *narrated* may be other than the first memory *remembered* by the teller, but it is the first one he chooses to include in his life story, the first one that, in Adler's words, has a "bearing on his situation" and thus may be even more significant for understanding this "situation."

Some life stories, however, do not include specific early episodes but general impressions from the teller's childhood. Can these be used as an "early memory," or should one keep looking for the distinctive first memory in the text? Such questions do not have simple solutions and require an interpretive strategy.

The method whereby life stories were obtained in the present study facilitated the search for early memories. Because the interviewee was asked to divide his or her life story into stages, and to relate an event or an experience that was typical of each one, I focused on responses to the first stage in the text. Several interviewees, however, could not recall a distinct early memory but reported about their early childhood in general terms. In David's interview, for example (pp. 50-60), the interviewer did not succeed in obtaining an early memory in spite of repeated attempts on her part.[4] He provided a general report: "I remember my childhood as being normal. A child, just a regular child, living in a good, nice home." Or "It was really a period of freedom from worries." In other cases, the narrators related more than one early episode, and I had to decide which one to select for the analysis.

My final decision was to look for the first distinct memory that appears in the text. By "distinct memory," I refer to any memory that stands out as a discrete episode rather than a generalized impression. Notwithstanding my preference for discrete episodes, I feel that general impressions about childhood may also provide insights about the whole story. Thus, when David asserts throughout his narrative that he was usual, mediocre, not an outstanding individual, for better or worse, it seems quite appropriate that he would use generalized statements of the same sort about his childhood— as in "I remember my childhood as being normal."

The decision regarding chronological or textual early memories was settled by the texts themselves; the organization of the interview led the narrators to construct a chronologically ordered story, and in most cases the first memory narrated was first on the time axis. In the unusual cases, when the time dimension was violated, as in Jacob's story to which I will refer later, the first narrated memory calls for special interpretation. Such examples would probably be more frequent when the organization of the interview allows for a freer construction of one's life story.

Sara:[5] Early Memories and
Their Meaning for the Life Story

The first distinct memory in Sara's life story concerns the death of her year-old sister, when Sara herself was a little girl in nursery school. She narrates this experience immediately when asked for a particular memory from her first life stage. Following Adler, I suggest that it is significant that this is the first memory that comes to her mind and that she narrates it in the way she does. In fact, she does not tell about her sister's death but about the experience of the *shiva*.[6] "I don't remember the period when she passed away, but I remember the shiva." Sara uses the term *experience* for this memory, and given that in Hebrew this term carries a positive connotation, she apologizes immediately: "the so-called experience," she corrects herself, not a pleasant memory.

The death of her sister introduced incomprehensible phenomena into Sara's home. Suddenly the house was filled with commotion—strange people coming and going, sitting on the floor—a threatening experience for a child, when no explanation is provided. The familiar home lost its security and became wide open to strangers. The normal family routines were disrupted, yet no adult offered an interpretation to Sara, who wandered outside in the neighborhood, in search of answers. Her narrative depicts the experience of a child who is lost in her own home, a sense of helplessness. "I even didn't understand what had happened," she says.

Without any prompting, Sara introduces a second early memory right after the first. These two memories seem to be associated in her mind. "So this was sort of a very traumatic experience. *That's it. Then,* towards first grade exactly we moved to a new apartment." The second memory is defined by Sara as very pleasant, yet in saying so she stops for a moment: "This was uh . . . a very pleasant experience," as if not quite sure about the appropriateness of her feelings. In this event, also, a little girl witnesses striking changes in her home without understanding what and why. This time, however, the girl is Sara's younger sister, not herself, while Sara is among those who understand, so she can recall the experience with humor (she laughs when telling about it). Her sister is 4 years old, about Sara's age when her baby sister had died. "She saw the whole house being packed, and thought that she would be left behind in kindergarten, and that we

wouldn't take her with us." The sister, then, experienced something similar
to what Sara herself went through during the shiva—an experience of loss,
lack of understanding, and helplessness. The personal belongings of the
family are packed and loaded, her parents seem to leave her behind, and no
explanation is provided.

The common denominator of the two episodes is that a fairly comforting
explanation for the strange occurrence does exist—not to the death, of
course, but to the mourning habits—yet is not provided to the girls, so that
they remain helpless. In both stories a girl is left alone, abandoned by her
parents, who forget her in the hassle of their adult lives. One sister suddenly
dies, another is left behind in kindergarten, and Sara herself is lost amidst
the commotion of traditional Jewish mourning.

Sara's first memories are highly interesting in the context of her story in
its entirety. It is possible to examine these memories from two perspectives:
Sara's description of her life at present and the central themes of her story.

I see Sara's first memory as representing the essence of her life at present
and will try to justify this claim in what follows. Throughout her narrative,
Sara tells a typical story of an Israeli secular woman in whose life religion
plays a minimal role. She was active in the youth movement, went to the
army, studied for a profession, lived as a single woman apart from her
parents, and so on. However, it was apparent to her interviewer that
currently Sara conducts her life in a Jewish Orthodox manner.[7] The interviewer's impressions (omitted from the text in Chapter 3) about the household where the interview took place, which do not match the contents of
the story, create some anticipatory tension: When did the transformation
take place, and why? What is the explanation for the changed lifestyle? The
solution of the mystery, however, is delayed to the very end of the story, as
if this part does not belong to the main plot of her life. Only after she has
completed her narrative does Sara comment: "Now, you probably want to
hear about my religious way of life." Similarly, in the outline proposed by
Sara for the chapters of her life story, the conversion does not mark a
separate life stage.

It is my contention that a parallel exists between Sara's first remembered
experience of the shiva—and the way she experiences the conversion of
her husband, followed by her own. D., Sara's husband, returned to the
Jewish Orthodox way of life after the death of his 16-year-old sister in a
car accident. Currently the whole family lives according to the Orthodox
Jewish way of life. Sara does not express any resistance to this change in
lifestyle; neither does she seem to have internalized it. Whispering, she
reveals to the interviewer that when she eats alone, she does not say grace
as required by Jewish law (again, omitted from the text). "I don't define

myself as 'religious,' " she says. She has not changed her job either, and continues to teach in a nonreligious school. Her husband's conversion—like the death of her sister—has led to the invasion of strange habits and regulations into Sara's home. The deaths of these two sisters have produced for Sara changes that she has neither fully understood nor internalized.

Consequently, Sara presents various justifications for her religious life-style—such as her ability to rest on the Shabat or the quality of education offered to her children in Orthodox schools—which are clearly not based on religious convictions or beliefs. Talking about the process of conversion, she repeatedly claims that it was bearable for her because it was gradual. She did not feel that D. forced anything on her because "there were no changes that happened all of a sudden." This process, so different from the sudden trauma of her sister's death, has served to mitigate her dread of the unintelligible. In her explanation of changing her lifestyle she says, "I care a lot about the family harmony." This stands out in contradistinction to her early memories of abandonment and family disintegration. Sara's conformity to her husband's conversion process, with all the changes entailed for the family, may thus be attributed to her early experiences; she will do anything to prevent the threat of family disintegration. In the early part of her interview she states, "A family was for me the . . . to this very day, I think, this is what seems to me the most important, all other things pale in comparison." Although uttered in a different context, "all other things" probably stands also for her husband's conversion. The value of family life is so high on Sara's scale that it justifies a lifestyle that is not based on deep, inner (incorporated) conviction.

Compared with Sara's life story, which greatly emphasizes the building of relationships and familial aspects, her early memories represent moments of loss and abandonment. Thus the experiences of being alone, and of not being able to make sense of changing reality, remain as a warning in Sara's consciousness. These are moments to which she certainly does not want to return. To establish her security within her family, so that she may not be forgotten once more, Sara defines herself mostly in the context of her home and family. She is the "firstborn," "the daughter of the home," a girl who receives a "lot of attention, a lot of love." When the interviewer presents a question that seems to threaten this position, concerning the gender issue, Sara hastens to deny that being a girl had any bearing on her status: "No, not at all." When the family moves to another location, Sara experiences a momentary threat to her sense of belonging. The children of the new neighborhood confront her: "What are you doing here? You don't belong here," as if as a girl separated from her home she has no place, which is experienced as having no identity. "And then I had to explain that I'd

moved," as if she had to reclaim her identity and existence based on the
fact that she did have a new home in the area.

In summary, Sara's insistent holding on to her family and home may
come from a deeper sense of insecurity in these respects, which is acutely
manifested in her early memories. The integrity of a family perhaps
becomes sacred when not entirely taken for granted.

Jacob: The Importance of First Memories in a Text

I decided to present Jacob's early memory as a second demonstration for
this section because it came first textually rather than chronologically.

Like all other interviewees, Jacob was asked to form a stage outline of
his life. While he was doing this, he told his interviewer the following
episode (from when he was 17), which is not an early childhood memory
but the first story he wanted to share.

> During 11th grade we had a tough experience, I did . . . I, personally, and
> my friends, too. That summer we went to a camp, a work camp in a kibbutz
> in the Valley. On the first day we got there, the kibbutz members greeted
> us happily, we were given our rooms and then, it was already evening, we
> were invited to a cookout near the fish ponds. They prepared lots of food,
> as much as I can remember—the trauma may have repressed some of the
> things I saw there—and then we went on a boat, a fishing boat, where one
> of the kibbutz members was rowing. He invited us to row in the fish pond.
> To remind you, nighttime, summer, a class, young boys and girls, each
> one calls the other to join, so this dilapidated fishing boat is filled with a
> relatively large number of kids, each one inviting his friends, and it's lots
> of fun. And then it turns out to be . . . In other words, my personal story
> is that I am sitting in the boat and I feel that the water flows in and . . . I
> won't be long, briefly, the boat sinks, drops to the bottom, and I sit there
> indifferent in the boat, since I am actually not concerned, I'll get wet, and
> it's summer so one can swim to shore, and what an experience! But this
> experience ends in tragedy, the death of the kibbutz member and the
> drowning of two soldiers, uh . . . two soldiers? (amazed), two students,
> two classmates. And here for the first time I find myself an adult, after
> being pushed into the water several times by his friends, he understands
> that actually there is someone fighting for their life here, that it's not the
> usual game of "drowning" as we used to play it in swimming pools or the
> beach, where you know the limit. And then I found myself . . . in a position
> of having to help my friends, take several people out of the water, one of
> them I pull out on the verge of—with us, or not with us. I, with another
> classmate, we turn him over and a huge quantity of water is coming out

of him, and he returns to himself, and then I understand that actually I
have faced for the first time a test of life and death, and I also helped
whoever I could to save lives. Uh . . . that's a difficult thing in itself, in
retrospect uh . . .

Jacob's story continues, describing his useless attempts to save another
classmate, who died, and he concludes,

I don't tell this as a . . . and take, God forbid, I don't take this as . . . as
my own responsibility, for the drowning, but all of a sudden I found myself
coping with a grown-up situation. That is, of fighters, of soldiers, as much
as I knew what a soldier or a fighter is.

Jacob's story is told vividly and dramatically, focusing mainly on his rescue
attempts. The event is presented as a turning point in his life, where he
became an adult and faced life-and-death problems for the first time. This
is further manifested in the stage outline of his story, where he elected to
divide his adolescent years in the unusual manner of 12-17 and 17-18 (most
of the interviewees divided 12-18, high school years). Jacob uses military
terms in this memory and, at one point, he has a slip of the tongue, when
the word *soldiers* replaces *students*—an error he corrects right away. His
concluding remark moves his story further into the military world—speaking
to the experience of soldiers and fighters.

Today, 42 years old, Jacob is a high-ranking officer in the Israeli Defense
Forces. He was released from obligatory service at 22 but returned for a
military career after his university graduation and marriage, at the age of
30. Reading his life story, it is clear that, like his first memory, Jacob's
whole narrative is deeply affected by the military experience. His two
earliest chronological memories depict a brave child who "isn't afraid of
anything." One episode describes a game of getting into a barrel, to be
rolled downhill at great speed. The second talks about looking for the
deepest rain puddles to dip into. Both of these memories are constructed
from the late vantage point of a military officer. In recalling the barrel slide
he says, "You get hit, you are all shaken—some good years later you will
do it inside a jeep or a tank." As for the puddles he says, "How did I dare
immerse myself in puddles when I had no idea what lay underneath . . . I
could have sunk right away." And he adds immediately: "I don't want to
associate this to the kibbutz event, I don't think it belongs." Saying so,
however, he himself indicates the connection. It seems plausible that had
he not become a career officer, whose main occupation was fighting and

rescue, the kibbutz memory would not have emerged so powerfully in his account and his whole childhood might have been narrated otherwise.

The effect of Jacob's present occupation on the way he constructs his childhood can be detected in other instances as well. When telling about an unsuccessful prank, he sums up: "It's a big insult, because actually you *failed the mission.*" Military terminology permeates another description, of stealing into the school storeroom, when he says, "It all amounted to two *skirmishes.*" When his mother caught him in some mischief he says, "Slowly I broke down *under interrogation* and confessed." Thus many of his childhood memories represent the initial sparks of his courage and the issue of facing challenges as an adult professional soldier.

The early memory about the kibbutz, however, is more significant than all the rest, which appeared later in his narrative, because it is the drowning episode that produced, according to Jacob's perception, his present life-style. It seems therefore the right place for beginning his life story, in spite of the fact that Jacob was already 17 at the time of its occurrence. One can describe his life as a circle, beginning in this episode at 17, continuing to mandatory service a year later, returning to the army as a professional until the present time, and going back to his childhood memories, restructuring them to fit his choices. "All my physical and mental difficulties," he says, "I experience them and continue the cycle I started somewhere in 11th grade—but let's not get carried away; they were entirely different."

Looking closely at Jacob's early memory, two themes seem to be present in the narrative: providing aid to and rescuing others, and a courageous position during struggle. These two elements are stressed in most of his childhood memories, which demonstrate his daring, on the one hand, and his altruism, on the other. When he is asked to characterize himself during childhood he says, "mischievous and helping others." As to his present self-image, in spite of his powerful position of high officer, he does not convey cold superiority but describes himself as a commander who is sensitive to the needs of his soldiers, who wants to help and educate them. This softer, warmer tendency is represented also in his childhood memory of his nursery school teacher, who was "like a big bird covering the nestling under her wings."

Jacob's life story was not fully presented in this book, yet the extracts used here may illustrate some of the possibilities for research on early memories when a self-narrative is obtained without specific instructions regarding its organization. In such cases the spontaneous choice of a first memory to be narrated—and not necessarily the earliest one—can be of great significance.

CONCLUDING REMARKS

In this chapter, two approaches to reading life stories from a content-holistic point of view were presented. In the first, in the tradition of the case study, a broad perspective of the general theme and emerging foci is used. In the second, a specific segment of the text is used to shed light on the story as a whole. Both demonstrations can be depicted as establishing links or associations within the entire story, whether from its beginning through the rest of it or across various periods and domains.

NOTES

1. This is not always the case. Some life stories are fragmented or describe great transitions. See the second section of Chapter 5. Even her religious conversion is not described as a drastic but a superficial change in her life. This also can be compared with the two life stories in the second section of Chapter 5.

2. The term *relational* refers to an emphasis on interpersonal dimensions rather than the separate self. For theoretical clarification of the term, see Gilligan (1982), Miller (1986), and Josselson (1992).

3. An excellent paper on this aspect of reading a narrative is Rogers et al. (in press), "An Interpretive Poetics of Languages of the Unsayable."

4. The reader should be reminded that David's interview was edited and somewhat abbreviated so that the repeated questions of the interviewer frequently were omitted from the text presented in Chapter 3.

5. It should be mentioned that the analysis of Sara's early memories was conducted by Michal Nachmias independently, without reading the former analysis, which was written by Amia Lieblich.

6. For an explanation of the term *shiva,* please refer to Note 3, Chapter 3.

7. Several external features identify a Jewish Orthodox home—among them the kind of books, ritual objects, and pictures that are displayed and the dress code of men, women, and children.

5

Holistic Analysis of Form

As in the previous chapter, here we focus on the analysis of the narrative as a whole. The goal in this case, however, is to demonstrate how narrative material may be used to learn about variations in structure. The working assumption in this cell of the model is that the formal aspects of structure, as much as content, express the identity, perceptions, and values of the storyteller. Analyzing the structure of a story will therefore reveal the individual's personal construction of his or her evolving life experience.

This chapter is divided to two sections: (a) structure analysis and (b) two-stage life stories: narratives of self-actualization. The first section uses a large number of life stories, while the second refers to the unusual form of two of our accumulated stories.

STRUCTURE ANALYSIS— STRATEGIES: RIVKA TUVAL-MASHIACH

Psychological inroads into the analysis of narrative structure have adopted a number of strategies from the field of literary criticism. Such strategies are based on consideration of narrative typology, progression of the narrative, and cohesiveness of the narrative.

A favored typology of four principal narrative types includes the romance, the comedy, the tragedy, and the satire. In the "romance," a hero faces a series of challenges en route to his goal and eventual victory, and the essence of the journey is the struggle itself. The goal of "comedy"[1] is the restoration of social order, and the hero must have the requisite social skills to overcome the hazards that threaten that order. In "tragedy," the hero is defeated by the forces of evil and ostracized from society. Finally, the "satire" provides a cynical perspective on social hegemony. (For more detailed readings, see Chanfrault-Duchet, 1991; M. Gergen, 1988; Murray, 1988.)

Progression of the narrative refers to the development of the plot over time. In a "progressive narrative," the story advances steadily (Figure 5.1). In a "regressive narrative," there is a course of deterioration or decline (Figure 5.2). In the "stable narrative," the plot is steady, and the graph does not change (Figure 5.3). These three basic formats can be combined to construct more complex plots (see Gergen & Gergen, 1988, for more detailed writings on the subject).

The third analytic strategy is concerned with the cohesiveness of the narrative. The elements of a well-constructed narrative (a "good story") include a story (or ongoing plot), a clearly defined objective, a series of events that progress toward that objective, and relations of sequence and causality among those events (Bruner, 1991).

Narrative research of autobiographies has suggested that men and women construct narratives differently. Men tend to devise clearly defined plots, which conform to the literary definition of the "good story" (Bruner, 1991), whereas women tend to "deviate" from literary norms and construct narratives along multiple dimensions (see Gergen, 1992). Research into such written narratives has not been complemented by research on oral narratives. The purpose of this chapter therefore is to consider the place of gender in the structure of oral narratives elicited in interviews with "ordinary" individuals. This is done by comparing the narrative structures of stories produced by men and women in our sample.

Structure Analysis:
Analysis of the Narrative as a Whole

The objective in this approach to narrative analysis is to sketch out a prototypical life course or structure for each gender group. This method entails careful reading of the story but also requires the researcher to bear in mind the stage outline provided by the interviewee.

The first phase of the analysis is to identify the axis of each stage, that is, the thematic focus for the development of the plot.[2] Here the researcher is interested in content, but only insofar as it provides raw material for the structure. While the plot axis may evolve along any theme or issue that is held to be important by the interviewee, the researcher is interested in the specific form and direction taken by this content. Thus comparisons between the structural graphs of the interviews focus on the development of themes and plots around which the structure is organized rather than on the themes and plots themselves. To give a more specific example, topics such

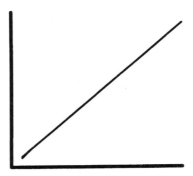

Figure 5.1. Narrative of Progress

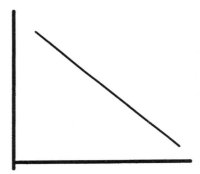

Figure 5.2. Narrative of Decline

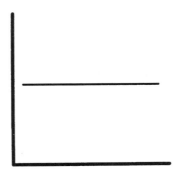

Figure 5.3. Steady Narrative

as the professional growth of the narrator or the development of social skills, independence, gender identity, and so on may be identified as thematic foci of the narrative, yet our analytic efforts will be to understand the course of this development rather than the content world in which this development takes place.

The second phase of the analysis is to identify the dynamics of the plot, which may be inferred from particular forms of speech. These forms may include (a) reflections on specific phases in the interviewee's life, such as "it was the worst time of my life," or "it was then that I first realized that I had to . . . " Evaluative comments may also refer to the interviewee's life as a whole. Thus, for example, the remark "my life has been a Cinderella story" refers to a narrative that moves from decline to triumph. The forms may also include (b) responses to a query about why the interviewee chose to end a stage at a given point in time (which was one of four questions asked about each of the stages). This question tends to elicit references to a turning point in the interviewee's life story (see McAdams, 1985, 1993). The forms may also include (c) use of terms that express the structural component of the narrative, for example, *crossroads, turning point, life course, route, progress,* or *staying in one place.*

Analysis of the narrative as a whole may also be enhanced by the researchers' personal perspective and evaluative impressions. Sensitivity on the part of the reader, for instance, to the detail and degree of emotion with which each stage is described or to discrepancies between different descriptions of the same stage may provide useful clues.

This demonstration of holistic-form analysis uses a subgroup of the total sample, namely, interviews with 22 midlife adults aged 42 (11 men, 11 women). The life stories of Ian and Mike, whose stories will be analyzed in the second part of the chapter, have not been included in this part. The interviews had been recorded in full and thus provided complete and verbatim records of the narratives. Following the procedure described above, I compiled a life-course graph for each interviewee, based on patterns of ascent, decline, and stability. Subsequently, I sought common denominators between the graphs of each gender group that would allow me to establish a prototypical graph for that group. In the last phase, the graphs of the groups were compared.

Gender Comparisons in the Interviews

Childhood. There were no differences in the shapes of the men's and women's graphs for this stage. Childhood was generally a stable period (straight line on the graph) and was often described as "normal," "ordinary," with "nothing of much importance." Most interviewees had good memories of their lives as children and described their home lives at this point in their histories as safe, warm, secure, and worry-free. Graphically, this could be plotted as a straight line in the center of the chart.

Transition to High School. The transition from elementary school to high school was universally experienced as a turning point. Although not all the interviewees delineated the period of transition as a stage in its own right, the prevailing tendency was one of movement at this point in the life course. The direction of movement on the graphs was shaped by the teller's particular experience with the academic, personal, and social exigencies of adolescence, which were generally age-appropriate.

Elias comments, "In a way it [going to high school] opened a door in my life, which determined everything that happened afterwards. I might have gone somewhere completely different—who knows? It might have been better or worse . . . but in any case I think it structured everything."

Army. For most of the interviewees, the periods of adolescence and army service were structurally quite similar. In terms of both content and direction, these years are depicted as an extension of the developmental axis that had begun in high school. Jacob, said, for instance,

> In the army I was always proving to myself that I could do just a bit more . . . I mean, all those physical challenges . . . then and even now I think I was just following the course I began, I guess, in grade 11 [when he discovered his leadership abilities; see second section of Chapter 4], but grade 11 was nothing compared to what I went through in the army.

The exceptions to this pattern were among those whose high school years had been experienced as a period of decline, generally members of the experimental, segregated program. For these interviewees, service in the army often provided a corrective experience. Some discovered hidden strengths or were able to begin spinning plans for the future. Libby said,

> In a way you could say that being in the army laid the foundations for what came later, for what I wanted to do with the rest of my life because

before then I used to think I'd want to study things that . . . I don't know what I could have done with them.

On the whole, the period of army service was more salient for the men.[3] Their descriptions of this stage are longer and more detailed than those of the women. This is not surprising given that for most of the interviewees, army service coincided with the Yom Kippur War[4] and the numerous painful experiences it entailed. Still, most of the interviewees do not recall this period in negative terms but as a phase in which they discovered skills and talents of which they had not been aware.

As in the previous stage, there are still more structural similarities than differences between the graphs of the men and the women. The prevailing trend is one of steady ascent that begins in a strong and stable childhood and peaks with the culmination of army service. This graph is relevant to most of the interviewees, with the exception, as noted above, of those who had a difficult time in the experimental high school program (which was the rationale for this study).

Early Adulthood. Early adulthood (age 20+) coincided, for most of the interviewees, with the period of study or career training with which this phase of life is generally associated among middle-class samples of this age. Thus for both men and women, the main thematic interest for this stage of the interview was the course of study chosen by the interviewee. As half of the women (six) married during their early twenties, family issues also begin to emerge for them at this stage.

Three distinct graph structures emerged for early adulthood: A graph of slow ascent represented interviewees who felt they had matured and developed during these years, assuming growing responsibilities as their horizons expanded (see Figure 5.1). A second group experienced early adulthood as a phase of search or even moratorium, which is represented as a dotted line on the graph (Figure 5.4). A third group is identified by their tendency to engage in brief endeavors prompting fresh changes of course. This period of trial and error is represented by a moderately wavy line on the graph (Figure 5.5).

It becomes increasingly difficult, as I progressed through the recollections of early adulthood, to establish a single prototypical graph for all the interviewees. Beyond the discrepancies between individual stories, and the split into the three structural types described above, a distinctly male graph structure, however, begins to emerge. This group is best represented by a career-related axis on the graph that climbs sometimes quickly, and some-

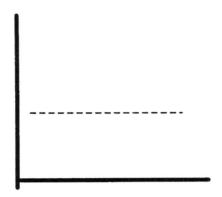

Figure 5.4. Moratorium

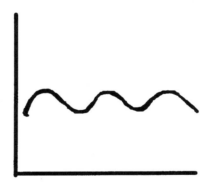

Figure 5.5. Trial and Error

times more doggedly, toward success. Even men whose graphs reflect
periods of stagnation focus on work and career-related issues, leaving
families and children in the margins rather than the centers of their narratives.

As is implied above, variations between the graphs of the men are
primarily related to the nature of their professional progress during this
period. The three variations, described below as distinct types, may also
merge and combine as individuals seek different strategies for solving
different problems. Interviewees in the first, "slowly but surely," group
(five men) describe slow advancement up the professional ladder toward
managerial and executive positions (Figure 5.6). Steve says, for instance,

Figure 5.6. Slowly Ascending

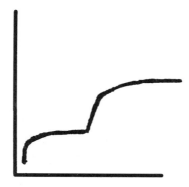

Figure 5.7. Risk and Gain

"I wouldn't say there were either sudden crises or movement by leaps and bounds. That's how it is for salaried workers. You move forward along a fairly standard course, and nothing ever happens too suddenly."

A second "sink or swim" group (four men) describe meteoric progress and assumption of responsibilities after plunging into highly challenging situations (Figure 5.7). David is one example of this type. Earnst is another, who says, "I more or less closed my eyes and jumped in over my head. Without knowing anything about the job, I suddenly found myself the office manager."

A third group find themselves retreating at an early stage of the game to cash in later. They describe situations of relinquishing status or job benefits

Figure 5.8. Descent and Gain

for the sake of prospective advancements. At times this translates into risking everything on a chance for a better future (Figure 5.8). Jacob says, for example, "You've caught me at an important juncture, just as I need to figure out what to do. To tell the truth, I'm not too bothered by all this. You can go far in any field if you really want to. I'm not afraid to retreat two steps in order to surge ahead later."

A prototypical graph for the women is far more elusive. This is because, first, a number of plot axes wind their way simultaneously through most of the women's narratives. These axes focus alternately or simultaneously on the worlds of work, family, and social relationships. Often it is difficult if not impossible to understand, as one does for the men, what the interviewee perceives as the central plot of her life story. Nor is it possible to represent the three axes in a single graph as the movement of each axis seems to be independent of the others.

A second issue is the intricacy of the plots on each axis. The women shift easily and constantly between topics and axes as they seek to clarify the salience of the issues they find important. It is difficult to follow the development of the plots, just as it is difficult to understand the progression of a pattern in which the significance of plot axes is constantly shifting.[5] Ruth's comments are typical of the multiplicity and complexity of such plot structures as she attempts to describe a period of her life between the ages of 28 and 33 when she began to work in a field far removed from her academic training:

> The transition period isn't a bad thing. It can be rather pleasant in fact, and wasn't at all stressful. I used to go to work, it was fine. I knew I was

doing something for my family, and I felt good about that. Maybe it wasn't the high point of my life. I wasn't fulfilling my dreams. I was disappointed that I wasn't going on with archaeology, but I knew I'd get there eventually.

Here the evaluations of the three plot axes diverge. Work on a daily basis is satisfying, if not fulfilling; family issues make Ruth feel good about herself, yet the frustration of her professional aspirations is a source of disappointment.

As in the male group, a number of general graph structures emerge for the women. These graphs are identifiable, however, by their emphases on one of a number of narrative strands rather than single plot trajectories. In one of these types, for instance (two women), career interests constitute a plot axis just as for the men, but the professional emphasis is only one of several trajectories on the graph. While the graphic representation of this type is reminiscent of the male examples, it tends to display more frequent diversions and digressions en route to the top.

A second group (three women), recalling Gergen and Gergen's "happily ever after" plots (1988), is characterized by the dominance of the family axes and stabilization of a plateau as the family begins to take shape. As in Sara's life story, an initial phase of trial and error in the women's lives comes to a close with the onset of marriage and child rearing. Although other plot axes continue to unfold in a minor key, establishing a family is experienced as the significant turning point. All subsequent progress along the graph is filtered through the experiences and development of the family as a whole. One interviewee comments, "You get into a routine. We're no longer the young couple just starting out. We both have jobs. There are the two kids—a family! Like one of my clients would say, a table with four sturdy legs. It really was a stable period in my life" (Libby).

For a third group (three women), the graph seems to have peaked in early adolescence and then declined as the women moved through the second and third decades of their lives. Now in their early forties, these women are slowly beginning to reclaim the freedom and independence that were temporarily lost during their child-rearing years. Beth reports,

Today I am more open than I used to be. Over the years you learn that nobody else is going to look after you if you don't do it yourself . . . In the final analysis, there's this period of your life where you're giving and giving all the time, having children—and really they always come first . . . suddenly you wake up and wonder . . . where did I get lost along the way?"

Among a quarter of the group (three women), no clear graph was discernible either because no single axis is predominant or no clear objective emerges from the structure of the story.

To summarize, the women's graphs differ from those of the men in a number of ways. Their lives are not structured by movement toward single clear objectives. No one domain is accentuated at the expense of all others. Yet with the absence of single-mindedness comes greater flexibility. Women divide their energies among different realms but have the freedom to choose which of these realms will be stressed.

The women also seem to adapt more easily to the twists and turns of fate. They seem to find it easier than men to accommodate themselves to changing realities, to define goals that befit their current situations (Bateson, 1989; Rabuzzi, 1988). A number of interviewees seem to bear out this hypothesis in their own reflections on their lives:

> I never knew what I'd be most suited to. I never had a master plan to do this or that . . . and on the way, you know, at every stage there are always new things to take into account and you think maybe this, maybe that. The truth is that I really didn't know what I was going to do. It was all so random, so unplanned. Things turned out the way they did and I just let them happen. . . . I didn't fight them, and they didn't get me down. (Joan)

And Ruth stresses, as she reflects on her past experience, that she wasn't always naturally assertive or goal directed. These characteristics only developed at a later stage of life.

> It was only at the age of 33 that I started to put things together for myself. Then, more than at other times in my life, I knew what I wanted. I mean I made things happen, instead of waiting for them to happen to me. . . . I was in control, choosing how my life would be, instead of letting my life control me.

Midlife. Two important considerations emerge from the interviewees' reflections on the current stage of their lives, that is, midlife. One is that during midlife, the structures of men's and women's stories begin to converge. Now women's lives also seem to be progressing along a central thematic axis. This phenomenon, which is based on the form analysis, conforms to Gutmann's theory (1987) as it relates to the content of men's and women's lives at midlife in his proposition that both genders become androgynous in their personalities. The second is that, for both men and women, this stage of life is viewed more positively than those that preceded it. Their narratives reflect themes of steady growth and/or stability. As Bill puts it:

> Very little has changed since then. Our lives are solid, well grounded, organized. Events proceed in a familiar routine . . . life keeps happening, and we go along with it, sometimes growing, sometimes just maintaining the status quo. Maybe in a few years' time we will retire and then things will begin to move.

Some interviewees (four men, two women) speak about wanting to change their lives or about feeling frustrated with their careers. Sara, for example, is burned out from years of teaching. Yet at this point in their lives, most of the interviewees seem to have made peace with themselves. While there is a sense of freedom to make choices or shift direction, these midlife adults are not in a hurry to make changes. John says,

> I think this is the best period of my life. I'm in my prime. I've matured in all areas of my life. I feel I understand, now, what life is all about, that I know what I didn't know when I was 20 or 30. Today I'm at my peak, whether in terms of my relations with other people, my own nature, my perceptions of myself and others, or my attitudes towards life in general.

Case Example: Sara and David

At this point, the method outlined above will be demonstrated in a brief analysis of the narratives of David and Sara. Readers are invited to return to their life stories and experiment for themselves.

Sara. In terms of content, Sara's story is typically "feminine" with a dominant relational axis (see the first section of Chapter 4). Objectives are framed first in terms of family and children, and professional advancement is clearly secondary to family concerns:

> At the end, most of us made progress, we were very successful, each of us has established a nice family and a career. You can see, you know, everyone has three children, four children, everyone has built a family and has a respected occupation.

Sara's story, it should be pointed out, is relatively more structured than those of most of the other women. Her life is stable up until her entry into high school, which she perceives as "something of a jump." The trajectory begins to rise sharply during high school. It continues to rise, if somewhat

Figure 5.9. Sara's Story

more moderately, during army service, dipping only briefly when she experiences disappointment at being stationed far from home. There are few changes until she marries. The graph climbs slightly at the beginning of each new stage (studies, work at GG, work on a kibbutz), only to drop when she begins to feel bored or socially isolated. The period before her marriage is, altogether, difficult to graph. Sara does not offer explanations for her choice of profession or for motives and plans that would clarify how her life evolved as it did. Career moves are elucidated in terms of social rather than professional considerations, and her reference to this stage of life as the period of "the work of teaching as a single woman" reinforces the sense that she is only marking time until she can establish a family. Marriage and children elicit a sharp rise in the graph (see Figure 5.9). The steady high plateau that her life subsequently achieves is hardly rocked by two major changes in her life: a move toward a more religious lifestyle and deliberations about a career change. She has adjusted gradually, she claims, to an observant lifestyle, and it is not a burden. The professional burnout that comes with 19 years of teaching experience is similarly muted as work issues are viewed through a filter of family concerns. If she has another child, she explains, then she will take a leave of absence.

Sara's narrative is, overall, the story of a woman who adapts. Events that might have been expected to upset the equilibrium are taken in stride. She looks on the bright side, particularly when potential disruptions serve family needs, as her life is construed in a context of commitment, above all, to the family. For Sara, maternal identity is the central one in her life, structuring the narrative in terms of both primary objectives and progress along the life course.

David. David's description of childhood conforms, like Sara's, to the norm established for the sample. There is "nothing special" beyond a few ups and downs: "There are times when a kid is more popular—then it was better for me, when you're less popular then . . . [it was worse]." Like Sara, David seems to experience relationships with others as central to his identity. Unlike her, however, he is far more invested in mapping out his place within the social and class hierarchies that define his social standing.

Two conflicting themes compete for ascendancy in this narrative: a drive to succeed and its antithesis, an obligation to curtail his own progress (by ensuring that he is always in second or third rather than first place). The struggle between these two motifs recurs at every stage of his life, shaping and determining the pace of his development.

The first turning point in David's life, during army service, is represented by a gradual rise in the graph subsequent to his decision to leave his peer group and strike out on a course of his own. Henceforth, the professional axis becomes central in his life and the graph follows his gradual upward progress. The climb, as he describes it, is often slow, belabored, and sometimes rife with obstacles to progress.

> I got a good promotion at work. From a simple clerk I was made vice-manager of my department and was put in charge of tourists' complaints [. . .]. It didn't take me long to see that I wouldn't be able to make an impact with the work I was doing [. . .] and so [. . .]. I started to look for another job. I wanted to work in a place where I would make a difference—not in a large organization like the one I had been in so far.

At only two points in the story does the graph rise sharply in response to professional choices on David's part. The first is when he initially decides to risk the hotel field (see Figure 5.10): "I went to work in the hotel. It was a tremendous leap for me, an ambitious leap, which is . . . a thing I think I always do. I got an important managerial job in a hotel although I knew nothing about hotels, aside from having been a guest." The second is when he agrees to leave Israel for a more challenging and risky hotel site in Africa.

David continuously offers detailed descriptions of the critical junctures in his professional history, dwelling on the alternatives that he might have taken, as if to secure the listener's understanding that his life could also have transpired differently. The extent to which he takes active steps to ensure his own professional progress—whether in his studies or his job searches—is very pronounced in the narrative:

Figure 5.10. David's Story

> I started to feel that this [the first hotel] was too small for me. I needed to
> learn more about hotels—it's a big world—and there are new methods
> developing all the time. Just at that time an American chain was opening
> a small new hotel . . . so I applied for a job there.

The movement of his narrative, in fact, is governed solely by professional
moves. The graph cycles through patterns of sharp ascent at the inception
of a new professional phase, more moderate upward movement for a time,
and then stability toward the conclusion of the phase, which prompts a
search for new venues and a fresh cycle of upward movement on the graph.
Family issues are evident at most stages of David's life and are clearly
important because of the special circumstances in David's story. Nonetheless, these concerns remain marginal in terms of the evolution of David's
narrative and are always peripheral to the content and the structure of the
story. The family axis progresses, for instance, but seems disconnected
from the primary career axis. David's claim, in response to a direct question
on the subject, that familial considerations also influenced his professional
choices is not borne out by the spontaneous version of his life story. Family
issues never provoke a shift of course. Even the difficulties he experiences
around the adoption of his first child, or anxieties about his son contracting
AIDS during a hotel stint in Africa, seem to have little bearing on the
development or direction of his professional progress or functioning.

David's identity, is, in summary, primarily professional, and his narrative
is structured by continuous movement toward professional goals. The most
salient features of his professional identity are ambitiousness, organizational ability, and willingness to assume challenges and risks. These aspects

of his identity are featured as much in the structure of his narrative as in their thematic content.

Discussion

This section of the chapter demonstrates the analysis of structural elements of narrative. I have compared the life stories of men and women in terms of plot structure of the whole story.

Before moving on to discussing the findings, a number of reservations should be raised about the analysis presented in the preceding pages and the use of structural analysis of life stories to understand identity: My conclusions are based on analysis of a small and specific sample of educated, middle-class, midlife men and women. The structural features of narratives produced by other groups of men and women may be quite different from those discovered in our sample.

The structural graph (described in the first part of the chapter) is an effective tool for presenting large quantities of narrative material in a clear, visually accessible format. Nonetheless, the artificial collapse of diverse material incurred by graphic representations of this type may be a deterrent to extensive use of the tool.

Our request to the participants to think about their life stories in terms of chapters may have invited a particular emphasis on turning points and important thresholds in their lives. Conceivably, the structure of life stories not organized according to temporal progression from the moment of birth, for example, would have differed from the structures elicited in our sample.

Despite these limitations, several important conclusions nonetheless can be drawn from the study. Analysis of the structure of the entire narrative was accomplished by creating a stage-by-stage representation of the life story. Although I had hoped to derive structural types that correspond to those represented in the literature (e.g., romance, comedy, satire, or tragedy), the structures from this analysis do not strictly correspond to the classic models. Nonetheless, if we return to the terms introduced at the beginning of this chapter, the narrative pattern of the male interviewees is roughly similar to the "romance" insofar as here too a hero contends with a series of conflicts and obstacles. The narrative of the female interviewees is, similarly, reminiscent of the "comedy" insofar as heroines combat obstacles to the restoration of social harmony and are most victorious when they are socially adept.

There are a number of structural similarities between the narratives of the men and the women. Both groups stress the importance of early stages in their lives (childhood, adolescence), and both describe a simple upward course up until early adulthood.

Differences, however, begin to emerge in early adulthood (age 20+). Men continue along an easily plotted career axis, which may assume various forms but generally reflects upward movement. Women's career axes, however, are not easily represented on a graph. For example, some women's lives take a downward turn after early adulthood. A more serious difficulty lies in creating a single graph to represent the multiple plot axes of the life structure. While women occasionally devote a single axis to family issues at the expense of all others, more often a number of simultaneous and equally important axes need to be represented on the graph.

It may be worth asking why—if there is a uniquely feminine life-story structure—the structural complexities of the feminine form begin to emerge only during early adulthood, and why they begin to stabilize during midlife? Moreover, given our assumption that relationships between story and identity, between life as told and life as lived, are bidirectional, how do the polyphonic narratives produced by the women relate to their identities?

A response to the first question may be sought in consideration of processes of socialization at different stages of life. During childhood and adolescence, boys and girls are all encouraged to develop in numerous directions, and freedom to choose and explore is granted regardless of gender. In structural terms, it can be said that multiple axes are open to every child and are viewed as viable future courses of development, regardless of whether the focus is on social skills, academic prowess, self-confidence, or independence. When youngsters reach adulthood, however, social norms begin to dictate their continued progress along certain axes, while others are turned to a lower flame. Boys are maneuvered in the direction of professional excellence and all that it entails. Girls are granted greater flexibility insofar as they are steered in the direction of family and child rearing yet retain options in the domains of social and family relations, career, and investment in the home (Levinson, 1996). This would explain the multiaxial features of their plot structures.[6]

During midlife, the gap between the graphs of the men and women closes once again. Possibly, the multiplicity of demands that have preoccupied women during young adulthood are beginning to diminish in intensity, and with the transition to midlife, women can once again focus on a single plot axis. Gutmann's (1980, 1987) conceptualization of the period of childbearing as an "emergency phase" in adult life is commensurate with this argument insofar as only after the crisis years of child rearing are adults, in his analysis, able to enjoy a higher quality of life and establish an emotional breathing space for themselves.

A response to the second question is more complex. Research into the use of narrative as a therapeutic tool has suggested that formal or structural "flaws" in a life story may reflect problematic aspects of self and identity.[7] This would imply that as the narratives of the women in our sample are "flawed" in terms of the structural criteria of good narrative (clear and logical organization of structure, objectives, and plot movement; Bruner, 1991; Omer, 1994), their identities are likewise impaired. Such a conclusion is problematic both because the women participants in the sample were all healthy, functioning adults, and because of the implication that half the human species is plagued by problems of identity. Clearly, as Mary Gergen (1992) concludes in her work, the flaw lies not with women's narratives but with a definition of the well-constructed narrative that is irrelevant to the life stories of female speakers.

Other writers and researchers of women's literature and autobiography have also documented the problems of attempting to understand women's writings according to the standard criteria of good narrative (e.g., Bateson, 1989; Belenky, Clinchy, Goldenberger, & Tarule, 1986; Duplessis, 1985; Heilbrun, 1989; Rabuzzi, 1988; Woolf, 1929/1957). More than one has protested that standards of good narrative established by men are relevant only to the stories, lives, and narratives of the male half of the human race (Mason, 1980; Woolf, 1929/1957).

Thus I conclude that analysis of the structure of a narrative may be an effective tool for understanding identity but that more flexible criteria for good narrative need to be employed in the analysis of women's narratives.

TWO-STAGE LIFE STORIES: NARRATIVES OF SELF-ACTUALIZATION: AMIA LIEBLICH, RIVKA TUVAL-MASHIACH, AND TAMAR ZILBER

The following section demonstrates a unique form, which was found in only two of the entire corpus of life stories, as described in the first section of this chapter. While the majority of our interviewees, in both the younger and the older cohorts, used the stage outline we suggested to divide their life stories into five to seven chronological chapters, each of them covering up to 10-year spans, two men from the midlife group (age 42) presented a two-stage structure (Lieblich, Zilber, & Tuval-Mashiach, 1995). In their

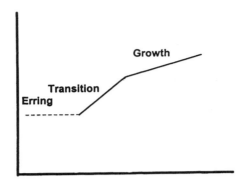

Figure 5.11. Structure of the Two Life Stories

interactions with the interviewers, they resisted suggestions to subdivide this scheme further and insisted that this structure not only suffices but most truly represents the story of their lives. Closer examination of the texts actually reveals three stages: "before" and "after" a major life change, with a much shorter mediating stage that could be called "the experience of transition" (Figure 5.11). The close similarity in form of the two stories was notable, in spite of the vast cultural and thematic differences between them. In the following section, we will use this pattern to briefly exemplify a narrative analysis based on form of the story as a whole.

Ian divided the story of his life at the age of 28, when he experienced conversion to an Orthodox[8] way of life. For Mike, the transformation occurred when he succeeded in producing his first full-length movie at the age of 35. We would like to propose these examples to demonstrate that the *structure* of the story may reflect the deeper personality of the teller—here as a "truth seeker" or "self-actualizer"—while the *contents* manifest the particular culture within which the story unfolds—in this case, where, and toward which goal, the search is taking place.

Both stories can be characterized as entirely dominated by a single idea, which provides the anchor for restructuring the tellers' memories. The first chapter, before their transition, is recalled as a long, relatively meaningless and undifferentiated period, a stage of trial and error or no progress at all. Details about this stage are blurred or missing, while many years and events are collapsed into a single mass. The middle stage of the active search and the transition itself, to which mystical significance is attributed, is described in great color and detail. The present chapter, of actualization since conversion, is depicted as a stage of mounting growth and satisfaction. The differences between the stages are thus manifested not only in their content but in the style of speech and the moods reflected in the narrative.

Let us examine the stories of Ian and Mike to demonstrate these points.

Before Transition

Ian recalls the vagueness of his former life: "I used to go, come all of a sudden, go there, and then see it wasn't it . . . so I returned here. Just like that, senseless."

Responding to the interviewer's request to clarify what he means, he says, "But all I did then was insignificant. . . . There's no difference between elementary school and high school or the army.[9]"

At a different point of the interview he says,

> The way I see it now, I used to live in a kind of a bubble. I wasn't . . . in general not . . . If someone would have asked me what I was, I would have said: I am not. Like this, nonexistent.—Like in outer space, (laughing) meaningless.

In several broken sentences, he covers years of the military service and various occupational attempts, all in one flow, without elaborating at all:

> In the army I was in an intelligence unit. Later . . . I wandered, that is, I wasn't part of anything. I tried to get into university, but I wasn't accepted. So I tried . . . I studied in all kinds of places. For example, I studied education and worked with street gangs, but after a while I left . . . I opened a video rental store, etc.

Notably, Ian's parents or siblings are totally absent from his life story. They are not mentioned before conversion because they cannot be remembered and are apparently insignificant, as they did not contribute to his current Jewish lifestyle, and after conversion because they did not convert together with him. This omission contributes a great deal to the sense of discontinuity in Ian's life story, as if he were "born again" at the moment of his conversion.

The evaluation of events in his life prior to his transition is fully determined by his present values. Among the few instances he describes from the first chapter of his life story, Ian tells about becoming unintentionally involved in a minor criminal action (something of an altogether Kafkaesque nature) and "gaining" a record of criminal conviction (which he labels a "spot"). Consequently, he couldn't become a policeman, as he had hoped for a short while later on. This misfortune, however, is reframed now as leading him to his transformation: "This spot seemed to stop me from many things I wanted to do in life, but on the other hand, today I realize it might have been predetermined. Because, had I gone to the police, where would I be today?"

While the stage before Ian's conversion can be characterized as one of aimless trial and error, Mike's description of this period is presented as preparatory to his success in realizing his artistic talents. In the beginning of the interview, when he named only one turning point in his story, that is, the production of his first film, he said the following about all the previous 35 years:

> I think that these chapters are mainly, more or less, from the point of the present, just a kind of almost identical routine [of many others like me], beyond first name, family name, family size, place—generally it is almost identical everywhere. The routes people travel here are all alike. I don't see anything making me exceptional.

As the story unfolds, however, it becomes evident that the turning point was not revolutionary or unexpected because from early on

> I always had some tendency towards the arts—I just didn't know how to channel this urge to write, and when I tried theater, I tried literature, I discovered that I was actually writing in pictures. My perception is totally visual. So I decided to study filmmaking, that is, to make films.

Mike describes himself as a very imaginative child and, as he is telling about this, he keeps exaggerating, reflects upon this trend, and corrects himself. When he talks about winning an encyclopedia in a school competition, for example, he says a few moments later, "By the way, I didn't get an encyclopedia, it was just a small book, I simply express myself this way." His life story, like a film plot, is thus presented as another imaginary production.

In construction of their narrative, the result of the total dedication in these men's lives to a single value—religion for Ian, and art for Mike—is that the first chapter before the transition is viewed only through the lenses of the later actualization. Ian sees his life without God as meaningless, and not worth a story, while Mike reconstructs his life before his transition as a complicated course of preparation for what might unfold in later years.

The Process of Transition

This short period of finding one's life goal, and stabilization of the trial-and-error phase, was not presented by our tellers as a distinct chapter. However, in spite of its brevity, this section stands out as very detailed and precise in comparison with the previous one.

In addition to a wealth of details and reflective terms such as *knowing, believing,* and so on, a sense of surprise emerges from Ian's story:

> And then, in that period, the essential questions about life began to awaken in me. Till I was walking one day in Jerusalem, and I saw an announcement hanging on a pole on King George Street, inviting the wide public to attend a lecture on the evolution of the Kabbalah.[10] I didn't know what it was, just that there was some mystical system in Judaism, so I went. The topic fascinated me. I didn't know, I didn't believe that Judaism deals with such spiritual subjects as ghosts, demons, astrology—it simply stunned me. So I began to go deeper into these subjects, and with knowledge, the external and internal change started to happen.

As he goes on, his story remains detailed and elaborated, reflecting a sense of astonishment and great joy at this newly discovered world.

For Mike also, care is given to the exact timing of the change, which is preceded by several events in the nature of omens: the birth of his first son and his return to Israel after a long stay in Europe: "Intuitively I felt that here I'd be able to produce more, that I had greater chances for realizing my dreams . . . I came and I got everything I have asked for."

Present Life as Self-Actualization

Life as a practicing Orthodox Jew has returned the spark to Ian's life and his story. In comparison with the absence of his parents from the story, his current rabbi-teacher is described in the story in great detail and with immense admiration. The story creates the impression that Ian's identity is totally merged with his religious ideology and that his private family is not really separate from his learning group and his rabbi, who even found him a bride.

The same enthusiasm and submission of private life to the chosen avocation is evident in Mike's representation of this stage. His face alight as he says, "And since then it's been a new film every two years, and that's the whole story to this very day." The remaining hour of the interview was dedicated almost completely to the plots and forms of his film creations, all of which may be considered to be alternate reconstructions of his life story.

Neither story presents the transition as a climax, with life in consequence declining in intensity or satisfaction, or reaching a plateau, as in the "happily ever after" plot. These are not stories of the kind usually labeled "romance" either—namely, of a quest that is answered by finding a single object or state—but of finding a *way,* a direction. Once it was found, the tellers keep progressing and developing in their tracks. Interesting parallels, with a strong influence of religion in the life of Ian and art in the life of Mike, exist also in the two heroes' stories about meeting their wives and raising their children. Thus the events of marriage and parenting do not divide the life story but are subsumed into the major quest.

CONCLUDING REMARKS

The two men's stories, titled self-actualization narratives, are different in content—one about finding meaning in religion, the other about success in art—yet very similar in form. This two-stage pattern can be viewed as a manifestation of the underlying personality rather than the specific cultural setting in which it is embedded. The form of the total life story is thus proposed as a key to understanding the personality of the teller on a level that is perhaps deeper than the manifest contents and probably given less to intentional falsification of different kinds. We may thus try to extract the commonalities of individuals who form their life story as a tragedy, comedy, or romance (Gergen & Gergen, 1986; see also Omer & Alon, 1997) to learn more about their deeper identity, just as in the current demonstration the two-stage form of the narrative has revealed an identity of a "truth seeker" or "self-actualizer."

As seen in the first part of this chapter, however, not all life stories lend themselves as easily as this form to structural characterization. In many cases, the approach to the teller's inner world via the contents of her or his life story, whether in a holistic or categorical manner, is more direct or accessible than via the formal aspects. This may be particularly true for those of us in the helping professions, trained to listen to others talking about their lives. None of the approaches described in our model, however, is as productive alone as in combination with the other ways of reading a life story.

NOTES

1. The terms *romance* and *comedy* should not be confused with their sense in everyday speech. Thus, for example, a story constructed as a "comedy" will not necessarily be amusing.

2. More detailed explanations of how the plot axis is recognized are provided in Chapter 4.

3. Military service is compulsory for both men and women in Israel, but most men have a longer and more strenuous service than most women.

4. See Note 26 in Chapter 3.

5. Associative leaps are also pronounced as women shift between recollections of childhood or historical anecdotes about families of origin, to reflections on their own children's lives, thus producing intricate narratives that weave present, past, and future into current understandings of themselves.

6. It would be interesting to speculate about the shape a life story might take in a traditional society or in prefeminist Western society. Conceivably, the absence of a potential career axis in the lives of women might give rise to a more distinct plot axis, focusing on family issues from an early age.

7. See, for example, White and Epston (1990).

8. The term *conversion* will be used in the following sections for a transition involving the adoption of a Jewish Orthodox way of life—and not for a change of religion, such as from Judaism to Christianity, as it is usually used. The Jewish Orthodox way of life entails many daily practices and rules that permeate all life spheres, from praying in public three times a day to a strict dress code.

9. In Israel, all Jewish citizens are required to serve in the army at the age of 18.

10. An esoteric traditional system of Jewish theosophy.

6

Categorical-Content
Perspective

In this chapter, the narrative materials of the life stories will be processed analytically, namely, by breaking the text into relatively small units of content and submitting them to either descriptive or statistical treatment. This is normally called "content analysis," which is, in fact, the classical method for doing research with narrative materials in psychology, sociology, and education (Manning & Cullum-Swan, 1994; Riessman, 1993). Two examples of content analysis from our own research will be presented in detail, and the chapter will conclude with a comparison of the two approaches.

The method of content analysis has many variations, depending on the purpose of the study and the nature of the narrative materials. Preference for one variation or another is also related to the researcher's adherence to criteria of objectivity and quantitative processing, on the one hand, as opposed to hermeneutic and qualitative perspectives, on the other. In this single chapter, we will neither introduce all the possibilities nor provide detailed instructions but, following a prototypical series of steps, concentrate on our research examples as models for the application of content analysis in reading a life story.

The steps taken in most of the variations of content analysis can be summarized as follows:

(1) Selection of the Subtext. On the basis of a research question or hypothesis, all the relevant sections of a text are marked and assembled to form a new file or subtext, which may be seen as the content universe of the area studied. For example, if the research hypothesis involves the family of the teller (as in the second part of this chapter), one should set apart all sections of the story that deal with the family while other parts of the text may be ignored. Characteristically, the selected sections of the subtext are withdrawn from the total context of the life story and are treated independently. Sometimes, however, interpretation of the results is validated or facilitated by parts of the interview material that remain

outside the selected subtext. In some studies, when the research question or hypothesis leads the researcher to choose a directive interview, namely, an interview that instructs the teller to focus on the "relevant" material (and not to provide a complete life story), all the obtained text can be taken as the data for the content analysis (Lieblich, 1986; Wiseman & Lieblich, 1992).

(2) Definition of the Content Categories. The categories are various themes or perspectives that cut across the selected subtext and provide a means of classifying its units—whether words, sentences, or groups of sentences. Categories can be predefined by a theory; Maslow's (1954) theory of human motives, for example, can direct the researcher to search the text for evidence of different needs. Similarly, Erikson's developmental theory can be used for identification of various stages and their typical dilemmas (Stewart, Franz, & Layton, 1988). Another method for the selection of categories, however, is to read the subtext as openly as possible and to define the major content categories that emerge from the reading. This process is closely linked to the next stage, of sorting the material into categories. In practice, it is a circular procedure that involves careful reading, suggesting categories, sorting the subtext into categories, generating ideas for additional categories or for refinement of the existing ones, and so on. The approaches that use predefined, theory-based categories as opposed to empirical categories, as suggested by the text, are not as different as they seem because readers' bringing their theoretical or commonsense assumptions to the reading of a text is unavoidable (Linde, 1993).

What is the optimal number of categories, and how extensive can they be? Answers to these questions naturally depend on research goals as well as practical considerations. The researcher aims to reach a balance between two very different tendencies. One is to define many, subtle categories that retain the richness and variation of the text but require meticulous sorting of the material. The other is to define a few, broad categories that are easy to use but do not do justice to the complexity of the text.

(3) Sorting the Material into the Categories. At this stage, separate sentences or utterances are assigned to relevant categories. While the utterances may all be from a single story, categories may also include utterances by several different individuals. This process—as well as the definition of content categories—can be performed by one or more researchers. When two or more judges are involved in sorting contents into categories, this can be done independently, to allow the calculation

of interjudge reliability, or jointly, to create higher sensitivity to the text and its meaning to different readers.

(4) Drawing Conclusions From the Results. The sentences in each category can be counted, tabulated, ordered by frequency, or subjected to various statistical computations—all in accordance with the research aims and questions and/or the researcher's preference. Alternately, the contents collected in each category can be used descriptively to formulate a picture of the content universe in certain groups of people or cultures. When specific hypotheses have been stated by the researcher, they can be tested at this stage.

While this procedure may seem clear-cut and simple to implement, dilemmas regarding each of the steps require complex decisions from the researcher. For example, which unit is to be counted—a partial or full sentence? A complete expression of an idea? Does one take into account the intensity of the utterance? Does one include several repetitions of the same expression, and how? As there are no foolproof solutions to any of these dilemmas, the precision of the analysis should never be taken for granted. When planning content analysis, the most significant consideration should be the concordance between the research goal and its method.

HIGH SCHOOL EXPERIENCES FROM
AN ADULT PERSPECTIVE: AMIA LIEBLICH

The question that shaped the content analysis to be presented below related to the distant memories and subjective impact[1] of the high school experience on the self in four groups of adults:[2]

1. Midlife adults (age 42), graduates of a segregated high school ($n = 19$)
2. Midlife adults (age 42), graduates of an integrated high school ($n = 17$)
3. Young adults (age 28), graduates of a segregated high school ($n = 12$)
4. Young adults (age 28), graduates of an integrated high school ($n = 12$)

The sources of the interview as well as the theoretical basis of its research question were described in Chapter 2. All of the 60 research participants whose accounts of this phase in life were complete enough were included in the analysis.

No specific hypotheses were proposed for this analysis. Rather, I was interested in comparing the four research groups on any high school-related dimension that might emerge from their accounts of this period in their lives.

The Process of the Content Analysis

1. All sentences relating to the high school experience, or the self vis-à-vis the high school, were highlighted on the verbatim transcriptions. These included references made to the topic throughout the interviews, not only during the description of the stage of adolescence in the life story.

2. From these subtexts, two readers chose the "principal sentences"— that is, utterances expressing new and distinct ideas or memories about the content universe. These were set apart as a file of the "principal sentences arrays" for each individual. The reader may note that this stage of analysis was not listed among the phases described in the outline of content analysis presented above. When the material is very rich in repetition and elaboration, however, concentration on "principal sentences" rather than the complete corpus is often advisable.

The material processed up to this point may already lead to several conclusions. All in all, 1,846 principal sentences were drawn for further processing. (Note that although the number of individuals in the study is not large, the number of units, namely, principal sentences, is very high and provides a large sample for inference.) The distribution of these sentences among the four research groups was not even. The average number of principal sentences for an individual per group was as follows: 34.8 for the segregated midlife, 24.3 for the integrated midlife, 37.2 for the segregated young, and 26.6 for the integrated young.

This distribution suggests that the experience of high school occupies a larger part of the life story in the accounts of both younger and older persons who studied in the segregated school as compared with those who studied in the integrated schools. In other words, it seems that the experience of high school left more traces—whether positive or negative will be revealed later—in the memories of those who participated in the experimental, segregated program. This conclusion is valid only because there were no systematic differences in total length of the interviews, or transcripts, of the four research groups.

3. Each "principal sentence" was judged as positive, negative, or neutral in its content, that is, the attitude it manifested toward high school or the

self in high school. The reader may note that such an evaluation is relevant to many content universes, when satisfaction versus dissatisfaction, attraction versus rejection, and so on can be discerned in the defined units of content.

Subsequently, each person's total array was judged as "positive" when it met our criterion of having more than three-quarters of its sentences judged positive, "negative" when more than three-quarters of the sentences were negative, or "ambivalent" when positive and negative sentences appeared in approximately equal proportion in the array. The selection of these particular criteria for the definition of positive, negative, or ambivalent is arbitrary, like many other decisions in such a process.

While no substantive differences in negative evaluation were found between the groups, graduates of the integrated schools were slightly more positive (53% and 67% for the older and younger groups of the integrated school versus 52% and 33% for the groups in the segregated school) and less ambivalent (29% and 25% versus 27% and 52%, respectively) regarding their high school experience. In terms of age, the older groups retained a slightly more positive memory and evaluated their experience better as compared with the younger groups.

4. Categories relevant to the content matter were suggested, based on the reading, for each person's array, and the sentences were divided into these categories. This stage was carried out by two judges[3] who discussed their decisions until a consensus was reached. The process was repeated for every interviewee within each one of the four research groups.

The consideration of the breadth of a content category, or its level of generality, became relevant in this stage and can be used here to demonstrate the impact of the research goals on decisions made in the processing of contents. Most frequent among the emerging categories were "teachers," "academic performance," or "class/school atmosphere." These are broad categories and comfortable sorting devices. However, on this level of generality, no differences would probably be found among the research groups—thus defeating the purpose of the research. It was decided therefore to sort the principal sentences into narrower categories, usually including an evaluation of the memory, such as "good teachers," "bad teachers," or "being a good student," "being a mediocre student." (More examples will be presented in Tables 6.1a, 6.1b, and 6.2.) Thus, while the categories themselves emerged from the subtexts, the aim of our study influenced their definition in terms of generality or breadth.

All in all, 35 categories emerged from the principal sentences arrays of all the interviewees. This total does not refer to categories that included

TABLE 6.1a

A Demonstration of the Selection of
Principal Sentences and Their Categorization: Sara

Sentences	Category	Comments
1. My high school was really good for me.	1. General positive evaluation of the school.	1. Her positive statement emphasizes good *for me*.
2. Our class was very cohesive.	2. Good social relations within the class.	2. Referring to her class, not to the school.
3. We formed a class within the best school in town.	3. Pride in school.	3. She omits "special" or "experimental" class.
4. They used to peep at us [. . .] as if we were monkeys in a zoo.	4. Stigmatization and isolation.	4. A very strong metaphor but can be accepted as humorous.
5. They wanted to see who were these new kids who had arrived.	5. Curiosity on the part of the regular students.	5. Saying "new" kids rather than "different" kids.
6. There were children who always felt disturbed by this, as if they were odd.	6. A sense of being inferior.	6. Excluding herself from the others, who had different and more painful reactions.
7. But I did not look at it this way.	7. Uniqueness of the self.	7. A different "look"— not a different feeling.
8. I think that this high school really invested in us above and beyond our expectations.	8. High investment on the part of the school.	8. Intensive statement— "really," "above and beyond."
9. We received help with our homework.	9. High investment on the part of the school.	9. Providing concrete examples for former statement.

only three sentences or less, representing extremely rare content materials, which, although individually intriguing, did not contribute to our analysis. Another major decision was undertaken at this stage: No category could be processed more than twice for each individual. In other words, if someone repeated an idea more than twice, it was still scored as 2 in the content analysis. Thus we were hoping to give less weight to the length of the interview or the eloquence of the speaker and focus on its expressed ideas.

TABLE 6.1b

A Demonstration of the Selection of
Principal Sentences and Their Categorization: David

Sentences	Category	Comments
1. I wasn't among the best in class.	1. Being a mediocre student.	1-2-3. Lightness, lack of seriousness in reference to high school.
2. I didn't even try.	2. Investing limited effort in studying.	
3. I went to B.D.—a mediocre school, reasonable.	3. Mediocre evaluation of the school.	
4. I stayed there [. . .], everything went well, and I graduated.	4. Success in school work.	4. No details given on this.
5. Socially it was easy, I was very popular, a member of the school council.	5. Positive social activities in school.	5. Participation in and contribution to the entire school.
6. At high school we also organized a radio system.	6. Positive social activity in school.	6. Providing a concrete example.
7. There are teachers that I remember but they weren't significant for my life.	7. Mediocre teachers.	7. Minimizing school's significance.

The number of times each category appeared in an individual record was therefore 2, 1, or 0. Other rules could have been adopted, naturally—for example, counting the frequency of each category as many times as it appeared in the text.

5. Because our research question related to group differences, the categories from all the individual accounts were collapsed for each of the four research groups (see Table 6.2). Thus a combined group list of categories emerged. No attempt was made to create identical lists of categories for each of the research groups. Rather, our aim was to study the specific

TABLE 6.2

Group Profiles of the Research Groups

Segregated	*Integrated*

Midlife

1. Good teachers and their investment in students	1. Positive social activities in school
2. Social problems—isolation and segregation	2. The heterogeneity of the student body and its integration
3. High academic level and success	3. A sense of freedom of choice
4. Class identity	4. General positive evaluation of the school
5. Doubts about personal identity	5. Good friends
6. Discrimination and stigmatization by the system	6. Good teachers
7. Belonging to an experimental project	7. Minimizing school's significance for life
8. Good social relationships within the class	8. Issues of personal identy
9. General positive evaluation of the school	9. Being a mediocre student
10. The heterogeneity of the student body, and my ability to fit in	10. Political activity in school

Young

1. Good social relationships within the class	1. Good social relationships within the school
2. Good teachers and their investment in students	2. Good teachers and their investment in students
3. Pride in school	3. A sense of freedom of choice
4. Discrimination and stigmatization by the system	4. Conflicts about discipline
5. Personal identity as a student	5. General positive evaluation of the school
6. Uniqueness of the self	6. Pride in success and in belonging to the school
7. Belonging to an experimental project	7. Investing limited effort in studying
8. General positive evaluation of the school	8. Positive evaluation of the vocational program
9. Social problems—isolation and a sense of inferiority	9. Good social activities in school
10. Investing much effort in studying	10. Successful integration in school

content universe for each group as represented in the slightly different category lists.

6. The number of times (2, 1, or 0) each category appeared in an individual record was summed across individuals within each group. Finally, the group order of categories by their relative frequency—or the *group profile of high school experience*—was determined separately for each of the four research groups.

Demonstration

Before the presentation of the results for the four groups, the reader may wish to attempt to compile the principal sentences arrays for Sara and David, evaluate them as positive, negative, or neutral, and sort them into content categories. As difficulties naturally will be encountered, more specific criteria should be developed for the processing stages, and working in teams may be advisable.

As can be easily observed, Sara dedicated a much larger proportion of her life story to her high school experience, while David was extremely laconic on the subject.[4] This represents well the group differences among graduates of the segregated versus integrated schools. Table 6.1a demonstrates the first steps of the content analysis using a short section from Sara's account on the subject, and Table 6.1b includes the entire account of high school in David's interview.

In the left column of the table, Sara's principal sentences array is presented for one paragraph of her account about high school, starting with the paragraph on page 37. The second column presents the content categories[5] proposed for these sentences. Some explanatory remarks are presented in the third column. A similar demonstration is repeated for David's account, using the paragraph in which he introduced his high school experience (see the paragraph on p. 51) and the only additional (two) sentences in which he spoke about high school later on.

The Group Profiles of High School Experience

In the following part of the chapter, the use of content analysis for comparing research groups will be demonstrated. Our main goal in the study was to investigate individuals who had studied at "Elite High School," which adopted an experimental method of segregating underprivileged students to teach them in a special enrichment program (see Chapter 2). We wished to study whether they would retain different memories, and describe different effects of their schooling in their lives, 24 and 10 years after graduation, than similar students who had attended regular, integrated schools. The group profiles that were obtained for each of the research groups provided the answer to this question.

The short profiles—using only the 10 most prevalent categories for each group—appear in Table 6.2. The first category in a profile is the most frequent, and the order of the categories is based on their frequency ranking. Because these are the 10 most frequent categories (out of 35), it should be noted that even the least frequent were quite popular—they appeared at least once in more than a third of the group.

These four profiles depict a rich and differential picture of the experience of high school as emerging from the life stories of the interviewees. Some—but not all—of the conclusions drawn from this analysis are presented below, including the process of inference whereby they were reached. Readers may stop here, go back to the general description of the aims of the study and the high schools chosen for the research in Chapter 2, and try to form their own summary of the results presented in Tables 6.1a and 6.1b.

Conclusions may be drawn both from the mere presence of certain content categories in a profile and from their ranking in comparison with other categories in each one of the profiles. The reader should bear in mind, as noted above, that no intentional attempts were made to arrive at identical content categories for the four groups, and the slight variations in the categories' label reflect nuances that appeared in the texts. Thus, for example, in the segregated young group, a category that emerged was "pride in school," whereas in the integrated young profile, we found "pride in success and in belonging to the school." These and similar differences are meaningful for an understanding of the school experience of the graduates. While some of the categories appear in all the four profiles (e.g., "general positive evaluation of the school"), an examination of their ranking reveals their relative salience in the graduates' memories (e.g., the rank of "general positive evaluation" is higher for students of the integrated schools than for those of the segregated school). Several categories are specific to the profiles of the integrated schools—such as "successful integration" or "a sense of freedom of choice," while others are specific to the profiles of the segregated school—"discrimination and stigmatization by the system."

The major issues that are clarified by the analysis will be examined in the next sections. In the process of interpretation, however, additional information stemming from the entire interview, or from less frequent categories that were not included in the profile, will often be used. It is our firm belief that content analysis of sections from a life story that completely ignores the context of the whole loses much of its power and meaning.

Discussion of the Results

What do we learn from the profiles presented above about the distant memories and reflections of the students who had encountered integrative or segregative[6] experiences in high school?

(1) Integration Versus Segregation: The Social Aspect. It is clear that both the older and the younger graduates of the segregated program portray a picture of minorities within an elite school. In both groups' profiles, social problems receive a high ranking; isolation, segregation, discrimination, stigmatization, and a sense of inferiority (categories 2 and 6 in older group, 4 and 9 in younger group) are all usually attributed, in the life stories, to negative attitudes on the part of the majority of the student body or the system in general. Of interest, activities undertaken by the school for the enrichment of the underprivileged students, such as afternoon classes or additional tutoring, are often depicted as discriminatory. When positive social memories are evoked, they refer to friendships *within* the class (category 1 in younger group) or to coping, in spite of the barriers, with the heterogeneity of the student body (category 10 in the older group).

The experience of the graduates of the integrated schools is entirely different; all references to the social aspects of their experience are positive (categories 1, 2, 5, 10[7] in the older group; 1, 9, 10 in the younger group) with respect to the school as a whole as well as the class. Thus we see that the differential experience of social integration versus segregation is clearly represented by the group profiles.

It is important to note that in all of the profiles, social aspects of high school, whether positive or negative, are extremely salient in the graduates' memories. This may imply that while most schools aim primarily to teach and educate, the impact they have on the personal narratives of graduates reflects the dominance of the social sphere.

(2) The Experience of Learning. Examining the profiles for reflections on academic life in school, we may focus on the ranking of categories related to evaluations of the teachers, learning tasks, and the student her- or himself in this context. Stories about the good teachers and their investment in students abound in the interview materials of the two groups that graduated from the segregated program (category 1 in

the older and 2 in the younger groups). Among graduates of the integrated schools, the same high evaluation for teachers appears in the younger group (category 2 in their profile), but in the older group, reference to "good teachers"—without specific recognition of their investment—appears only in the sixth rank. Furthermore, the category "conflicts about discipline," which usually entails tension between teachers and students, appears only in the profile of the younger graduates of the integrative school (category 4). Among the less frequent categories that were not included in the group profile, "bad teachers" or "insignificant teachers" were also mentioned only by graduates of the integrative schools—a category exemplified in David's array in Table 6.1b. In general, therefore, graduates of the segregated program provide a warmer, more positive, and more harmonious evaluation of their high school teachers.

Both profiles of the graduates from the segregated program include references to the academic requirements in school: In the adult group, the stress is on the high academic level of the program and the experience of succeeding in it (category 3), while among the younger graduates, the same issue appears in recollections of how much effort was required to study in the program (category 10). The picture that emerges from the comparison with the integrated schools is clearly different. The older group's profile includes references to being mediocre students (category 9), and the younger's, to investing limited effort in studying (category 7)—both exemplified by David's array in Table 6.1b. On the other hand, graduates of the integrative schools recall the freedom of choice of academic subjects (category 3 in the two profiles)—something that is missing from the memories of the segregated program's graduates. Only graduates of the integrative schools mention their positive evaluation of the vocational subjects that were offered (e.g., electronics). We may thus conclude that the academic program of the integrative schools is recalled as permitting greater freedom of choice and making fewer demands, while in the segregated school, it is depicted as being more restricting but also more challenging for the students.

So far we have seen that while graduates' satisfaction with the social climate of their high school favors the interviewees from the integrated schools, satisfaction with academic aspects is more emphasized among graduates of the segregated program.

(3) General Evaluation of the School Experience. Many of the interviewees provided a spontaneous general evaluation of their high school. The large majority of these evaluations were positive, but this category

appears in higher ranking for the integrated than for the segregated schools' graduates (categories 9 and 8 in the segregated, and 4 and 5 in the integrated). A similar content category expresses pride in high school; this also appears in the profiles of the younger groups, but with a slightly different connotation. While graduates of the segregated program expressed general pride in their high school—because it is "the best high school in town"—without referring directly to themselves as part of it, the interviewees from the integrative school talked about two aspects that caused them pride—their success in their studies and their affiliation with this particular school.

Negative general evaluation was too rare to be included among the 10 most frequent categories for any of the research groups, although "minimizing school's significance for life" (category 7) can be found among the older graduates of the integrated school. The sense from this category was that, in spite of the good memories retained from school, from the perspective of adulthood the high school experience does not seem to have contributed much to one's achievements and development. Such a concept is entirely missing in the remaining profiles and would be in stark contradiction to the story told by the graduates of the segregated program, who, even if school was difficult and painful, described it as having a formative influence on their lives. The general context of the story, as well as the place of each category among the others, is thus highly influential to our understanding of the results of the content analysis.

(4) Issues of Individual and Collective Identity. In the discussion of the content categories relevant to the three topics discussed above—social relations, studies, and general evaluation—we have already referred to most of the information summarized in Table 6.2.[8] Only seven categories remain to be discussed, all of them dealing with personal and collective identity—prominent issues in the world of adolescents (Erikson, 1968). These categories do not always relate directly to the school experience but to the self vis-à-vis the class or the school as a whole.

Although identity issues seem to be common to all adolescents, they appear much more frequently in the life stories of the graduates of the segregated school program (categories 4, 5, 7 for the older group; 5, 6, 7 for the younger group) than in those of the integrated schools (category 8 for the older, and none for the younger groups).This finding can be interpreted in many ways. Various aspects of the "rehabilitative teaching" program (e.g., the small size of the class, intensive teacher-student relations, alienation from one's natural surroundings) may have caused the students to become more aware of identity dilemmas, more introspective or reflective. Moreover, if students felt, or were told, that they were participating in an "experimental project" (category 7 for both of the segregated groups), and that they were concentrated in a special classroom with many students of "their kind" (category 4 in the older segregated group profile), this naturally led to speculation about their identity as minorities, or as underprivileged, compared with the rest of the students in "regular" classes. This is a powerful aspect of Sara's account of her high school experience (as can be seen on pp. 37-41). Many other interviewees who had belonged to the segregated school expressed negative sentiments regarding their placement in the experimental project and tried to assert their uniqueness (category 6 in the segregated young profile). As an outcome of the confrontation between the individual and the school system, many retained doubts about their "real" identity (category 5 in the segregated older profile). Such issues are almost completely absent in the accounts of graduates of the integrative schools, indicating that they were probably not an important part of their high school memories.

Summary of the Findings

The part played by high school memories within the individual life story was greater for individuals who had studied in a segregated program. The content analysis of the interview material reveals meaningful differences in their outlooks on the social and academic reality of school as well as their identity dilemmas. The general evaluation of the high school experience as positive was more prevalent among graduates of the integrated schools. This reinforces findings from the simple classification of all principal sentences into positive, negative, or ambivalent, according to which accounts of the graduates of the integrated schools were found to be slightly more positive and less ambivalent than those of students of the segregated program. In other words, the objective life attainments of the segregated programs' graduates, as impressive as they may be,[9] were earned at the expense of a less enriching social experience in high school and perhaps also lingering doubts about their identity.

General Conclusion

An analysis of the impact of high school memories on four groups of adults has been presented as a demonstration of how content analysis may proceed and what kind of inferences may be drawn from it. The stages of selecting the subtext relevant to a particular research question—defining content categories, sorting utterances into these categories, and ranking them according to frequency—have been described and shown in practice. While the procedure may seem clear and precise, many dilemmas must be tackled, especially in the selection of content categories and the tasks of sorting and counting. Each decision that is made should be based on careful consideration of the research goals as well as the feasibility of different options.

Focusing on a "categorical" rather than a "holistic" perspective means extracting parts of the life story out of the whole and disregarding contextual factors. This may be problematic; when interpretations are proposed, one should also try to take into account holistic and contextual factors.

Similarly, in paying attention to "content" and not to "form," an important source of information may be lost. In the analysis demonstrated above, additional support for the emerging picture could be drawn from the length, detail, intensity, and emotional tonality of the utterances, for example, when students who had graduated from the segregated school spoke about their experience of segregation or their positive evaluation of their teachers. This can be discerned in Sara's life story (see pp. 37-41) and the short sentence array presented in Table 6.1a. This exposes the shortcoming of the described content analysis in its ability to convey the richness and depth of the narrative material unless additional information is taken into consideration.[10]

ADULTS AND THEIR FAMILIES:
RIVKA TUVAL-MASHIACH

Another demonstration of content analysis from our research is presented in the following part of this chapter, which focuses on the interviewees vis-à-vis their families. The units for the analysis are sections of the complete text, chosen for their contents. While references to the experience of high school in the previous illustration were often concentrated in the interviewees' accounts about adolescence, the utterances that form the present subtexts were gathered from the entire transcript, and not from a specific stage or period in the tellers' life stories. In addition, the present content analysis differs from the former in two main aspects: (a) Its aim is a description of the content universe rather than group comparisons and (b) it is more impressionistic-interpretive and less quantitative than our high school example.

To understand the research question leading to this analysis, a brief introduction is necessary. All the participants of the reported research belong to a highly mobile social-cultural subgroup in Israel (see pp. 21-24 for a description of the sample). Almost all had been born to new immigrants from Moslem countries who had reached Israel in the early 1950s and whose initial socioeconomic status in Israel was low. As a result of a general process of social and economic mobility in the population, and of these subgroups in particular, these families' offspring typically can be found in higher classes than their parents' some 40 years after immigration. Several studies (e.g., Lissak, 1984) have demonstrated this mobility in terms of the educational, occupational, and income levels of the first versus the second generation of immigrants.[11] At the same time, Israeli society is highly family oriented, and generational closeness—both emotional and geographic—is very common (Peres & Katz, 1991).

Intrigued by the impressive mobility obtained by our interviewees, my research questions focused on the place of the interviewees' families of origin in their life stories. I wanted to explore their attitudes toward their family of origin, their parents, and the environment in which they grew up. Furthermore, I was interested in exploring questions such as the following: How do the self-images of the tellers and their experience of life transitions relate to their perceptions of their families? Do the participants view themselves as continuing or discontinuing their parents' way of life, and how do they feel about this?

To study these questions, 36 complete interviews of the midlife group (age = 42) of research participants were content-analyzed.

The first stage was reading the entire transcripts to highlight the subtext, namely, all the sections in which the teller referred to his or her parents and family. Such references could be found throughout the interview, and not only in the narration of childhood memories. They appeared spontaneously in the story and also in response to one of the leading questions asked about every stage: "Who were significant people for you during this stage" (see Chapter 2).

The definition of the content categories resulted from an ongoing interpretive dialogue with the text, a process I would like to exemplify in this section. When I began my work, using a conceptual analysis of the term *individual-family relationship,* I formulated two major categories: perception of the parents and continuity versus change. For each of these categories, I had several subcategories in mind. In the process, however, while the two major categories were indeed useful for my analysis, reading the subtext led to two kinds of changes and refinements in the preconceived subcategories: Some of the categories that I had hoped to find were not

TABLE 6.3

Content Categories for the Adult and His or Her Family

Perceptions of Parents	Continuity Versus Change
Issues	Contribution of parents to teller's education
Differentiation	Significant figures in addition to one's parents
Dynamics	Teller-siblings similarity
	Family history and roots
	The teller and his or her children—attitudes
	—involvement

referred to in the transcripts, whereas others unexpectedly emerged. For example, I had expected to find direct statements regarding continuity between the narrators and their parents, such as "in this respect I try to do as my parents did." These were almost entirely absent from the transcripts. On the other hand, initially I did not include reference to family roots as a possible index for continuity, but it emerged from the text. Table 6.3 presents the content categories that were finally chosen for exploring the research questions.

For the analysis, all utterances of the subtext were divided into the major categories of "perception of parents" and "continuity,"[12] and further examined as described below.

Perception of Parents

This broad category consists of three subcategories that emerged from the texts:

1. *Issues:* The subjects or themes to which the teller refers when talking about his/her parents
2. *Differentiation:* Reference to both parents or to one of them
3. *Dynamics:* Changes that may be detected in the perception of parents in different periods, in terms of their evaluation

Method

All utterances concerning perception of parents were carefully read. Topics that were brought up about the parents were listed and examined. These same utterances were examined regarding the differentiation and dynamics they reflected.

Main Findings

(1) Issues. Several main issues were mentioned by the tellers, among them parents' educational impact, the narrators' feelings toward parents' mentality, and power relationships between the narrator and his or her parents. At different stages of life, the salience of these issues changed.

The educational impact of the parents, how they compelled the narrators to study, was the topic most emphasized in the perception of parents during *childhood.* Parents, and especially fathers, were consistently described as aspiring to see their children make progress and succeed in their studies. Even illiterate parents, unable to help their children in school, still managed to instill high motivation to study in their children.

Following this topic in frequency were interviewees' references to emotional and material input from their parents and the resulting feelings toward them. Although most of the participants praised their parents in this respect, in the social or cultural sphere perceptions of parents were not always positive. Several interviewees remembered being ashamed of their immigrant parents because of their poor homes or "primitive mentalities." Two narrators recalled being ashamed of their mothers, who were "always pregnant." Others were critical of their parents' restrictive rules of conduct, stemming from what they saw then as outdated traditions.

The perception of parents shifts and becomes ambivalent or negative when the participants talk about *adolescence.* The transition to high school, often in another neighborhood outside their familiar environment, was experienced as a cultural change. Being exposed to the new culture made it possible for the tellers to observe and reflect on their parental home and family tradition. They became aware of social-economical rifts as well as ethnic differences[13] between themselves and other students in high school. The following brief conversation demonstrates this transition:

Jack: That's where it all started [at high school]. Classical music . . .
Interviewer: You think that you got it there?
Jack: Sure, absolutely. It doesn't matter that I developed this later, I took some classes in music appreciation at the university, but it had to begin somewhere. It started with my willingness to encounter [new] things, and to cope with them. Even if it doesn't belong to you, if it's another culture.

For other interviewees, the selection of high school was calculated—often jointly with the parents—to prevent a gap between the ambience of the school and their home environment, as explained by Ben, one of the participants:

I was an excellent student, and supposed to go to X high school, but then I felt as if the social group of X students is sort of distant from me. I understood that there were vast differences between the Ashkenazic and Sephardic,[14] the rich and the poor, and that it would be very difficult for me to study in a school of the social and economical elite. So I preferred to go to a school where it would be socially easier, and I'd have friends of my own kind.

While many of the interviewees disclosed conflicts with their parents during adolescence, Sara's life story (see, e.g., p. 41) is an exception in this respect. She says:

I really think it's a matter of one's character. I almost didn't have [conflicts] because I am obedient by nature. I wasn't the type who goes out and disappears either. When I went to the youth movement they trusted me. I almost never had confrontations with my parents, I really didn't.

When the participants talked about their present *adulthood and midlife* concerns, their perceptions of their parents were focused on the shift in power relations—the parent being the weaker side as compared with the teller. In the spirit of midlife reflectiveness and introspection (Gould, 1978; Neugarten, 1968), some of the tellers raised the issue of the origin of their traits and values, and asked themselves which parts of their adult selves were actually "inherited" from or influenced by their parents.

(2) Differentiation. The utterances that belong to this category mostly stem from the interview question regarding significant people in the teller's life during the different stages. Answers to this question provide information that could be used in comparisons within a person's life story, across the life stages, and also between individuals.

Parents were selected as "significant figures" especially during the earlier stages of life, yet people interpreted the adjective *significant* in a variety of ways. Some of the interviewees identified *significant* with *dominant;* some differentiated between the parent who was significant and the one they resembled or with whom they identified; others distinguished between "positively" or "negatively" significant (e.g., people who were mean or rejecting toward them). Most often, however, the tellers interpreted *significant* as either emotionally nourishing, loving, and patient or as a dominant authority at home with greater involvement in the child's education.[15]

For those interviewees who chose their parents as significant in childhood, my findings revealed that in terms of quantity, the differences between the selection of mothers or fathers was very small (mothers were selected 13 times; fathers, 11). When fathers were selected, however, it was due to their authority and influence in driving the interviewee to study and move forward, whereas when mothers were selected, it was explained in terms of their warmth, care, and the creation of a warm home atmosphere. It is interesting to note that even tellers whose mothers had careers tended to chose their fathers as more significant to their personal advancement.

(3) Dynamics. As can be seen, different content categories emerged regarding the different stages of the narrators' lives. It was evident that the perception of parents in the texts was dynamic, namely, it varied over the different life stages. Because the narrators made evaluations while talking about their parents, it is possible to conceive of this variation as resembling a U-curve: Good and significant relationships are described during childhood, a decline in the quality of relationship appears during adolescence,[16] and a renewed closeness or a more balanced, integrated perception of parents characterizes adulthood (from early adulthood to the present).

Two specific points emerged from the developmental perspective:

1. At present, many of the interviewees describe a process of becoming the support figures for parents, who are weaker, sick, or in need of assistance. This is accompanied by a change in the perception of parents parallel to their aging.

2. While the U-pattern is most frequent among our interviewees, a smaller group of life stories can be described as a "moderately ascending trajectory" from negative to positive perception. These stories described childhoods of indifference, neglect, or even physical abuse of the child by the parent(s), with a growing move, later, to a state of closeness, acceptance, and understanding at the present time.

The current positive perception of parents was often attributed to changes that occurred when the teller became a parent and could better appreciate the efforts of his or her parents in the past, under conditions of hardship. This is demonstrated by the next quote from Alex:

> I understand my parents much better now that I have had a child. I began to understand them more, not only mine, but parents in general—the parent-child relationships, the worries, the need for advice . . . Once you

have a child you appreciate your parents all the more. It makes me sad [that it happened so late].

Continuity Versus Change

The second broad category in the adult-parent realm dealt with the degree of continuity of parental heritage and lifestyle as reflected in the collected narratives. The operational definition of this concept is not simple, as almost none of our interviewees referred to this subject directly in his or her life story, and all the indexes were indirectly inferred. The analysis of continuity versus change in our data may therefore provide an example for the use of more complex categories in qualitative content analysis, where the act of interpretation becomes central and a more sophisticated approach to the text is required.

It should be emphasized, again, that objectively speaking—in terms of occupation, income, family size, and so on—the research participants were significantly different from their parents.[17] Therefore, the following content analysis solely involves the subjective experience of continuity. In any case, continuity should not be defined as a dichotomy, manifesting continuity or not, but as a continuum composed of several indexes or subcategories. Alternately, individuals may have a "continuity profile" based on their scores for each of these indexes.

Because no direct reference to this category was found in the material, my choice of subcategories, following careful reading of the subtext, was as follows:

(1) Contribution of Parents to Teller's Education. This attribution of parental input to the present status of the interviewees was the most direct reference to the broad category of continuity. In general, the more frequent such references were in the interview, the greater the continuity.

(2) Reference to "Significant Figures" That Are Not One's Parents. This shows that other people provided care or enrichment to the teller in areas where parents' input was insufficient. In general, the more frequent such references, the less there was continuity.

(3) Similarity of the Teller to His or Her Siblings. Similarity or dissimilarity can be mentioned regarding talents, learning and achievement, being loved and cared for, being close to parents, present lifestyle, and so on. In general, the closer the similarity, the greater the continuity.

(4) Family History or Roots. How much information about family origins is revealed in the interview? The more history is revealed, the greater the continuity.

(5) The Tellers and Their Children (in particular, similarity between their attitudes toward and expectations of their children) and Their Memories of Parental Attitudes and Expectations During Childhood. This was further subdivided into attitudes and expectations toward one's children and active involvement in their lives. In general, the closer the similarity, the greater the continuity.

Reading and Processing

Reading the selected subtext, I looked for manifestations of the five categories as defined above. Each subcategory was scored between 0 and 5, according to the number of relevant utterances that appeared in the narrative (reversing the score of the second subcategory). The score 5 was assigned whenever the number of utterances was five or more. The total score of this category was therefore between 0 and 25. Finally, these scores were averaged, so that the highest score for continuity was 5. Lower scores indicate a lower level of continuity, or a higher degree of change in the interviewee's life story. These judgments are clearly complex and require careful deliberation, as will be demonstrated below. The judgment process may include more than one judge but, as in the present case, can be also carried out by a single "expert" who gains experience by rereading the text from the defined perspectives and refining her understanding of the topic.

Results

General. The quantitative processing of my content analysis led to the following distribution:

High continuity (scores 4 and 5): 15 participants
Moderate continuity (score 3): 7 participants
Low continuity (scores 1 and 2): 12 participants
Not scored because of little information: 2 participants

It can be concluded that, in light of the great mobility and the low objective continuity with parents' lifestyle in our sample, the experienced continuity, as revealed in the life stories, is quite high.

Let us examine the subcategories more qualitatively, namely, by looking at detailed contents that emerged in the reading as well as some additional, unexpected findings.

(1) Contribution of Parents to Teller's Education. Many interviewees tended to see themselves as continuing their parents' traditions in the area of education, in spite of the fact that, objectively, they had obtained a much higher standard of education. This sense of continuity is based on two reasons:

a. By getting an education, the narrator fulfills his or her parents' expectations.

> You have to understand, that I was the first son to go to high school. Not only the first son [from my small family], but [the first] in a broader sense. Perhaps that's why there were many expectations, I don't know . . . really, there were many expectations of me in the family. (Steve)

b. One of the parents, usually the father, is described as possessing a high, yet unfulfilled, potential for further education. Thus the perceived gap between the teller and his or her parent can be minimized, as in the case of Sara: "My father was always terrific in mathematical calculations, and he had a fantastic memory for facts and figures. I could ask him anything and he answered me right away."

(2) Reference to "Significant Figures" Who Are Not One's Parents. While, as presented above, most of the interviewees mentioned their parents as the significant figures of their childhood, some preferred to name others in this role. The most frequent choices were as follows:

a. Teachers in kindergarten or elementary school, especially the first teacher the teller encountered outside home, were indicated. In these cases, the chosen figure was used as a role model.

b. Grandmothers, and less frequently grandfathers, were chosen for their care and nurturing (see, for example, Sara's life story, pp. 36-37), particularly when the mother worked outside the home. When this was the figure chosen as the significant other, it was *not* interpreted as indicating discontinuity with the family.

c. Friends or the peer group were chosen as significant in early child-hood by several individuals, all from poor families. In these cases, good friends seemed to compensate for the absence of positive models within the family. For example: " I don't think there were any significant people, perhaps my friends—We were like a group of our own, not connected to parents. The parents were there, they did what they could, but it was very limited" (Earnst).

(3) Similarity of the Teller to His or Her Siblings. Discontinuity between the individual and his or her family background is sometimes indicated by presentation of the self as very different from other siblings in traits, achievements, or relationships with the parents. Not all the interviewees provided this information in their life stories. The descrip-tion of the self as unique within their families was apparent in many cases, however, as can be exemplified by Sara's depiction of herself as a firstborn. This type of uniqueness—similar to the presentation of other interviewees as the only male child or the youngest in their families—does not, by itself, manifest discontinuity; it depends on the meaning of the utterance. Most relevant were the cases (eight among our group) in which the teller described himself as the only one in the family who had a high school diploma or received a college education.

(4) Family History or Roots. Many of the interviewees provided a family history, in spite of the fact that they were not asked to do so. Often they came from immigrant families, and the family history relates to life in another country and culture. By telling about the family history prior to immigration, the person often suggested that, in the old country, the family had been more affluent and socially respected than in Israel. Furthermore, many of the anecdotes depicted the teller's parent as rebellious against his own parents, as if founding the first generation in a chain of change. In this manner, these interviewees provided indirect justification for their own discontinuous life choices. In any case, the introduction of family roots into one's life story proved to be important for maintaining one's sense of continuity in spite of change.

(5) The Teller and His or Her Children.

(a) Attitudes and Expectations. All in this group of participants were parents and, in comparing themselves with their children, disclosed

aspects of their own selves. This sometimes happened when the child's experience was presented in contrast to one's own remembered childhood and could be categorized as manifesting discontinuity. A striking example is presented in the following dialogue between the interviewer and Jack:

Jack: But it is a pleasure to see how he (narrator's son) belongs.
Interviewer: Belongs to what?
Jack: Belongs to something, something which accompanies him for the rest of his life, which doesn't disturb him . . . And it's his, before him and after him . . . It's good for him. Belonging is a tremendous thing.

This "belonging" is something the narrator himself never felt, given that in his childhood and adolescence he felt alienated from his environment, like "a plant that dies to reach the ground, but you say, look, I didn't find ground."

In other cases, the comparison reveals a sense of continuity, especially when the present parent perceives himself as pushing his child toward achievements as much as his parents did:

I remember my father waking me up at 6:00 to practice my music, it was so stressful, and I used to cry and hate it. Now, there are many things that I apply to my children today [in their sport training] . . . I am definitely affected by this approach. (Earnst)

A smaller number of participants refer to an opposite trend and describe themselves as giving their children more freedom of choice than they experienced in their homes: "I don't want for them anything they don't want for themselves . . . and I don't see myself as an educator either" (Mike).

Some of the interviewees remember childhood feelings and episodes that help them to understand their children, as in the case of David (see p. 51):

There were naturally also periods of feeling more introverted, and more . . . Now, that I have my own children, I see this is as all normal, crises that everyone experiences. I remember these moods somehow, however, and I think that it helps me today with my kids.

(b) Parental Involvement. In the majority of the life stories, the interviewees presented themselves as more involved and actively engaged in their children's lives than their own parents were willing or able to be. This was raised more frequently by men, whose male parent

models, their own fathers, were remembered as being absent from home and taking almost no part in the daily life of the family. As much as the men of our sample were also very busy with their careers, they described their actual involvement in their children's life as being very significant, as reported by David: "I am always available [to my kids] on the phone, I cook for them, feed them, play with them."

Continuity Types

In the process of reading and interpreting the sections that were relevant to the subject of continuity and change, another characterization of the data emerged. It seemed that the narrators could be classified into five different groups according to the type of continuity they exhibited in their stories, as follows:

(a) Intentional Continuity. People belonged to this group if their stories revealed that they made conscious choices to continue the family tradition by making decisions regarding occupation, religiosity, residence, and so on that manifest similarity or closeness to their parents. This pattern was rare in our group and included only three men, all of them from relatively well-off families.

(b) Unintentional Continuity. This group of people declared that they were trying to be different from their parents, but, in fact, their life stories exposed much similarity between them. There were three men of that type among the interviewees.

(c) Continuing Without Awareness. In their interviews, this group of people did not refer one way or another to continuing their family tradition. However, their stories reveal that they manifest continuity in many areas. Most of our interviewees, including Sara (see pp. 29-50), belong to this group.

(d) Revolutionaries. This group includes people who declare that it is their intention to break away from family traditions, and their life stories reflect this choice. Three individuals among the research participants can be placed in this group.

(e) Self-Made Individuals. These people attribute their entire development, and the choices they made, to themselves. They rarely present their parents in their story or among the significant figures in the

different stages. There were two such individuals in the research group, one of whom is David (see pp. 50-60), who said about his childhood: "When I had problems, I preferred to tackle them all alone, I didn't share them with my family."

Summary of the Findings

In this part of the chapter, two broad categories were explored to evaluate the relationship between the participants' notable mobility and the place of their family of origin in their life stories. The analysis implied that, in spite of large objective differences from their parents, the interviewees' perceptions of their families of origin are mainly favorable, especially at present, and that the experience of continuity between their life choices and values with those of their family of origin is quite high. To arrive at these conclusions, a complex process of interpretive content analysis was demonstrated. The selection of subcategories, their definition within an interpretive framework, and their use in understanding the interviewees' presentations of themselves exemplify how profound and sophisticated the process of content analysis can become.

CONCLUDING REMARKS

Three main dimensions or choices clarify the comparison of the two demonstrations of content analysis provided in this chapter, all of them relevant to the objective-subjective continuum:

1. Does the researcher use a well-defined subtext of utterances, or does she include in the process inferences from the context, from the unsaid, and/or the comparative placement of one section versus another and so on?
2. In sorting the material into categories, how much interpretive or impressionistic work actually takes place?
3. Are the units of analysis processed quantitatively or in a freer, more descriptive manner?

While the more accurate or objective method of content analysis, as in the first part of the chapter, is easier to report on, replicate, and criticize, we have indicated that many decisions taken in this process are also often arbitrary. The more subjective, hermeneutic approach takes more training to apply and defend yet, like other nonpositivistic approaches to scientific inquiry, can reach more profound realms of understanding lives and experiences.

NOTES

1. The *subjective* impact refers to the personal evaluation of the high school experience from the standpoint of the teller. The present chapter is not concerned with comparisons of the "real" or "objective" attainments of the four research groups.

2. For a complete description of the samples and their high school experience, please refer to pages 21-24.

3. The author and Mrs. Sara Blank Ha-Ramati, a clinical psychologist who also participated at the interviewing stage. I would like to extend my deepest thanks to Sara for her contribution to the research.

4. As mentioned at the beginning of Chapter 3, the transcriptions of Sara's and David's interviews were edited slightly. Nevertheless, the texts can be used for this demonstration.

5. For a list of the categories proposed for the four research groups, please see Table 6.2.

6. While the terms *segregation* and *integration* are used repeatedly in this chapter, in the context of Israeli society the terms relate only to separation or integration in schools according to the socioeconomic status of the family and do not carry the connotation of racial differences as in the United States. For further background about the educational policy regarding school integration in Israel, please refer to Chapter 2 and also to Lieblich (1995) and Amir et al. (1984).

7. "Political activity in school" refers to belonging to a youth organization for or against major issues in the politics of Israeli society, going to demonstrations, signing petitions, and so on. This therefore can be counted as social activity that took place within the school.

8. The use of colored markers for the different tasks of content analysis is recommended. Here, for example, I highlighted each topic of the content categories in a different color.

9. Presenting the comparative objective outcome is out of the scope of this chapter (Lieblich, Tuval, & Zilber, 1995, in Hebrew). It may be interesting to note here that the final conclusion of this question remained controversial because no clear indication for the initial equality of the students who were admitted to the different high schools could be obtained.

10. For a proposed analysis of the emotional aspects in a spoken or written narrative, see the second part of Chapter 7.

11. This is true for the general Israeli population except for the lowest SES groups, a small minority who, due to extreme poverty or lack of parental care, had no educational channels opened to their offspring.

12. There is naturally some conscious and unconscious relationship between parents' perception and a sense of continuity, although not always a simple one.

13. In Israel, *ethnic differences* is a term used to describe cultural-geographic origins of the family. The major distinction is between "Ashkenazee," who originate from

Christian countries in Europe or America, and "Sephardee," who originate from Moslem countries in North Africa and the Middle East.

14. See Note 5.

15. This distinction is very similar to the famous distinction made by Bales (1958) about "instrumental" versus "expressive" leadership types.

16. This pattern is similar to what is usually found in Western societies, namely, that adolescence is an age of rebellion against parental authority, with an increase in the significance of the peer group (Erikson, 1959).

17. Information about the objective mobility of the narrators in terms of their comparison with their parents in education and occupation was summarized in a Hebrew research report (Lieblich, Tuval, & Zilber, 1995).

7

Categorical-Form Analysis

In this chapter, the use of categorical-form analysis to examine oral narrative will be demonstrated with two examples. The purpose of the analysis is to learn something about the speaker that might not have been apparent from examination of content alone. The chapter opens with a detailed example demonstrating how cognitive skills may be reflected in oral narrative. A second and more concise example of categorical-form analysis demonstrates how emotions are reflected in the telling of significant events in a speaker's life.

ANALYSIS OF COGNITIVE FUNCTIONING
AS REFLECTED IN NARRATIVE DATA:
TAMAR ZILBER

In the following analysis, I will be looking at differences between the genders in terms of cognitive ability as defined in Carl Frankenstein's conceptual framework.[1] In doing so, I will share with you the internal dialogue of the researcher as she attempts to construct a new research tool.

Assumptions

The study of cognitive functions through life-story analysis presupposes an assumption that the manner in which life stories are presented reflects thought processes. Previous research has made use of spontaneous verbal productions to analyze cognitive styles (e.g., Gottschalk, 1994) or decision-making processes (e.g., Tetlock, 1991). The present research, however, is based on the work of C. Frankenstein, who established the educational program that was the subject of our original study (see Chapter 2). In his books *Liberating Thinking From Its Bondages* (1972) and *They Think Again* (1981), Frankenstein presents analysis of material from classes taught according to his method of rehabilitative teaching. Excerpts from students' verbal and/or written material are brought to demonstrate faulty thinking in some cases, and, in others, the use of new cognitive capacities attained through exposure to the rehabilitative teaching method. As such, the emphasis of his work is on thought processes rather than contents.

Given Frankenstein's contention that efficient thinking or the lack thereof is manifested in all areas of life, it is reasonable to assume that both efficient and faulty thinking will be reflected in the way life stories are told. It is, however, advisable to bear in mind that efficient thinking does not constitute the entire domain of cognitive ability, and therefore my conclusions regarding cognitive functions cannot be generalized to all cognitive processes. Narration of a life story highlights, in particular, those aspects of thought that are verbal, related to the self, emotionally charged, and that take place in the context of interpersonal communication.

Cognitive Skills: Theoretical Framework

As opposed to the attributes of "effective thinking" (Frankenstein, 1981), Frankenstein has specified four types of faulty thinking that are characteristic of secondary retardation (Frankenstein, 1970b, 1972, 1981):

1. *Irrational thinking* is reflected in
   a. thought patterns characterized by uncontrollable associations and emotionality;
   b. preference for concretizations over abstractions (examples rather than generalities and laws, specific rather than general concepts, identification of values with their concrete manifestations and of feelings with their external expressions);
   c. preference for concrete symbols over concepts.

2. *Inadequate differentiation* is reflected in
   a. inability to use analogies and to keep in mind their "as-if" character or to differentiate between analogy and reality;
   b. dichotomization;
   c. use of stereotypes and of scientific terms that are not adequately understood.

3. *Lack of responsibility for the acts of thinking and learning* is reflected in
   a. passive reliance on authoritative figures (e.g., teacher or book).

4. *Inability to maintain simultaneous perceptions* is reflected in
   a. inability to see several aspects of a problem, a task, or phenomenon at one and the same time;
   b. inability to follow two or more directions simultaneously.

For each category of faulty thinking, there is a contrasting ability that is characteristic of effective thinking. Effective thinking is therefore primarily rational, differentiating, responsible, and capable of maintaining simultaneous perceptions.

Due to space limitations, only the three first types of efficient thinking will be demonstrated in the following sections.

Data

The analysis presented in this chapter is based on the life stories of 12 men and women from the younger adult research sample. For the purpose of demonstration, I will be using Sara's and David's interviews although they were not included in my sample. As I worked, it soon became clear that analysis of all 12 interviews would be lengthy and unwieldy, given the precision of the analysis and its emphasis on details. Thus I decided to limit myself to the first stages of the life stories. I assumed that cognitive skills would be equally well reflected by any given section of the life stories.

As will be recalled, participants were requested to divide their lives into stages from birth up the present. To maintain a consistent time framework, I decided to work with the accounts of the first 12-13 years of life, which many of our interviewees regarded as one or two stages. This decision reflects a preference for an objective (and somewhat arbitrary) criterion, which more or less corresponds to the subjective stage breakdowns provided by the participants themselves.

Participants were asked four standard questions about each of their life stages (see Chapter 2). The structured nature of the procedure ensured that there would be some similarity between the interviews, especially in their content categories. Nonetheless, it was inevitable that there would be inter- interviewer variability in the framing of the questions, the handling of the interview, and the extent to which procedural interview guidelines were followed. This variability can be assumed to have influenced the interviewees and contributed to the natural variance between their responses. It is clear that such contextual differences will be reflected in the findings of my analysis.

Operationalization: Measures

The measures for assessing efficient versus faulty thinking were developed through a dialectic process between Frankenstein's theoretical framework and the stories themselves. I began by attempting, on a purely intuitive basis, to translate Frankenstein's explanations and examples (1970a, 1970b, 1972, 1981) into measures that could be accurately applied to the life-story texts. Returning to the stories, I tested these measures against the material, used what I'd learned to sharpen the measures, and once again returned to the texts. This was a lengthy process that required numerous rereadings of the interview material. A measure was considered serviceable only when it could be clearly defined and was applicable to any random textual example. This internal dialogue (which I also could have carried out in a group setting) ultimately generated tools that were compatible with the issues of standardization and quantification and could be satisfactorily implemented. The cyclical movement from Frankenstein's theoretical material to the data of the interviews themselves, to create a measure that is rooted in both, is reminiscent of the process of evolving grounded theory (Glaser & Strauss, 1967).

Assessment of Rational Thinking

According to Frankenstein (1970b, 1972), rational thinking reflects a capacity for abstract and/or symbolic conceptualization that is free from the influence of uncontrollable and unrestrained associations, whereas irrational thinking is reflected in a preference for concrete and particular examples. I chose to assess rational thinking by looking specifically at abstract as opposed to concrete thinking. I found that if a particular statement could elicit the question, "Could you give me an example of that?" it was indicative of a high level of abstractness, whereas if a statement could elicit the question, "What is the interviewee trying to tell me?" it was indicative of an extreme concreteness. This may be better understood with the help of the following two excerpts.

Sara, describing the death of her younger sister, says "and then really only ah . . . I asked more questions." Here her discourse is completely abstract, and I found myself wondering about concrete details, that is, "What exactly did she ask." When she describes moving to a new home, however, she says,

> And then we moved to a new apartment, and there was also this experience of children from my class who suddenly saw me in the new neighborhood:

What are you doing here? You don't belong here. And then I had to explain that I'd moved.

Here I found myself unsure of what she was trying to convey in her description. The concreteness with which Sara describes the situation reflects her own inability to abstract more comprehensive understanding from a confusing and unsettling experience.

These two examples are extreme cases of abstraction and concreteness. In the absence of concrete details, it is clear that the first passage is abstract, while the second passage is concrete by virtue of its nonabstractness. In most cases, however, such a distinction is problematic insofar as we are referring to a continuous, and not a categorical, aspect of thinking. Assessment of the abstractness or the concreteness of a given statement therefore can usually be made only in relation to another more or less abstract or concrete expression.

To solve this problem, I decided to focus on transitions between concrete and abstract expressions rather than to treat this aspect as a dichotomy. This tactic also proved useful for the evaluation of cognitive development. Although abstract thinking is viewed as more advanced than concrete thinking (according to Frankenstein as well as cognitive developmental theorists such as Kohlberg, 1976; Perry, 1968; Piaget, 1955), the capacity to conceive of a subject in both concrete and abstract terms, and to move easily between these two types of perception, is also indicative of a high level of cognitive development and can be viewed as an aspect of cognitive complexity and effective thinking (Goldstein & Scheerer, 1941).

As in the identification of abstractness and concreteness per se, the search for transitions between abstractness and concreteness is facilitated by the kinds of phrases that can be elicited by the material. If a certain passage can be prefaced by key phrases such as *the principal of the matter is* or *for example,* a transition between concreteness and complexity is generally occurring in the text. David says of his childhood, "But it was really a period of freedom from worries [for example], I don't know, going to the beach, picking wild grapes, spending time with other kids." Here David begins in an abstract mode and speaks of "a period of freedom from worries," and then makes the transition to a more concrete mode with specific examples of typical childhood activities.

On occasion, the transition is signaled only after the concrete examples in the form of a summation. Sara, for example, reflecting about her schooldays, gives concrete examples of her enjoyment of that period: a trip to the zoo, her childhood partner, a play in which she participated. It is only several sentences later that she returns to summarize this period in more abstract terms: "First and second grade were really a special experience, really."

At times speakers may use a conjunction to signal a transition to a different level of concreteness. David says, for example, "We had a teacher who educated us in real values—*like,* not cheating on exams, and friendship and mutual aid," and elsewhere, "Our family relationships were warm and good but not too open. *In other words,* when I had problems I preferred to tackle them all alone." Such linkages suggest that the speaker is aware of having to explain the sense of what is being said. There are, however, numerous examples of transition between levels of abstraction that are not announced by the speaker. For example, David recalls his family moving to another city when he was 8 years old: "Suddenly my whole life changed. I remember the class, the new kids, the structure of the school, which was different. The weather was somewhat different." Here David moves from an abstract statement to concrete examples without reporting the transition.

Identification of transitions is not always as clear-cut as in the above examples. The following are some of the more problematic cases. Sara, for instance, recalls, "I have very good memories from kindergarten (. . .) I even really remember the names of my teachers because I enjoyed myself so much there." Here I wondered whether remembering the names of her teachers signaled a transition to a more concrete mode. Eventually I concluded that Sara had remained at the same level of abstraction and was simply restating her abstract understanding of her enjoyment of kindergarten; that is, it was so enjoyable that she could remember the names of her teachers and other good things (which she also does not specify in concrete detail).

Similarly, David, describing himself as a child says, "I was shy, I think, I was sensitive, I was a cry-baby, that is, who easily took offense." While *shy, sensitive,* and a *cry-baby* are all linguistically at the same level, I wondered if the use of *easily insulted* represented a restatement of all the other qualities or a move to a lower level of abstraction. I wondered about David's use of the words *that is* and whether they might have indicated his intention of giving an example. Here, too, I concluded that the use of the phrase *that is* did not signal a move to a different level of abstraction, because for each of these descriptions we could have requested an example, suggesting that they are all abstract.

Such examples emphasize the personal-interpretive and subjective aspects of this type of analysis. Often the decisions are based on the context in which a statement was made and/or on personal attributes of the speaker, such as fluency of expression.

There are different kinds of transitions. For instance, Sara says, "I always used to come back to a home full of joy, with a cooked meal and a mom who's home, who's there for us, welcomes us." In contrast is Sara's description of the death of her baby sister (see pp. 31-32 in Chapter 3). In the first example, Sara moves from a high level of abstraction ("home full of joy") to more concrete examples of her experience. These examples, however, are still abstract in their own right insofar as they invite more detailed descriptions of her memories of coming home, of specific kinds of food, for instance. In the second example, in contrast, Sara moves from extreme abstraction ("very unpleasant memory") to a particularly concrete description of the house and people she recalls from that time. The latter is an example of final transition—the level of discourse cannot become any more concrete than it already has. The former is an example of partial transition—the level of discourse becomes more concrete, but there is room for even more concreteness.

To conclude, then, I found that the number of transitions from abstraction to concreteness (and vice versa) could be used as a measure of the capacity for abstract thinking. Such transitions may be signaled by conjunctions where the transition is a conscious one. While a distinction may be made between final and partial transitions, my analysis did not indicate the existence of differences between the groups for this variable, and thus it was not explored further in later stages of analysis.

Initially I counted the number of transitions between levels of abstraction for each interviewee and summed the results across gender groups. In total there were 39 such transitions for the men as opposed to 33 for the women. Such comparisons are justified only when the texts of the groups (e.g., women and men) that are analyzed are of equal length. This was the case in the present analysis. Moreover, within each of the groups, the distribution was about equal.

On the face of things, it seems that the higher number of transitions for men is indicative of a greater capacity for abstract thinking. Closer reading of the protocols, however, revealed that often transitions were precipitated by questions on the part of the interviewer. There were interventions of two types:

Often, an interviewer requested an example and thus elicited a transition from abstraction to concreteness. For example, when Danny says, "I was a live wire. Judging from the stories I was pretty wild . . . ," the interviewer prompts, "for example?" and Danny responds with a story he's been told of how at the age of 2 he crawled several hundred meters, and across the street, to his grandfather's house to get candy.

A second type of intervention elicited a transition from concreteness to greater abstraction. For instance, when Sara describes being loved and spoiled as the eldest daughter in the family, the following dialogue between the interviewer and Sara took place:

I: So if you had to characterize yourself at this first age you would describe yourself as a child, a preferred child?
S: I think that, I think yes, at every age, really at every age.
I: Yes.
S: In Spanish we say *Bechorika*—the beloved firstborn girl that . . .

In this case, however, the interviewee provides the concrete examples, and it is the interviewer who supplies the more abstract term.

Although such interventions do not always generate a transition between levels, they may convey to the interviewee a sense of what is expected in the interview situation, which affects the further course of the interview. Without examining the interviews in their entirety, however, it is difficult to ascertain whether interventions intended to elicit such transitions induce the interviewee to use more transitions.[2] For this reason, I conducted another count of transitions that were not initiated by interviewer interventions. I found 23 such transitions among the men and 27 among the women, indicating that when interviewer effects are taken into account, the picture in terms of gender differences is reversed.

Assessment of Capacity for Differentiation

Frankenstein (1970b, 1981) defines *differentiation* as the ability to identify similarities and distinctions between different phenomena (personal attributes, events, objects), to perceive relative and objective dimensions of reality, and to remain uninfluenced by preconceptions, stereotypes, and patterns of cognitive and evaluative activity. I chose to investigate this capacity via analysis of the tendency to generalize. Generalization is the inclusion of something in a category of other things. Generalization requires us to temporarily ignore the complexity and differences among all those other things for the sake of inclusion in a mutual category. My premise is that minimal use of generalizations and/or a preference for qualified generalizations are indicative of a capacity for differentiation. As opposed to other measures I have used, this measure is defined in terms of a negation, primarily because generalizations are easier to identify than differentiations.

Although identification of generalizations may invite speculations about their truth-value (particularly in the case of stereotypes), I attempted to focus on the *act* of generalization as a measure of differentiating thought. One example of a generalization is from David's description of himself as a child: "but there were naturally also periods of feeling more introverted, and more . . . Now that I have my own children, I see this as all normal crises, that everyone experiences." There is no indication of how David has reached the conclusion that everyone undergoes similar experiences. Nor is there any basis for determining whether David is right or wrong. Both of these issues are irrelevant to our interest in David's thought processes here, that is, his decision to attribute shared qualities to all members of a larger group—"everyone."

As I have suggested above, a distinction should be made between generalizations and qualified generalizations. The former, as in the above example, assume that the generalization holds true in all cases. An example of a qualified generalization is taken from Danny, who describes how he had to be coaxed to eat and says, "*I imagine* all kids have their things where you have to coax them into doing something." In this case Danny makes no claim that all children are difficult eaters, and the preface of his statement with "I imagine" makes it clear that what we are hearing is his own perception rather than a statement of universal principals. Phrases such as *I imagine, I would guess that, as far as I know* are all indicative of the speaker's uncertainty about the claim he or she is making.

Another type of qualification is the demarcation of the range to which the generalization applies. Expressions such as *usually* or *for the most part* signal this type of qualification and indicate that the speaker is aware of the limitations of his generalization. Lory, for instance, describes how easily she blushes, adding, "but *usually* only naive people blush, and I don't belong in that category."

To determine if there were differences in the capacity for differentiating thought between the two groups, I compared them across two dimensions:

1. *Frequency of generalizations:* Men made 28 generalizations as opposed to 34 among the women.
2. Frequency of qualified generalizations: Men made 10 qualified generalizations as opposed to 13 among the women

According to these findings, women generalized more than men. Both groups use similar proportions of qualified generalizations (approximately one-third of all generalizations).

Assessment of Responsible Thinking

Frankenstein (1970b, 1972, 1981) defines *responsible thinking* as freedom from reliance on authority (i.e., authoritative figures or books) and the ability to recognize the internal laws of phenomena, actions, and processes. Deficiencies in responsible thinking will be evident in failures to see beyond the concreteness and immediacy of given situations, and in a tendency to infer the veracity of critical judgments from the authoritativeness of their source.

I looked for evidence of responsible thinking in the critical statements made by the interviewees. I defined *critical statements* as allegations in defiance of apparent fact. These may refer to any circumstance (e.g., parenting style) so long as they denote judgment or evaluative activity on the part of the speaker. Allegations of this type reflect critical judgment and as such can be classified as responsible thinking. They are responsible insofar as the speaker exercises an ability to independently assess and evaluate events rather than passively accepting them at face value. Expression of a critical opinion, particularly when it refers to figures of authority (such as parents, teachers), is assumed to be indicative of freedom from reliance on authority.

An initial reading of the material from the perspective of responsible thinking suggested that distinctions should be made among descriptions, evaluations, and criticisms:

Description Versus Evaluation. Although it may be argued that no descriptions are free of evaluative activity on the part of the speaker, what is relevant here is that, linguistically, one can distinguish between descriptive and evaluative statements. A description answers an implicit question about what transpired whereas an evaluation answers an implicit question about the speaker's opinions on events, people, or behavior. David, for example, describes his functioning in school: "I was very obedient, a good kid, doing my homework, but not making too much effort (. . . .) I was average." If he had said only that he was obedient and did his homework without much effort, his remarks would have been classified as description. The evaluative element in "a good kid" and "I was average, " however, is what marks this as evaluation.

Distinctions between descriptions and evaluations are not always clearcut. A term may be seem descriptive yet assume evaluative dimensions in a certain context. Mary, for instance, describes her first-grade teacher, saying, "I remember that she also really loved us (. . .) she got carried away with her feelings for us (. . .)." While the phrase *she really loved us* seems descriptive, being carried away by these feelings of love introduces negative connotations of being involved against one's will or better sense. There is therefore reason to speculate that this statement was evaluative or even critical, and an examination of context confirms this speculation. Mary, on closer reading, is offering a careful and subtle criticism that springs from her own perception of a conflict between the distance she maintains from students and her former teacher's submission to her emotions. She says,

> I remember that she also really loved us. It was mutual, and as a teacher I know today how easily this can happen, I mean there are classes that you get really attached to as a group, not for the individual children. I try to retain a distance. I remember that she got carried away with her feelings for us, I know today that can happen. (. . .)

As will be evident below in the section on criticism, a careful evaluation such as Mary's can also be characterized as implicit criticism.

As can be seen from the above, evaluations, unlike descriptions, are also abstract statements. The difficulty of distinguishing between descriptions and evaluations, as well as the extensive overlap between evaluations and abstract statements (as described in a previous section), were seen as reason to drop this category from the analysis. I chose instead to focus on a more stringent measure of responsible thinking, specifically criticisms.

Criticisms are either proclamations of agreement/disagreement with a given state of affairs, or they are statements of opinion based on deliberation and extensive consideration of all possible options. They differ from evaluations, which make value judgments often without express awareness of their evaluative content, and offer opinions without elucidation of the reasoning behind them. Within the category of criticisms, distinctions can be made between direct as opposed to implicit criticism and between full-scale as opposed to restrained criticism.

Direct criticisms are simply critical opinions that are expressed publicly. Sara, for instance, makes it clear that she disparages the decision made by the educational system that had characterized her as underprivileged according to criteria that still seem senseless to her.

> At that time, they called children of this class "underprivileged"—I don't know if my parents belong to this category, maybe since my father never

studied. You know the definition of underprivileged was based on the
education of the parents, and the second criterion was origin of the
parents, I think. Today I don't agree to this at all.

And she goes on to describe her father's talent for mathematics and her
mother's love of books.

Implicit criticisms are not spoken openly but can be inferred from the
content of what is being said. Usually the criticism is conveyed by way of
a contradiction between two behaviors or by careful choice of vocabulary.
Sara says, for example, "and I remember us going there all the time, that's
we used to go there a lot, taking the bus with not much uh . . . great joy—we
were not spoiled then." Sara's comments suggest a disparity between
behaviors—those of the children of those times who rode the bus uncom-
plainingly and those of today's spoiled children.

Restrained criticism reflects awareness of context and suggests that the
speaker is ready to soften the judgment in light of the circumstances. Danny
says, in describing the *cheder*[3] where he studied,

(. . .) I would guess that it wasn't just my parents who found it easier,
that there were perhaps other parents who found it simpler to put their
children there at such a young age. At that age, to start learning the
alphabet, and discipline, and whatever in that alienating environment,
such a long day, from morning to nightfall.

Here Danny expresses his implicit critical opinions through his choice of
the words *alienating environment* or *such a long day.* His censure of his
parents, moreover, is moderated by his reference to other parents, which
serves to soften the judgment against the individual parents by sharing
responsibility among all parents who lived according to his parents' norms.

It should be noted that while a critical attitude may be either positive or
negative, speakers did not make the effort to explain their opinions when
they were positive. Only negative criticisms were presented as opinions,
whereas positive evaluations were offered without explanations and presented as descriptive, so that they could not be included within the measure
of responsible thinking as I defined it earlier.

A question also arises as to whether differences in type of criticism are
relevant to an evaluation of a capacity for responsible thinking as defined
by Frankenstein. Are such differences simply a product of individual
differences in the expression of critical opinions, or do they reflect more
fundamental differences in underlying thought processes? My own opinion
is that both direct and implicit criticism are independent thought processes

of equal value. Direct expression of criticism requires a "braver" speaker who is willing to defend his or her opinion rather than retreat behind excuses of having been misunderstood. This may mean taking greater responsibility for one's thoughts but is not necessarily related to the capacity to think independently. In the case of restrained criticism, consideration of the contextual aspects of a situation may diminish the critical element, but it also indicates that a measured and considered process has been involved in the consolidation of the opinion. Thus a restrained criticism is no indication of lesser cognitive skills. It is instead a proof that a criticism is upheld, despite the speaker's reservations, and that those reservations have been brought into play in a considered thought process.

The use of criticism as a measure of responsible thinking, however, requires further clarification. First, the fact that an adult is capable of criticizing how his parents or teachers treated him as a child does not mean that he is independent of the authoritative figures who are currently important to him. This problem, however, is specific to the use of the measure in looking at an earlier chapter in the speaker's life and is not inherent to the measure itself. Second, failure to express an opinion may be indicative of an absence of appropriate opportunities to express that opinion rather than an absence of critical opinions altogether. While this reservation could be targeted at all the measures discussed in this chapter, it should be recalled that a premise of this kind of analysis is that the life story is a valid representation of personal identity in which tendencies to consolidate and express well-founded opinions will find expression.[4]

Thus, to assess responsible thinking, I examined the interviewee's critical statements. A critical statement was defined as one that expresses an opinion of agreement or disagreement about an activity or a person in an open or implicit and/or restrained manner.

Altogether, the interviewees made 37 critical statements with respect to the period of childhood, 20 among the men and 17 among the women. Half of the men's criticisms were direct and half were implicit, whereas among the women, more than half were implicit and only one-third were direct. Men tended more to qualification of their criticism (one-half of their statements as opposed to one-eighth of women's statements).

Discussion

The analysis cannot be brought to a close without a discussion of some of its limitations. In the work presented above, selected sections of the interview texts have been analyzed and interpreted in terms of three measures, each representing one of the cognitive skills conceptualized by

Frankenstein. For the purposes of this analysis, Frankenstein's theory was taken at face value, and no attempt was made to consider, compare, or contrast it with other cognitive and educational theories.

Furthermore, it is clear that different operational measures might have been suggested for each of the three cognitive skills. For instance, it would have been possible to look at frequency of comparisons made by the interviewees as indicative of the capacity to assess differences and similarities. Or it would have been possible to view the extent to which interviewees explain occurrences in terms of general laws or principles as indicative of a capacity for evaluation as opposed to description.

It is also clear that none of these measures can singly distinguish between differences in the cognitive skills of men and women, given the presence of additional factors that might have influenced the interviewee's thought processes (such as the identity of the interviewer and the manner in which the interview was organized).

Such limitations, though important to voice, do not diminish the value of the measures that have been developed for the purpose of this analysis. All cognitive skills and all assessments of intelligence are influenced by factors other than intelligence itself. The use of more than one measure to assess the variable in question is, in fact, one way of contending with such influences.

To summarize my findings regarding gender and efficient thinking, no major differences were detected in comparing women and men on the various measures developed in this section. When differences have been found, it is still impossible to determine whether they are due to cognitive ability or, as some recent studies propose (Belenky et al., 1986; Goldberger et al., 1996; Tannen, 1990), to preferred style of verbal expression.

USING LINGUISTIC FEATURES OF
THE NARRATIVE TO RECOGNIZE AND
ASSESS ITS EMOTIONAL CONTENT:
TAMAR ZILBER

Various aspects of narrative can yield insight into the emotional experience with which a narrative is charged. The most direct method of assessing an interviewee's emotions is to listen for direct expressions of feeling, whether in content ("I am sad") or in paralinguistic terms (tears). Careful reading for content can also teach us about the speaker's feeling in an indirect way (e.g., what is not said; see the example in the analysis of the importance of marriage in Sara's life in Chapter 4). In content analysis, conclusions are drawn on the basis of empathic and sensitive readings of the text. The following section of this chapter demonstrates a third method, specifically the use of a formal measure for assessing to what extent the narrative of a speaker is emotionally charged. In this case, conclusions are drawn on the basis of linguistic features of the narrative.

Interest in this issue is located at the intersection between the analysis of narrative in both linguistic and psychological research. Linguistic researchers study how language expresses emotion. They assume that lexical, grammatical, and structural aspects of discourse can be guides to the nature and magnitude of expressed emotion. Writers/speakers of narrative create texts according to conventions of discourse, and an audience of readers/listeners interpret these texts accordingly (Ochs, 1989).

Writers in the field of psychology have also characterized psychological states on the basis of linguistic factors. Here the assumption is that events evoke emotions, human beings attempt to deal with those emotions, and their coping mechanisms are reflected in the linguistic features of their discourse. Spence (1983), for instance, aspires to define the linguistic features of stress denial. Capps and Ochs (1995) have studied the linguistic features of the autobiographical narrative that reveal mechanisms for coping with emotions such as fear and helplessness. Heizner (1994) has looked at linguistic expressions of helplessness in trauma narratives. These researchers have focused on linguistic features that are related to the symptoms and perceptions of psychological distress. Thus, for example, in narratives of agoraphobia, the focus is on adverbials emphasizing the element of unexpectedness and on passive forms of verbs reflecting the speaker's sense of helplessness (Capps & Ochs, 1995).

In the example that follows, I will consider how formal aspects of emotionally charged narrative can be used as a tool for understanding an episode of the life story.

Measure

In this study we collected narratives from healthy and functional men and women with no apparent psychological disorders. Although it can be argued that all narratives express emotion (Wigren, 1994), I have chosen to focus on difficult aspects of our interviewees' lives on the assumption that they will yield more clear examples of emotion. As ordinary life-course traumas and difficulties occur in all of our lives, I decided to focus on the formal aspects of descriptions of such moments in the interviewees' stories.

On the basis of the research cited above, as well as other studies (Biber & Finegan, 1989; Ochs & Schieffelin, 1989), a list was compiled of the formal aspects of emotional or mental disturbance. These are not all expected to appear in the narratives, nor is it to be anticipated that they will feature with equal intensity and/or frequency. The list serves only as a guide to formal elements that may appear in an emotionally charged narrative. The following is a partial list of formal features, presented for illustrative purposes alone.

- Adverbials such as *suddenly* may be indicative of how expected or unexpected an event may be.

- Mental verbs such as *I thought, I understood,* and *I noticed* may be indicative of the extent to which an experience is in consciousness and is undergoing mental processing.

- Denotations of time and place may be indicative of attempts to distance an event or bring it closer to the narrator.

- Past, present, or future forms of verbs, and the transitions between them, may be indicative of a speaker's sense of identification with the events being described.

- Transitions between first-person, second-person, and third-person speakers may be indicative of a split between the speaking self and the experiencing self due to the difficulty of reencountering a difficult experience.

- Passive and active forms of verbs may be indicative of the speaker's perception of agency.

- Intensifiers such as *really* or *very* or deintensifiers such as *maybe* or *like* raise questions about whether intensifiers consistently appear in connection with markers of the magnitude of an experience and whether deintensifiers always appear in conjunction with expressions of helplessness and inability to cope.

- Breaking the chronological or causal progression of events by way of regressions, digressions, leaps in time, or silences may be indicative of attempts to avoid discussing a difficult experience.

- Repetitions of parts of the discourse (syllables, words, sentences, ideas) may indicate that the subject of discussion elicits an emotional charge in the speaker's narrative.

- Detailed descriptions of events may be indicative of reluctance to describe difficult emotions.

Method

For the purposes of this demonstration, I decided to use the life stories of our adult women sample. Rereading their life stories, I marked all difficult episodes. "Difficult episodes" included experiences of loss (death, separation) and painful life events (accidents, infertility). I attended to the accounts of the actual occurrence of such episodes rather than to the speakers' evaluations of their experience.

One problem at this stage of analysis was that, as the life stories had been collected in the context of interviews, their formal aspects may have been influenced by the interaction between interviewer and interviewee. Some of the interviewers were clinical psychologists by training, and their questions tended to stress the emotional elements of the interviewee's experiences. The sense of identification experienced by these interviewers, and their tendency to express empathy when hearing an emotionally charged narrative, may have affected the emotional state of the speaker and thus influenced formal qualities of the discourse as well.

For this reason, I chose to focus mainly on the part of the narrative that was told before the interviewer entered the conversation, either by expressing identification or by asking for more details. As much as I could, I removed dialogical influences from the analysis. It should be noted that the impact of nonverbal communication could not, however, be assessed.

Another problem was the quality of the transcripts. As was noted in Chapter 3, different types of analysis require different levels of precision in the written record of the interview. Categorical-form analysis requires particularly detailed transcription. Although linguistic researchers may go as far as recording the length of silences, intonations, and so forth, in this case I settled for complete protocols without extraverbal details.

After identifying the narrative of a difficult episode, I looked for the formal linguistic aspects listed above. The following are two brief examples of this work.

Example 1

We got married just after the army, and as a young couple we settled in G^5—it was just beginning to be populated. A lot of Zionism,[6] and a lot, . . . and just nine months after the marriage, **we're involved in an accident,** a terrible car accident, and it was exactly the Yom Kippur War. We got married in March, in October there was the war, and in December we were hit. At the time, the war was still going on in the Golan Heights, it was really still war. **And an armored troop carrier was coming along the road,** it was eight in the morning, and I mean it **swerved out of its lane.** What can you do against something like that? We really. I don't remember, but witnesses said that we managed to stop, there was nothing we could do. It just **drove into us.** And Sem was driving, together with us in the car there were two friends from G, we were driving from the north to G after a weekend in H. Sem is from H, and they were in M and we picked them up and drove down beside R. It happened, and then **Sem** really for 10 days he was unconscious, and **he was hurt very badly, and I was close to death** because in fact the ribs broke into the lungs and there was complication of all that. And all kinds of dramatic stories. During that year, it was really, operations, operations, of all kinds, and it changes the reality of our life because in the near future a trip abroad had been planned, you know, a long trip, and everything and it was all getting organized in anticipation, all kinds of brochures and things, and it was canceled, of course, and we spend a year being rehabilitated more or less, with me very short-tempered, I'm really in an advanced state of anxiety, with no patience for anything, I mean it is very clear to me, and I refuse to stay in bed too much, I refuse to be a cripple, and I need to walk with a cast for half a year (Sharon).

The actual events, the "facts of the accident," are marked in the example in bold. The speaker begins by noting the time, as preface to the telling of the episode, and then swerves from her topic to describe the period more fully and locate the incident in terms of timing and context. She returns to a description of the accident, diverges to what happened from the perspective of the witnesses, and then describes the accident itself. Once again she veers away from a description of the accident to mention who the driver was, who the passengers were, and why they were there that morning, and only then returns to tell what happened, who was hurt, how badly, and the consequent changes in the plans of the young couple.

There are, altogether, three deviations from the course of the narrative, each at a painful moment in the story. The first two delay the necessity of talking about the accident itself—the actual collision between two vehicles. The third defers a description of the extent of the injury to the speaker and her spouse.

On the one hand, the information presented during these digressions is important; on the other, it can be assumed that the digressions are timed to postpone the recollection of painful memories. Thus, for example, the speaker leaves the story to tell about the two friends who had joined them in the car—who they were, where they had been picked up—but then doesn't refer to them again, not even to say if they were hurt or not. Thus, at first glance, it seems that they are irrelevant to the story, and that they serve only a function of deferral. Yet later, in the context of a dialogue between the interviewer and interviewee (not included here), we learn that one of them had been killed and the other badly hurt. It is certainly possible that she mentions them so briefly because it is difficult to come to terms with what happened to them and, perhaps, out of a sense of guilt that her husband had been the driver. Here we see how familiarity with the whole narrative is clearly important in the analysis of sections of a life story.

A number of words and phrases recur several times in the text: *marriage/married* (2), *accident* (2), *war* (4), *nothing to be done* (2), *operations* (2), *I don't agree* (2). The theme of the speaker's inability to come to terms with the accident also recurs several times. Such repetitions yield insight into key moments in the story and the extent to which they are emotionally charged. The emphasis on the war—ostensibly in the context of the story—infuses it with the tensions, pain, and loss that the experience of war usually conveys. It is also linked to the outcome of the accident—a battle for health and for life. Once again this is an illustration of the importance of context—in this case, social context and its impact on the linguistic conventions of the speaker. The Yom Kippur War, in October 1973, is perceived as a moment of breakdown in Israeli society. The war was difficult, incurred many losses, and in retrospect could have been averted or, at least, better anticipated. As such it represents a rupture in the relations of trust between the government and the nation. The use of the term *war* suggests a parallel between the calamity of the national war and that of the couple's personal disaster. It also might suggest a corresponding breakdown of trust between the speaker and her spouse.

The accident is presented as an unavoidable event over which the passengers in the car had no control ("what can you do against something like that," "there was nothing we could do"). The same defenselessness is evident in the speaker's reference to the interruption of their plans ("a trip abroad had been planned," "everything was getting organized in anticipation"). The use of the third-person passive in these references suggests the speaker's sense of an inability to take responsibility for the way her life unfolds. She regains control, however, in her response to her injuries and in her rejection of the status of patient ("I refuse to be a cripple"). Similarly, in a later part of the dialogue, she tells the interviewer how she rushed from university to university on her crutches to register for the upcoming year of studies.

The actual description of the accident is distanced and alienated from the speaker's point of view. She says, "And the armored troop carrier was coming along the road," "it just swerved out of its lane"—referring only to the other car. When she turns to a description of her side, she needs to distance the experience from herself and thus transfers the perspective to witnesses.

The speaker uses several intensifiers—*I mean, really, very*—to emphasize the severity of the accident. She also uses the word *really* when she attributes the blame to the other vehicle rather than to her husband. It is significant that first she attributes the blame to the army vehicle and stresses that the accident was unavoidable, and only later mentions that her husband was driving their car. Certainly after such a difficult accident, it is important for her to be certain herself, and to make it clear to others, that her husband was not the responsible party. We can speculate therefore that her third digression, just after the information that her husband had been driving, is intended to mark a boundary between her husband as driver of the car and the description of the damage.

It is also interesting to note the transitions between verb tenses. The speaker begins in the continuous present ("we're involved in a car accident"), moves to the past tense, and returns—in her description of the outcome of the accident and her attempts to deal with the injury—to the continuous present. It seems quite clear that the period before and after the accident are more concrete to her than the accident itself. Indeed, she doesn't even remember the moment of impact, suggesting just how difficult it is for her to cope with the experience.

A final comment about the passage is that the speaker turns to the listener with rhetorical questions or comments such as "What can you do against something like that?" or "you know." It seems that the direct appeal to the interviewer reflects the speaker's wish to share the experience with her and to elicit her identification and empathy. Making a direct appeal to the listener, and using rhetorical questions, are both features of feminine discourse (see Lakoff, 1975, 1990). Thus the consideration of text in social context includes sensitivity to the use of different linguistic conventions in the discourse of men and women.

Example 2

The second example is from Sara's life story and her description of the death of her baby sister.[7]

S: "Something very, that is a thing, an experience, an experience in quotation marks, which was very unpleasant. That . . . I think I was then really in kindergarten still, yes when **a sister was born** to us, and I don't remember, she was a year old, or about, **she passed away.** I don't remember the period when she passed away, but I remember the *shiva,*[8] which remained a very unpleasant memory for me, what I remember is that . . . the commotion, it was a small house in an immigrants' housing project, before we moved to another flat, and I remember the experience, the so-called "experience," again I'm saying, a house full of people —

I: Was she already 1 year old?

S: She was about a year old when she passed away, I think 10 months or a year, the girl. As much as I remember from my mother, she passed away **of some disease** actually, a children's disease which probably developed into something more that it, so—it's not really clear what, hepatitis if I'm not mistaken, if I remember correctly. So [I recall] **the commotion of lots of people lying on the floor, coming and going, and I'm pretty much lost within all this and I go out to play in the neighborhood,** and then I even didn't understand what had happened, and then **one of the older girls of the neighborhood then said to me: " Do you know why your home was full of people—because your sister died."** And this was such a shock to me, and then really only uh . . . I asked more questions.

Sara's preface to the story is relatively long and includes an evaluation of her experience ("an experience"). The introduction also includes unfinished sentences ("something very," "that is a thing"), which are not usually evident in Sara's speech. This latter is another example of the importance of context, that is, the consideration of a linguistic expression in the context of the speaker's individual style of speaking. Both of these features may be indicative of the emotion with which this narrative is infused and of the difficulty of entering into a narrative mode when such a traumatic event is being recalled.

After introducing the incident, Sara locates the story in time, hesitates ("I don't remember"), and reports that her sister had been born and died. Once again she claims a failure of memory and then begins to describe the *shiva.* Here she pauses (indicated as . . .), digresses to a description of the house and the family's subsequent move to a new home, and then consciously returns to her topic ("again I'm saying"). The interviewer's question, at this point, prompts a short digression from the story. Sara answers and returns to where she left off, describes the crowd and the experience of lying on the floor. She digresses to describe her own state of mind at the time, to twice recall her confusion ("and I'm pretty much lost within all this," "and then I even didn't understand what had happened,"), and then arrives at the apparent climax of the story—going out to play and learning about the death of her sister from an older girl in the neighborhood.

All this suggests that Sara's emotion is attached not to the death of her sister but to the manner in which she learned of the death. She was, after all, a small child at the time, and her sister died before they had time to become acquainted. What is also suggested is that, as an adult, Sara is angered by her parents' failure to be honest and to tell her about the tragedy themselves.

In this example, too, repetition of words and phrases is indicative of the emotion with which the memories are infused. Her repetition 11 times of phrases related to memory is particularly significant ("I remember," "I don't remember," "I think I was then really in . . . "). The recurring sense of ignorance may be indicative of her literal ignorance as a child of what was going on ("I even didn't understand") and of her sense of being lost ("I'm pretty much lost"). Rereading of the entire transcript of Sara's interview reveals that Sara often tends to emphasize whether or not she recalls a given incident clearly, yet her use of such terms in this passage is particularly extreme, illustrating why it is important to consider the speaker's usual style of speaking. Of particular interest, also, is Sara's involvement in the event, which seems almost equivalent to a reexperiencing of the incident, when she refers to being lost in the continuous present and not in the past. This hypothesis is strengthened by the fact that Sara describes what her friend told her as if she were hearing it now.

Discussion

The two examples that have been presented above illustrate how detailed analysis of the formal aspects of a story can be indicative of the emotional content of a story. Although close and sensitive reading of the texts may also have elicited a sense of the emotional charge of the narrative, the use of the measure gives a further grounding in formal and linguistic features of the text for what is more intuitively evoked by careful reading.

The measure presented here may be used in different contexts. It can be used to assess and confirm the extent to which a narrative is emotionally charged, particularly when a text refers to a speaker's own life experience. This can be the case even when a speaker is unaware of, or denies, the emotional weight of an experience. The measure can also be used in therapeutic settings to identify gaps between distanced speech and hidden levels of emotion. Similarly, the measure can be used to assess to what extent individuals are connected to their emotions.

CONCLUDING REMARKS

The emphasis in this chapter has been on analysis of form. Although in theory it is important to distinguish between form and content, in practice it is worthwhile to consider both of them. Synthesis between form analysis and content analysis can prove very fruitful. Form analysis requires the researcher to engage in definition of criteria, classifications, and examination of the deep structures of a text, while consideration of these categories in terms of content often highlights dimensions and distinctions that would not have arisen from purely structural analysis.

Content analysis of generalizations in the interview texts, for instance (in the first part of this chapter), suggested that in terms of content there were two types of generalizations:

1. *Generalizations about people* occur when the speaker claims that a trait characterizes a large population, such as a certain age group. "I think that at that age one is more interested in friends than in family" (Mary).

2. *Generalizations about law* occur when the speaker claims that a law or principle is always true. For example, Mary explaining why her class was more successful than the parallel class makes an assumption about a general law from her own personal experiences: "That's how it always is. When there are two classes, one is always better than the other. It always happens that way."

I examined the differences between men and women with regard to the two types of generalizations, having two possible outcomes in mind. On the one hand, women—more attuned to relationships—would generalize more about people, while men would generalize more about laws. On the other hand, if women are more sensitive to interpersonal differences, they may be less likely to make generalizations about large groups. I found that two-thirds of women's generalizations referred to people and one-third to laws, while among the men, four-fifths of the generalizations referred to people and only one-fifth to laws. Although the proportional differences are small, it is notable that although women generalize more than men, and generalize more altogether about laws, they generalize less about people than do men. While I cannot necessarily explain, at this point, why such differences arose, it is important to point out that they wouldn't have been evident at all in a pure analysis of form whereas analysis of content did bring them to light.

In the same vein, the examples in the second part of this chapter stress the importance of context in categorical analysis. Specifically, we saw how familiarity with the content of the entire life story, the speaker's linguistic style, and the broader social context are essential for analyzing sections of the life story.

NOTES

1. The research project during which the current data were collected (see Chapter 2) compared graduates of the special learning program with graduates from ordinary high school, in each age group. Here the comparison will be between men and women.

2. The frequency and nature of interventions is certainly influenced by the tendencies of the interviewers and their interactions with the interviewees. Although I did not engage in a systematic investigation of this issue, my impression is that interviewers with a clinical orientation were more likely to use such intervention techniques.

3. *Cheder* is a religious elementary school.

4. It is advisable to investigate to what extent the interviewer's attitudes and openness to criticism affect this measure. Although this was not systematically investigated, on the face of things there were no such influences.

5. All letters stand for places.

6. Zionism was the Jewish national movement to restore a national territorial entity in the land of Israel. After the establishment of the state of Israel (1948), for an Israeli to be a "Zionist" means, among other things, to be willing to make an effort and contribute to one's country. The speaker gives the ideological motive for her settling in G, a new communal settlement (kibbutz).

7. It should be mentioned that the analysis of Sara's memories of her sister's death was conducted by Tamar Zilber independently, without reading the former analyses written by Amia Lieblich and Michal Nachmias (Chapter 3).

8. For *shiva,* see Note 3 in Chapter 3.

8

Discussion: Choices and Evaluation in Narrative Research

In this final chapter, we would like to return to some of the basic issues that underlie many of the themes and illustrative passages presented throughout the book. This chapter is largely about choice: the options and dilemmas facing researchers at almost every step of their inquiry. Having provided the reader with a model for various methods of reading, analyzing, and interpreting narrative materials, and shown how this model can be used, we would like to "complicate" and "deconstruct" matters at this stage by opening up some of the questions that, for the sake of clarity, we have put aside so far.

When approaching any new study, the researcher is faced with many dilemmas regarding the choice of research question and approach, but these are rarely elucidated. In fact, this choice is determined by a multitude of factors—and their interaction—concerning the domain and the study, on the one hand, and the researcher, on the other. Most important is the concordance between the research goals and its methods, yet practical considerations and personal preference have their own impact on this complicated decision process. We believe that psychology today is characterized by pluralism, both in theory and in method. Moreover, this pluralism encompasses both pure extremes based on a single theory or method of inquiry (as we have attempted to show for our demonstrations in Chapter 1) and many more cases that blend and amalgamate new or existing elements.

ON TEXT, READING, AND INTERPRETATION

First on a long list of dichotomies that this chapter is now about to blur or disrupt is that of "text" and its "reading," and consequently "reading" and "interpretation." As the hermeneutic school argues (Widdershoven,

1993), we found in our own work that no reading is free of interpretation and, in fact, that even at the stage of procuring the text, especially in the dialogical act of conducting a life-story interview, explicit and implicit processes of communicating, understanding, and explaining constantly take place. The illusion that we have a static text of narrative material, and then begin a separate process of reading and interpreting it, is far from the truth. This is related to a dilemma that we have called "levels of interpretation" (see pp. 76-77), namely, the role of theory in listening to and explaining an account. Is the interviewer a naive listener attuned only to the phenomenological world of the narrator as presented? Or does she constantly question, doubt, and look for gaps, contradictions, silences, and the unsaid? (On an approach to narrative research of the "unsayable," see Rogers et al., in press.) Can one take a middle course between these ends? Can one do both at the same time? This choice is as relevant to the acts of interviewing and listening as to the acts of interpreting and making conclusions from a life story. Based on our experience, our claim is that in the mere acts of being together in a room, stating the purpose of the encounter, asking questions, relating to the responses, and participating in the creation of an atmosphere, some interpretive choices have already been made. Yet, for the sake of the individual study or of instruction in various research "steps," we often ignore such shady matters in practical work, perhaps because it would be too difficult to keep them in mind and "learn about doing research" at the same time. Narrative studies, however, may profit from the researchers' sensitivity to and awareness of these subtle processes and their willingness to share them with the reader.

ON PLURALISM:
QUALITATIVE AND/OR
QUANTITATIVE APPROACHES

A frequent distinction is made between quantitative and qualitative methods. These research methods usually belong to different paradigms in the social sciences and represent different general perspectives about the world and hence the nature of science. In terms of our concern in this book, quantitative research deals mainly with numbers and statistics while qualitative research deals with discourse and its interpretation. However, as Hammersley (1992) succinctly argues in his discussion of current ethnography, the qualitative-quantitative divide can be easily deconstructed because "a large proportion of research reports (including many that are regarded as qualitative) combine the two" (p. 161). This is certainly true for the analyses reported in previous chapters, which greatly vary as to the place of counting and computing within each. More accurately, therefore, the researcher is faced with a range of possibilities rather than a dichotomy. For data collection, she has to decide how precise the data should be, how objective, reproducible, and replicable. Another set of questions is how personal, authentic, and contextual the sought-after data should be.

The necessity of choosing (a questionnaire versus an unstructured interview, for example) does not end at this stage, however. As we have demonstrated, when narrative data are selected for inquiry, their analysis also can be more quantitative, as exemplified in the first sections of Chapters 6 and 7, or mainly qualitative, as in Chapter 4. We have pointed out, however, that no less than qualitative processing, the quantitative treatment of verbal texts requires a great number of (what may be justly considered) arbitrary definitions and decisions along the way to the final table of results. These simply turn the objectivity of such procedures, in our view, into an illusion. Processes that seem to be systematic and precise do not render an interpretation objective. Therefore, it is perhaps no less "accurate" to read a text with an open mind, and to fully record one's impressions of its meaning for the narrator, as well as for the reader, using no figures at all. Our basic position is, however, that there is ample place for all of these approaches and methods, and that our understanding of a question, a person, or a culture is enriched by this pluralism.

Our own work, which has been demonstrated in previous chapters, clearly is closer to the subjective, narrative end of the range. We repeatedly returned to the same data, our collected corpus of about 80 life stories, armed with different hearing aids and lenses, which produced myriad readings. From this variety of angles, we elected to concentrate as much as possible on two life stories, or even some episodes or sections within them. Most notably, the reader encountered three interpretations of the memory of the death of Sara's infant sister in her childhood, conducted independently by several researchers. While this may have seemed, at times, redundant or repetitive, these readings were never identical. Each unique reading revealed some new facets of the remembered episode. We may consider checking these interpretations for contradictions among them: What would such inconsistencies teach us? Our belief is that life stories and their readings are as multilayered and complex as human identity, so that—as in psychotherapy—conflicts and contradictions consist as part and parcel of narrative inquiries. We hope to have proven how rich and revealing such a multiplicity of readings can be in understanding an individual.

THE CHOICE OF LIFE STORY AS
A MEANS FOR THE STUDY OF IDENTITY

Indeed, we started out on our route from an assumption regarding the linkage between life story and identity or personality, stating our interest in understanding the inner world, or the world of meanings, of women and men in their culture. It was our choice and intention to explore this world by listening to the voices of people telling their life stories, knowing that people create stories out of the building blocks of their life histories and culture, and at the same time, that these stories construct their lives, provide them with meanings and goals, and tie them to their culture. Therefore, no story is unidimensional in its voice. A story may have melody, pitch, and loudness or, in our terms, content and form—content, which comprises many interwoven, sometimes conflicting, themes, and form, which may be characterized by structure, style, coherence, and other attributes.

Our next question for this discussion then may be as follows: Which is a reflection of the narrator's identity? We may reach the conclusion that both story and identity are complex and multifaceted or, as Bakhtin (1981) writes, dialogical and polyphonic (see also Hermans et al., 1993). Like stories, as we saw in Sara's and David's narratives, identity has many components and layers. The various components may interact to create a whole; often they are in dialogue that remains conflictual; and sometimes there is no dialogue at all. Regarding the concept of layers, we would like to propose that, in comparison with the quest for identity through contents of the life story, the structural aspects of a narrative are more attuned to the deeper levels of personality, less easy to manipulate, and perhaps more revealing. At the same time, we would like to repeat here that the distinction between form and content is not as clear-cut as it seems, which brings us to the discussion of our model and the choices it offers to researchers.

REFLECTIONS ON OUR PROPOSED MODEL

Our two-by-two model has been presented as a device for ordering the growing number of methods and ideas for reading a life story. We believe that it has heuristic value for thought and discourse about methods of narrative inquiry and can be used with a great variety of materials: verbal, whether oral or written, and perhaps also visual. Having proposed and used the model, however, we would like to conclude this book with a cautionary note. This model has perhaps created dichotomizations that should now be softened or retracted, as already suggested at various points in the previous chapters. Our "four cells" model—whole-content, category-content, whole-form, category-form—was certainly instructive for the beginning of the book, yet, taken at face value, it may be misleading. Preferably, the reader should conceive of the model as consisting of two continua. At the ends of each one are rare but very clear examples of an either-or nature, while most proposed reading methods would consist of more balanced mixtures.

As much as it initially may be helpful to think about methods of analysis separately, and the organization of narrative reading methods into four cells, this conceptualization masks finer distinctions and combinations. Analyses that "belong" to the same cell are often far from similar, as in our example of the two content analyses provided in Chapter 6, or the two categorical-form analyses presented in Chapter 7. While the first, regarding the impact of high school, attempted to be accurate in counting utterances and rank-ordering categories by frequency, the second, relating to the narrators and their families, was more interpretive and impressionistic in its treatment of the data. Using the term *intersubjectivity,* the second content analysis exemplifies subjective listening of the researcher to the subjective voices of the tellers. This may lead to fine and profound conclusions, otherwise ignored. The differences between various methods that belong to the same "cell" are often not simple to characterize and need additional dimensions for their elaboration.

At the same time, as was amply demonstrated in our examples, the major distinctions created by our model frequently oversimplify the practice of conducting narrative research. When aiming to concentrate on the form of a story, globally or categorically, the content of the narrative could not be ignored. On the contrary, the content of the plot or its segments is essential for characterizing and understanding its form. The separation of "whole" from "category" is, in reality, not clearer than that between "content" and "form." Again, this is not a dichotomy. The determination of the size of the part or the breadth of a category is another of the relevant choices facing investigators. We have demonstrated how detailed and meticulous one may be in breaking a text into minute and precise units, or how illuminating can be the use of broader issues, motifs, or themes. As in a figure-and-ground relationship, a relatively short segment of a life story (such as a stage or a chapter in our data) may be considered as a "whole" in which a smaller component is embedded. Moreover, when reading the entire life story, utterances or single episodes stand out and create a focus for the reading of the whole. On the other hand, it is, in our view, quite rare for content analysis to reach meaningful conclusions when it disregards the context of utterances or discards insights that come from understanding the person and her or his story as a whole. We therefore offer, at this stage, to liberate our readers from adherence to these dichotomies and use the terms to express ideal polarities that define the domain yet very rarely materialize in their pure form.

ARE WE WISER REGARDING "HOW TO DO" NARRATIVE RESEARCH?

Excluding traditional methods of "content analysis," which are often even computerized today,[1] among the many remaining approaches for reading and interpretation there are few manuals or prescriptive guides for conducting research work step by step. This is, in our view, not only the result of the relative infancy of this type of methodology in psychology and other social sciences but a consequence of the very nature of such research work, which is similar to literary readings of a poem or a novel. We strongly believe, however, that narrative analysis is not a form of art or a given talent. Nor is it a mere "technique." It is a skill that requires great patience and dedication, and can be academically learned, refined, and improved. Reading of detailed examples, as we hope to have provided in this book, is one of the avenues for achieving better results on one's own.

Passive exposure, however, to the perfect model of research, if there is one, is not always a productive means of instruction. For this purpose, we have tried, throughout the chapters of this book, to activate the reader. Moreover, we have made an effort to elucidate the dilemmas and considerations that entered the researcher's dialogue with herself or with her research associates (topics that are almost never presented in research reports) en route to reaching a final destination—that is, of "how to" perform the chosen procedure. This is always a fascinating, sometimes aggravating, process of weighing pros and cons, reaching and revising feasible, optimal rules, and often making compromises for the sake of practical limitations. Yet, as demonstrated particularly in the first part of Chapter 7, in the analysis of the cognitive level of the narrators as displayed by their stories, this process need not curb the academic excellence of the final, chosen procedure and its application. The shared reflexivity and open disclosure of the researcher's dilemmas guarantee a fair, mature, and critical dialogue between scholars and their readers, a dialogue that gives the field of narrative research its energy and drives us all forward.

Consideration of progress or models for research brings us to an important issue in narrative research, namely, its judgment and evaluation. With our study in mind, as demonstrated so far, we will close the book with this final discussion.

CRITERIA FOR QUALITATIVE RESEARCH

The "old" criteria for evaluation of research were, basically, reliability, validity, objectivity, and replicability. These criteria were mainly quantitative, namely, expressed in coefficients of correlation or similar measures. While some scholars believe that the same should apply for all research, including narrative (or qualitative) research, this position is practically difficult—or impossible—to maintain (Altheide & Johnson, 1994). Moreover, it contradicts the very nature of the narrative approach, which, starting from an interpretive viewpoint, asserts that narrative materials—like reality itself—can be read, understood, and analyzed in extremely diverse ways, and that reaching alternative narrative accounts is by no means an indication of inadequate scholarship but a manifestation of the wealth of such material and the range of sensitivities of different readers—as amply demonstrated in this book.

What then can be offered as criteria for the quality of narrative research? How should we distinguish a good study from a bad one? How can we offer guidelines for the improvement of narrative analysis? Pluralism seems to characterize this issue as well given that the questions stated above have received a variety of answers in recent work in the field. We now offer a sample of these propositions to our readers as issues to be applied to the former chapters of this book as well as future guidelines for reading and performing narrative research.

In his summary of previous attempts to deal with evaluation of case studies, Runyan (1984) distinguished between internal criteria, such as style, vividness, coherence, and apparent plausibility, and external criteria, namely, correspondence with external sources of information about the subject. "To be complete, the process of evaluation cannot be carried out solely by reading the case itself, but also must involve judgments by people who either know the subject or are familiar with other sources of evidence"

(p. 150). Based on his review, he suggests seven criteria for evaluating a case study. We present them fully below, as they also may be taken as research goals for the individual embarking on a narrative inquiry or as reasons for deciding to conduct one.

> 1. Providing "insight" into the person, clarifying the previously meaningless or incomprehensible, suggesting previously unseen connections;
> 2. Providing a feel for the person, conveying the experience of having known or met him or her;
> 3. Helping us to understand the inner or subjective world of the person, how he or she thinks about their own experience, situation, problems, life;
> 4. Deepening our sympathy or empathy for the subject;
> 5. Effectively portraying the social and historical world that the person is living in;
> 6. Illuminating the causes (and meanings) of relevant events, experiences, and conditions; and
> 7. Being vivid, evocative, emotionally compelling to read. (p. 152)

This profound and extensive list has focused only on single case studies and has not exhausted the issue. In the spirit of pluralism, on the one hand, we may find radical views, such as expressed by Smith (1984), who contends that assessment of qualitative, interpretive research stands in stark contradiction to the basic characteristics and values of this kind of scholarship. On the other hand, new, more concise lists and definitions of criteria have been offered. In a most recent work, Rogers et al. (in press) modestly proposed that "in qualitative research, a fundamental criterion of validity requires that interpretations and conclusions follow a trail of evidence that originate in the text" (p. 5). Hammersley (1992) proposed two very general criteria: validity, which asks how truthful, plausible, and credible an account is (p. 69), and relevance, which asks whether an account is important and contributes to the field, previous findings, methods, theory, or social policy (p. 73). Using another perspective, Mishler (1990) proposed two different criteria for evaluating narrative research, namely, trustworthiness and authenticity. Of the two, trustworthiness refers to the evaluation of a community of researchers. Mishler argues as follows: "Focusing on trustworthiness rather than truth displaces validation from its traditional location in a presumably objective, non-reactive, and neutral reality and moves it to the social world—a world constructed in and through our discourse, and actions, through praxis" (p. 420).

Based on all of the above, and our experience as researchers of life stories, we found the following four criteria helpful for our evaluation of narrative studies:

(1) Width: The Comprehensiveness of Evidence. This dimension refers to the quality of the interview or the observations as well as to the proposed interpretation or analysis. Numerous quotations in reporting narrative studies, as well as suggestions of alternative explanations, should be provided for the reader's judgment of the evidence and its interpretation.

(2) Coherence: The Way Different Parts of the Interpretation Create a Complete and Meaningful Picture. Coherence can be evaluated both internally, in terms of how the parts fit together, and externally, namely, against existing theories and previous research.

(3) Insightfulness: The Sense of Innovation or Originality in the Presentation of the Story and Its Analysis. Close to this criterion is the question of whether reading the analysis of the life story of an "other" has resulted in greater comprehension and insight regarding the reader's own life.

(4) Parsimony: The Ability to Provide an Analysis Based on a Small Number of Concepts, and Elegance or Aesthetic Appeal (which relate to the literary merits of written or oral presentations of the story and its analysis; see Blauner, 1987; Richardson, 1994).

Similarly to Mishler (1990) and Rogers et al. (in press), we do not refer directly to the truth-value of a narrative study but propose that a process of consensual validation—namely, sharing one's views and conclusions and making sense in the eyes of a community of researchers and interested, informed individuals—is of the highest significance in narrative inquiry. Much has been said in this book about the importance of dialogues between researchers as well as being aware of internal dialogues and sharing them.

The reader has probably realized by now, however, that having a "list" does not necessarily guarantee smooth decisions or agreements. Compared with the quantitative measures of reliability and validity, the criteria proposed above are qualitative in nature, that is, they consist of judgments that cannot be expressed in scales or numbers. The field of narrative research should and can strive for better work, as assessed by consensual evaluation, yet by its very nature, its products cannot be reduced to simple formulas or numerical values.

To recapitulate our words in this discussion as well as the book as a whole, it is our contention that there are good and bad narrative studies. There are ways of learning to improve skills of reading, analysis, and interpretation of life stories. Yet narrative studies are not, in any absolute way, better than statistical or experimental studies. Each approach is more suitable for some purposes than for others; reading and interpretation can be conducted in myriad ways. As Denzin and Lincoln state in their book (1994): "The processes of analysis, evaluation, and interpretation are neither terminal nor mechanical. They are always emergent, unpredictable, and unfinished" (p. 479).

NOTE

1. The subject of software for computerized content analysis has not been included among the topics of this book. Having as our research data life stories in Hebrew, none of the computerized programs was available for us. We see this situation as somewhat of a blessing, however, because it forced us to face the texts without any technical aids. For readings about computerized content or discourse analysis, please refer to Richards and Richards (1994), who have also an appendix with a list of software developers (p. 461). In addition, the following books deal with computerized analysis: Fielding and Lee (1991), Miles and Huberman (1994), Weitzman and Miles (1995), Kelle, Prein, and Bird (1995).

References

Adler, A. (1929a). *The practice and theory of individual psychology.* New York: Harcourt & Brace.

Adler, A. (1929b). *The science of living.* London: Low & Brydone.

Adler, A. (1931). *What life should mean to you.* Boston: Little Brown.

Adler, A. (1956). *The individual psychology of Alfred Adler.* New York: Basic Books.

Alasuutari, P. (1997). The discursive construction of personality. *Narrative Study of Lives, 5,* 1-20.

Allport, G. W. (1962). The general and the unique in psychological science. *Journal of Personality, 30,* 405- 422.

Altheide, D. L., & Johnson, J. M. (1994). Criteria for assessing interpretive validity in qualitative research. In N. K. Denzin. & Y. S. Lincoln (Eds.), *Handbook of qualitative research* (pp. 485-499). Thousand Oaks, CA: Sage.

Amir, Y., Sharan, S., & Ben Ari, R. (1984). Why integration? In Y. Amir & S. Sharan (Eds.), *School desegregation* (pp. 1-20). London: LEA.

Bakan, D. (1966). *The duality of human existence.* Boston: Beacon.

Bakhtin, M. M. (1981). *The dialogic imagination.* Austin: University of Texas Press.

Bales, R. F. (1958). Task roles and social roles in problem solving groups. In E. E. Maccoby, T. M. Newcomb, & E. L. Hartly (Eds.), *Reading in social psychology* (pp. 437-447). New York: Holt.

Barnett, W. S. (1993). Benefit cost analysis of preschool education: Finding from a 25-year follow-up. *American Journal of Orthopsychiatry, 63*(4), 500-508.

Bateson, M. C. (1989). *Composing a life.* New York: Atlantic Monthly Press.

Belenky, M. F., Clinchy, B. M., Goldenberger, N., & Tarule, J. M. (1986). *Women's way of knowing: The development of self, voice, and mind.* New York: Basic Books.

Biber, D., & Finegan, E. (1989). Styles of stance in English: Lexical and grammatical marking of evidentiality and affect. *Text, 9*(1), 93-124.

Bickman, L., & Rog, D. J. (Eds.). (1998). *Handbook of applied social research methods.* Thousand Oaks, CA: Sage.

Bishop, D. R. (1993). Applying psychometric principles to the clinical use of early recollection. *Individual Psychology, 49,* 153-165.

Blauner, B. (1987). Problems of editing "first person" Sociology. *Qualitative Sociology, 10,* 46-64.

Brown, L. M., Argyris, D., Attanucci, J., Bardige, B., Gilligan, C., Johnston, K., Miller, B., Osborne, D., Ward, J., Wigginns, G., & Wilcox, D. (1988). *A guide to reading narratives of conflict and choice for self and voice.* Cambridge, MA: Harvard University Press.

Bruhn, A. R. (1985). Using early memories as a projective technique: The cognitive perceptual method. *Journal of Personality Assessment, 49,* 587-597.

Bruner, J. (1986). *Actual minds, possible words.* Cambridge, MA: Harvard University Press.

Bruner, J. (1990). *Acts of meaning.* Cambridge, MA: Harvard University Press.

Bruner, J. (1991). The narrative construction of reality. *Critical Inquiry, 18,* 1-21.

Bruner, J. (1996). *The culture of education.* Cambridge, MA: Harvard University Press.

Capps, L., & Ochs, E. (1995). *Constructing panic: The discourse of agoraphobia.* Cambridge: Cambridge University Press.

Chambon, A. S. (1995). Life history as a dialogical activity: "If you ask me the right questions, I would tell you." *Current Sociology, 43,* 125-135.

Chanfrault-Duchet, M. F. (1991). Narrative structures, social models and symbolic representation in the life story. In S. B. Gluck & D. Patai (Eds.), *Women's words: The feminist practice of oral history* (pp. 63-75). New York: Routledge & Kegan Paul.

Crabtree, R. F., & Miller, W. L. (1982). *Doing qualitative research.* London: Sage.

Curtis, W. (Ed.). (1988). *Revelations: A collection of gay male coming out stories.* Boston: Alyson.

Denzin, N. K. (1978). The sociological interview. In N. K. Denzin (Ed.), *The research act* (pp. 112-134). New York: McGraw-Hill.

Denzin, N. K. (1989). *Interpretive interactionism* (Applied Social Research Methods Series, Vol. 16). Newbury Park, CA: Sage.

Denzin, N. K., & Lincoln, Y. S. (Eds.). (1994). *Handbook of qualitative research.* Newbury Park, CA: Sage.

Duplessis, R. B. (1985). *Writing beyond the ending.* Bloomington: Indiana University Press.

Eiger, H. (1975). *Rehabilitative teaching for underprivileged students* [in Hebrew]. Tel-Aviv: Sifriat Poalim.

Eiger, H., & Amir, M. (1987). Rehabilitative teaching for underprivileged students: Psychoeducational aspects. In U. Last (Ed.), *Psychological work in school* [in Hebrew] (pp. 174-204). Jerusalem: Magness.

Epston, D., White, M., & Murray, K. D. (1992). A proposal for the authoring therapy. In S. McNamee & K. J. Gergen (Eds.), *Therapy as social construction.* London: Sage.

Erikson, E. H. (1959). *Identity and the life cycle.* New York: Norton.

Erikson, E. H. (1968). *Identity: Youth and crisis.* New York: Norton.

Eshel, Y., & Klein, Z. (1995). Elementary school integration and open education: Long-term effects of early intervention. In G. Ben-Shakhar & A. Lieblich (Eds.), *Studies in psychology in honor of Solomon Kugelmass* (pp. 155-175). Jerusalem: Magness.

Farrell, M. P., Rosenberg, S., & Rosenberg, H. J. (1993). Changing texts of male identity from early to late middle age: On the emergent prominence of fatherhood. In J. Demick., K. Bursick., & R. DiBiase (Eds.), *Parental development* (pp. 203-224). Hillsdale, NJ: Lawrence Erlbaum.

Feldman, C., Bruner, J., & Kalmar, B. (1993). Plot, plight and dramatism: Interpretation at three ages. *Human Development, 36*(6), 327-342.

Fielding, N. G., & Lee, R. M. (1991). *Using computers in qualitative research.* London: Sage.

Fisher-Rosenthal, W. (1995). The problem with identity: Biography as solution to some (post) modernist dilemmas. *Comenius, Utrecht, 3,* 250-265.

Fontana, A., & Frey, J. H. (1994). Interviewing: The art of science. In N. K. Denzin & Y. S. Lincoln (Eds.), *Handbook of qualitative research* (pp. 362-376). Thousand Oaks, CA: Sage.

Frankenstein, C. (1970a). *Impaired intelligence.* New York: Gordon & Reach.

Frankenstein, C. (1970b). *Rehabilitating damaged intelligence* [in Hebrew]. Jerusalem: Hebrew University, School of Education.

Frankenstein, C. (1972). *Liberating thinking from its bondages* [in Hebrew]. Jerusalem: Hebrew University, School of Education.

Frankenstein, C. (1981). *They think again* [in Hebrew]. Tel-Aviv: Am Oved.

Freud, S. (1950). *Screen memories.* In J. Strachey (Ed. & Trans.), *Standard edition of the complete works of Sigmund Freud* (Vol. 3, pp. 301-322). London: Hogarth. (Original work published 1899)

Freud, S. (1960). Childhood memories and screen memories. In J. Strachey (Ed. & Trans.), *Standard edition of the complete works of Sigmund Freud* (Vol. 6, pp. 43-52). London: Hogarth. (Original work published 1901)

Frye, N. (1957). *Anatomy of criticism.* Princeton, NJ: Princeton University Press.

Gergen, K. J. (1991). *The saturated self: Dilemmas of identity in contemporary life.* New York: Basic Books.

Gergen, K. J. (1994a). *Realities and relationships: Soundings in social construction.* Cambridge, MA: Harvard University Press.

Gergen, K. J. (1994b). Mind, text and society: Self memory in social context. In U. Neisser & R. Fivush (Eds.), *The remembering self* (pp. 78-104). New York: Cambridge University Press.

Gergen, K. J., & Gergen, M. M. (1986). Narrative form and the construction of psychological science. In T. R. Sarbin (Ed.), *Narrative psychology: The storied nature of human conduct* (pp. 22-44). New York: Praeger.

Gergen, K. J., & Gergen, M. M. (1988). Narrative and the self as relationship. In L. Berkowitz (Ed.), *Advances in experimental social psychology* (Vol. 21). San Diego, CA: Academic Press.

Gergen, M. M. (1988). *Feminist thought and structure of knowledge.* New York: New York University Press.

Gergen, M. M. (1992). Life stories: Pieces of a dream. In G. C. Rosenwald & R. L. Ochberg (Eds.), *Storied lives: The cultural politics of self-understanding* (pp. 127-144). New-Haven, CT: Yale University Press.

Giddens, A. (1991). *Modernity and self identity: Self and society in the late modern age.* Stanford, CA: Stanford University Press.

Gilligan, C. (1982). *In a different voice: Psychological theory and women's development.* Cambridge, MA: Harvard University Press.

Gilligan, C., Lyons, N. P., & Hammer, T. G. (1990). *Making connections: The relational worlds of adolescent girls at Emma Willard School.* Cambridge, MA: Harvard University Press.

Gilligan, C., Rogers, A.G., & Tolman, D. L. (Eds.). (1991). *Women, girls & psychotherapy: Reframing resistance.* New York: Harrington Park.

Glaser, B., & Strauss, A. (1967). *The discovery of grounded theory.* Chicago: Aldine.

Gluck, S. B., & Patai, D. (Eds.). (1991). *Women's words: The feminist practice of oral history.* New York: Routledge & Kegan Paul.

Goldberger, N., Tarule, J., Clinchy, B., & Belenky, M. (Eds.). (1996). *Knowledge, difference and power: Essays inspired by women's way of knowing.* New York: Basic Books.

Goldstein, K., & Scheerer, M. (1941). Abstract and concrete behavior. *Psychological Monographs, 53*(2), 1-151.

Gorkin, M., & Othman, R. (1996). *Three mothers three daughters: Palestinian women's stories.* Berkeley: University of California Press.

Gottschalk, L. A. (1994). The development, validation, and applications of a computerized measurement of cognitive impairment from the content analysis of verbal behavior. *Journal of Clinical Psychology, 54*(3), 349-361.

Gould, R. (1978). *Transformation: Growth and change in adult life.* New York: Simon & Schuster.

Greene, J. C. (1994). Qualitative program evaluation: Practice and promise. In N. K. Denzin & Y. S. Lincoln (Eds.), *Handbook of qualitative research* (pp. 530-544). Thousand Oaks, CA: Sage.

Gutmann, D. (1980).The post parental years: Clinical problems and developmental possibilities. In W. H. Norman & T. J. Scarmella. (Eds.), *Mid-life: Developmental and clinical issues.* New York: Brunner/Mazel.

Gutmann, D. (1987). *Reclaimed powers: Men and women in later life.* Evanston, IL: Northwestern University Press.

Hammersley, M. (1992). *What's wrong with ethnography? Methodological exploration.* London: Routledge & Kegan Paul.

Hartley, L. L., & Jensen, P. L. (1991). Narrative and procedural discourse after closed head injury. *Brain Injury, 5,* 267-285.

Heilbrun, C. G. (1989). *Writing a woman's life.* New York: Ballantine.

Heizner, Z. (1994). *The rhetoric of trauma.* Unpublished doctoral dissertation, Hebrew University, Jerusalem.

Herman, J. L. (1992). *Trauma and recovery.* New York: Basic Books.

Hermans, H. J. M., Rijks. T. I., Harry, J. G., & Kempen, H. J. G. (1993). Imaginal dialogue in the self: Theory and method. *Journal of Personality, 61*(2), 207-236.

Hevern, V. W. (1997). *Resources for narrative psychology: Guide and annotated bibliography* [on-line]. Syracuse, NY: Author. (Available through http://maple.lemoyne.edu/Ehevern/nrmaster.html).

Howard, G. S. (1991). Culture tales: A narrative approach to thinking cross cultural psychology and psychotherapy. *American Psychologist, 46,* 187-197.

Josselson, R. (1987). *Finding herself: Pathways to identity development in women.* San Francisco: Jossey-Bass.

Josselson, R. (1992). *The space between us: Exploring the dimensions of human relationship.* San Francisco: Jossey-Bass.

Josselson, R. (Ed.). (1996a). *The narrative study of lives: Vol. 4. Ethics and process.* Thousand Oaks, CA: Sage.

Josselson, R. (1996b). *Revising herself: The story of women's identity from college to mid-life.* New York: Oxford University Press.

Josselson, R., & Lieblich, A. (Eds.). (1993). *The narrative study of lives* (Vol. 1). Newbury Park, CA: Sage.

Josselson, R., & Lieblich, A. (Eds.). (1995). *The narrative study of lives: Vol. 3. Interpreting experience.* Thousand Oaks, CA: Sage.

Josselson, R., Lieblich, A., Sharabany, R., & Wiseman, H. (1997). *Conversation as method: Analyzing the relational world of people who were raised communally.* Thousand Oaks, CA: Sage.

Kelle, U., Prein, G., & Bird, K. (1995). *Computer aided qualitative data analysis: Theory, methods, and practice.* Thousand Oaks, CA: Sage.

Kemper, S., Rash, S., Kynette, D., & Norman, S. (1990). Telling stories: The structure of adults' narratives. [Special issue: Cognitive gerontology]. *European Journal of Cognitive Psychology, 2,* 205-228.

Klein, Z., & Eshel, Y. (1980). *Integrating Jerusalem schools.* New York: Academic Press.

Kobasa, S. C. (1982). The hardy personality: Toward a social psychology of stress and health. In J. M. Suls & G. Sanders (Eds.), *Social psychology of health and illness* (pp. 3-33). Hillsdale, NJ: Lawrence Erlbaum.

Koch, T. (1990). *Mirrored lives: Aging children and elderly parents.* New York: Praeger.

Kohlberg, L. (1976). Moral development and moralization: The cognitive development approach. In T. Lickona (Ed.), *Moral development and behavior: Theory, research, and social issues.* New York: Holt, Rinehart & Winston.

Kuale, S. (1983). The qualitative research interview: A phenomenological and a hermeneutical understanding. *Journal of Phenomenological Psychology, 14,* 171-196.

Labov, W., & Waletzky, J. (1967). Narrative analysis: Oral versions of personal experience. In J. Helm (Ed.), *Essays on the verbal and visual arts* (pp. 12-44). Seattle: University of Washington Press.

Lakoff, R. T. (1975). *Language and women's place.* New York: Harper & Row.

Lakoff, R. T. (1990). *Talking power: The politics of language in our lives.* New York: Basic Books.

LaRossa, R. (1989). In depth interviewing in family medicine research. In N. Ramsey Jr. (Ed.), *Family system in medicine* (pp. 227-240). New York: Guilford.

Levinson, D. (1996). *The seasons of a woman's life.* New York: Knopf.

Lieblich, A. (1986). Successful career women at mid-life: Crises and human development. *International Journal of Aging and Human Development, 23*(4), 301-312.

Lieblich, A. (1993). Looking at change: Natasha, 21: New immigrant from Russia to Israel. *Narrative Study of Lives, 1,* 92-129.

Lieblich, A. (1995). A preliminary exploration of high school experience and its effects on graduates of the rehabilitative teaching project at the high school adjunct to the Hebrew University of Jerusalem. In G. Ben-Shakhar & A. Lieblich (Eds.), *Studies in psychology in honor of Solomon Kugelmass* (pp. 176-201). Jerusalem: Magness.

Lieblich, A., & Josselson, R. (Eds.). (1994). *The narrative study of lives: Vol. 2. Exploring identity and gender.* Thousand Oaks, CA: Sage.

Lieblich, A., & Josselson, R. (Eds.). (1997). *The narrative study of lives* (Vol. 5). Thousand Oaks, CA: Sage.

Lieblich, A., Tuval, R., & Zilber, T. (1995). *Long term follow-up of the educational work of the rehabilitative teaching within the "project" of the Hebrew University School in Jerusalem* [in Hebrew]. Scientific report, the Israeli Foundations Trustees.

Lieblich, A., Zilber, T., & Tuval-Machiah, R. (1995). Seekers and finders: Generalization and differentiation in life stories [in Hebrew]. *Psychology, 5*(1), 84-95.

Linde, C. (1993). *Life stories: The creation of coherence.* New York: Oxford University Press.

Lissak, M. (1984). The ethnic organization in the Jewish community in Palestine [in Hebrew]. *Megamoth, 28*(2-3), 295-315.

Mahler, M., Pine, F., & Bergman, A. (1975). *The psychological birth of the human infant.* New York: Basic Books.

Manning, P. K., & Cullum-Swan, B. (1994). Narrative, content, and scientific analysis. In N. K. Denzin & Y. S. Lincoln (Eds.), *Handbook of qualitative research* (pp. 463-477). Thousand Oaks, CA: Sage.

Marcia, J. E. (1966). Development and validation of ego identity status. *Journal of Personality and Social Psychology, 3,* 551-558.

Maslow, A. H. (1954). *Motivation and personality.* New York: Harper & Row.

Mason, M. G. (1980). Autobiographies of women writers. In J. Olney (Ed.), *Autobiography essays: Theoretical and critical.* Princeton, NJ: Princeton University Press.

Maxwell, J. A. (1996). *Qualitative research design: An interactive approach* (Applied Social Research Methods Series, Vol. 41). Thousand Oaks, CA: Sage.

Maxwell, J. A., & Miller, B. A. (in press). Categorization and contextualisation as components of qualitative data analysis. *Qualitative Sociology.*

McAdams, D. P. (1985). *Power, intimacy, and life story: Personological inquiries into identity.* New York: Guilford.

McAdams, D. P. (1990). *The person: An introduction to personality psychology.* Orlando, FL: Harcourt Brace.

McAdams, D. P. (1993). *The stories we live by: Personal myths and the making of the self.* New York: William Morrow.

McAdams, D. P., Hoffman, B. J., Mansfield, E. D., & Day, R. (1996). Themes of agency and communion in significant autobiographical scenes. *Journal of Personality, 64,* 339-377.

McCracken, G. (1988). *The long interview.* Beverly Hills, CA: Sage.

Miles, M. B., & Huberman, A. M. (1994). *Qualitative data analysis: An expanded source book* (2nd ed.). Thousand Oaks, CA: Sage.

Miller, J. B. (1986). *What do we mean by relationship?* (Work in progress, Working Paper Series, 22). Wellesley, MA: Stone Center.

Mishler, E. G. (1986a). The analysis of interview-narratives. In T. R. Sarbin (Ed.), *Narrative psychology: The storied nature of human conduct* (pp. 233-255). New York: Praeger.

Mishler, E. G. (1986b). *Research interviewing: Context and narrative.* Cambridge, MA: Harvard University Press.

Mishler, E. G. (1990). Validation in inquiry-guided research: The role of exemplars in narrative studies. *Harvard Educational Review, 60,* 415-442.

Mishler, E. G. (1995). Models of narrative analysis: A typology. *Journal of Narrative and Life History, 5,* 87-123.

Mitchell, W. J. T. (Ed.). (1981). *On narrative.* Chicago: University of Chicago Press.

Mosak, H. H. (1958). Early recollections as a projective technique. *Journal of Projective Techniques, 22,* 302-311.

Murray, K. D. (1988). The construction of identity in narrative of romance and comedy. In J. Shotter & K. Gergen (Eds.), *Texts of identity.* London: Sage.

Murray, K. D. (1992). The construction of a moral career in medicine. In R. Young & A. Collins (Eds.), *Interpreting career: Hermeneutical studies of lives in context* (pp. 31-47). New York: Praeger.

Neisser, U., & Fivush, R. (1994). *The remembering self: Construction and accuracy in the self narrative.* New York: Cambridge University Press.

Nelson, K. (1989). *Narratives from the crib.* Cambridge, MA: Harvard University Press.

Neugarten, B. L. (1968). *Middle age and aging.* Chicago: University of Chicago Press.

Ochberg, R. L. (1994). Life stories and storied lives. *Narrative Study of Lives, 2,* 113-144.

Ochs, E. (1989). The pragmatics of affect: An introduction [Special issue]. *Text, 9*(1), 1-5.

Ochs, E., & Capps, L. (1996). Narrating the self. *Annual Review of Anthropology, 25,* 19-43.

Ochs, E., & Schieffelin, B. (1989). Language has a heart. *Text, 9*(1), 7-25.

Omer, H., & Alon, N. (1997). *Constructing therapeutic narratives.* Northvale, NJ: Jason Aronson.

Omer, H. (1994). *Critical interventions in psychotherapy.* New York: Norton.

Peres, J., & Katz, R. (1991). The family in Israel: Change and continuity. In L. Shamgar-Hendelman & R. Bar Yosef (Eds.), *Families in Israel* [in Hebrew] (pp. 9-32). Jerusalem: Academon.

Perry, W. G. (1968). *Forms of intellectual and ethical development in the college years.* New York: Holt, Rinehart & Winston.

Personal Narratives Group. (Eds.). (1989). *Interpreting women's lives: Feminist theory and personal narratives.* Bloomington: Indiana University Press.

Piaget, J. (1955). *The child's construction of reality*. London: Routledge & Kegan Paul.

Plummer, K. (1995). *Telling sexual stories: Power, change and social worlds*. New York: Routledge & Kegan Paul.

Polkinghorne, D. E. (1988). *Narrative knowing and the human sciences*. Albany: State University of New York Press.

Polkinghorne, D. E. (1991). Narrative and self concept. *Journal of Narrative and Life History, 1*, 135-154.

Rabuzzi, K. A. (1988). A theory of multiple-case research. *Journal of Personality, 56*, 239-264.

Richards, T. J., & Richards, L. (1994). Using computers in qualitative research. In N. K. Denzin & Y. S. Lincoln (Eds.), *Handbook of qualitative research* (pp. 445-462). Thousand Oaks, CA: Sage.

Richardson, L. (1994). Writing: A method of inquiry. In N. K. Denzin & Y. S. Lincoln (Eds.), *Handbook of qualitative research* (pp. 516-529). Thousand Oaks, CA: Sage.

Riessman, C. K. (1990). *Divorce talk: Women and men make sense of personal relationship*. New Brunswick, NJ: Rutgers University Press.

Riessman, C. K. (1993). *Narrative analysis* (Qualitative Research Methods Series, Vol. 30). Newbury Park, CA: Sage.

Rimmon-Keenan, S. (1989). *Narrative fiction: Contemporary poetics*. London: Methuen.

Rogers, A. G., Casey, M. E., Ekert, J., Holland, J., Nakkula, V., & Sheinberg, N. (in press). An interpretive poetics of languages of the unsayable. *Narrative Study of Lives*.

Rosenthal, G. (1993). Reconstruction of life stories: Principles of selection in generating stories for narrative biographical interviews. *Narrative Study of Lives, 1*, 55-91.

Rosenthal, G. (1997). National identity or multicultural autobiography. *Narrative Study of Lives, 5*, 1-20.

Rosenwald, G. C., & Ochberg, R. L. (1992). *Storied lives: The cultural politics of self understanding*. New Haven, CT: Yale University Press.

Rotenberg, M. (1987). *Re-biographing and deviance: Psychotherapeutic narrativism and the midrash*. New York: Praeger.

Rotter, J. B. (1966). Generalized expectancies for internal vs. external control of reinforcement. *Psychological Monograph, 80*(Whole no. 609).

Runyan, W. M. C. (1984). *Life histories and psychobiography: Explorations in theory and method*. New York: Oxford University Press.

Sarbin, T. R. (Ed.). (1986). *Narrative psychology: The storied nature of human conduct*. New York: Praeger.

Scarf, M. (1981). *Unfinished business: Pressure points in the lives of women*. New York: Ballantine.

Schafer, R. (1983). *The analytic attitude*. New York: Basic Books.

Schulman, P., Castellon, C., & Seligman, M. E. P. (1989). Assessing explanatory style: The content analysis of verbatim explanations and attributional style questionnaire. In *Behavioral research and therapy* (pp. 505-512). Oxford: Pergamon.

Schwartz, S. H., & Bilsky, W. (1987). Towards a psychological structure of human values. *Journal of Personality and Social Psychology, 53*, 550-562.

Smith, J. K. (1984). The problem of criteria for judging interpretive inquiry. *Educational Evaluation and Policy Analysis, 6*, 379-391.

Spence, D. P. (1982). *Narrative truth and historical truth: Meaning and interpretation in psychoanalysis*. New York: Norton.

Spence, D. P. (1983). The paradox of denial. In S. Breznitz (Ed.), *The denial of stress*. New York: International Universities Press.

Spence, D. P. (1986). Narrative smoothing and clinical wisdom. In T. R. Sarbin (Ed.), *Narrative psychology: The storied nature of human conduct* (pp. 211-232). New York: Praeger.

Spence, J. T., Helmreich, R., & Stapp, J. (1975). Ratings of self and peers on sex role attributes and their relation to self esteem and conceptions of masculinity and femininity. *Journal of Personality and Social Psychology, 32,* 29-39.

Spradley, J. P. (1979). *The ethnographic interview.* New York: Holt, Rinehart & Winston.

Stewart, A. J., Franz, C., & Layton, L. (1988). The changing self: Using personal documents to study lives. *Journal of Personality, 56*(1), 41-74.

Sutton-Smith, B. (1986). The development of fictional narrative performances. *Topics in Language Disorder, 7*(1), 1-10.

Tannen, D. (1990). *You just don't understand.* New York: William Morrow.

Tetlock, P. E. (1991). An alternative metaphor in the study of judgment and choice: People as politicians. *Theory and Psychology, 1*(4), 451-477.

Tetlock, P. E., & Suedfeld, P. (1988). Integrative complexity coding of verbal behavior. In C. Antaki (Ed.), *Analyzing everyday explanation: A casebook of method* (pp. 43-59). London: Sage.

Thompson, S. (1994).Changing lives, changing genres: Teenage girls' narratives about sex and romance, 1978-1986. In A. S. Rossi (Ed.), *Sexuality across the life course* (pp. 209-232) (John D. and Catherine T. MacArthur Foundation Series on Mental Health and Development: Studies on Successful Mid-Life Development). Chicago: University of Chicago Press.

Van-Langenhove, L., & Harre, R. (1993). Positioning and autobiography: Telling your life. In N. Coupland & J. F. Nussbaum (Eds.), *Discourse and lifespan identity: Vol. 1. Language and language behaviors* (pp. 81-99). Newbury Park, CA: Sage.

Watkins, C. E. (1992). Adlerian-oriented early memory research: What does it tell us? *Journal of Personality Assessment, 59*(2), 248-263.

Webster's Third International Dictionary. (1966). Springfield, MA: Merriam-Webster.

Weitzman, E. A., & Miles, M. B. (1995). *Computer programs for qualitative data analysis: A software source book* (2nd ed.). Thousand Oaks, CA: Sage.

White, M., & Epston, D. (1990). *Narrative means to therapeutic ends.* New York: Norton.

Widdershoven, G. A. M. (1993). The story of life: Hermeneutic perspectives on the relationship between narrative and life history. *Narrative Study of Lives, 1,* 1-20.

Wigren, J. (1994). Narrative completion in the treatment of trauma. *Psychotherapy, 31*(3), 415-423.

Wiersma, J. (1988). The press release: Symbolic communication in life history interviewing. *Journal of Personality, 56*(1), 205-238.

Wiseman, H., & Lieblich, A. (1992). Individuation in a collective community. In S. C. Feinstein (Ed.), *Adolescent Psychiatry: Developmental and Clinical Studies, 18,* 156-179.

Woolf, V. (1957). *A room of one's own.* New York: Harcourt Brace Jovanovich. (Original work published 1929)

Yin, B. K. (1984). *Case study research design and methods* (Applied Social Research Methods Series, Vol. 5). Newbury Park, CA: Sage.

Zigler, E., & Valentine, J. (Eds.). (1979). *Project Head Start: A legacy of the war on poverty.* New York: Free Press.

INDEX

APPLIED SOCIAL RESEARCH
METHODS SERIES

Series Editors
LEONARD BICKMAN, Peabody College, Vanderbilt University, Nashville
DEBRA J. ROG, Vanderbilt University, Washington, DC

Other volumes in this series are listed on the series page

About the Authors

Amia Lieblich is Professor of Psychology at the Hebrew University of Jerusalem, where she served as a chairperson from 1982 to 1985. Her books have presented an oral history of Israeli society, dealing with the war, POWs, military service, and the kibbutz. With Ruthellen Josselson, she is the editor of the Narrative Study of Lives annual series (published by Sage from 1993). For the past few years, she has been teaching courses on life stories and narratives as a psychological research method.

Rivka Tuval-Mashiach is a clinical psychologist at Hadassa Hospital, Jerusalem, and a Ph.D. candidate at the Hebrew University, where she also supervises students in their first experiences in psychotherapy and teaches a course on adult development. Her thesis research explores the narratives women and men tell about their lives.

Tamar Zilber is an organizational psychologist. She has recently submitted her Ph.D. thesis, at the Hebrew University of Jerusalem, on ambiguity as a coping mechanism of an organization. Her study combines an anthropological participant-observation method with analysis of the narratives of the organization. Currently she is teaching a course on culture and organization from critical and feminist perspectives.